Caring Spaces, Learning Places:

Children's Environments That Work

By Jim Greenman

Foreword by Elizabeth Prescott

Illustrations by Charles Murphy

Photographs by Jean Wallech, Nancy P. Alexander, Shawn Connell, and Francis Wardle

Published by Exchange Press Inc.

Dedication

To Emma and the zest she carries with her into my life

Cover Photos
(left to right) Jean Wallech, Francis Wardle, Jean Wallech

Masculine and feminine pronoun references in this book are used randomly for simplicity and in no way reflect stereotyped concepts of children or adults.

— Foreword —

It has been said that *fish can tell you little about water*. In our research, we have found, similarly, that people can tell you little about their physical environment. Patterns of responding to the physical world remain largely nonverbal. Consequently, you may read **Caring Spaces, Learning Places: Children's Environments That Work**, savoring its content, without realizing what an accomplishment it is to have gotten all these insights about environments into such a readable framework.

When our research staff first sought to identify materials and information about early childhood environments, we found very little. There were licensing codes of regulatory agencies that spelled out standards for square footage, amount of light, numbers of toilets, and fire safety. Their purpose was to set minimums for early childhood programs, not to define the optimum in program quality. However, their very existence provided a statement about the correspondence between the environment and the well-being of children.

There was also the input of educators. These ranged from the carefully crafted ideas of Maria Montessori about appropriate environment and materials to the plethora of cute or often faddish offerings in commercial catalogues.

Architects were clearly an appropriate source though we have been sobered by our contacts in this field. The concepts taught in professional schools do not easily translate into good design when knowledge of young children and their caregivers are lacking.

These most obvious contributors to children's environments had, for the most part, specific practical goals. Increasingly, we began to discover threads that connected adults' fondest memories of such things as spider webs, bread dough, sand, cozy hiding places, sorting and sorting buttons to the meaning that they ascribed to their particular life cycle in a particular culture. We also began to see that these first experiences with the world of things that could

be seen, touched, and felt provided the firm foundation for the powerful leaps in thought from the concrete to the conceptual. With this discovery we began to see art, poetry, novels, and theory building in a new light.

The significance of this book lies in Jim Greenman's skill in showing how the ordinary, everyday work with children which is often deemed dull and burdensome can be transformed into meaning that can last a lifetime. This is an important book to read, and I hope each reader will see the physical world through new eyes.

Elizabeth Prescott

Pacific Oaks College
Pasadena, California

Acknowledgements

This book reflects the practical wisdom of the teachers and directors in the programs I have worked with and visited over the years. Their open and generous sharing of ideas and creations made this book possible.

For the generous use of their wonderful photographs, two years of support, and detailed comments about the text, I am very grateful to Francis Wardle and Nancy Alexander.

Janice Krick, Molly Greenman, Mary Asper and Margaret Toth read the manuscript in various forms and provided numerous helpful criticisms.

Photographers Jean Wallech and Shawn Connell deserve extra-credit for traipsing around with me and sensitively capturing on film both programs and people.

Illustrator Charles Murphy proved easy to work with and greatly improved upon the vaguely articulated images I gave him to work from.

Working with Exchange Press has been a delight, with few of those uneasy moments of ego and right-eousness between author and publisher. This book is a true collaboration, and I am grateful to Bonnie and Roger Neugebauer for the opportunity to work together. I also appreciate the efforts of Sandy Brown, Sue Epeneter, Dennis Brown, Ute Kidder, and Louise Schon.

Living with someone who is writing a book on the side is akin to living with a bag lady. One has to endure preoccupations with bits and pieces: strings of words, packs of photographs, sudden searches for obscure facts; and also live with frustration-induced flashes of anger and despondency. Emma Green-man and Annerhe and Jan Krick managed to survive the worst and throughout provided all sorts of support and generous forbearance that kept me going.

— Preface —

"To live in an environment that has to be endured or ignored rather than enjoyed is to be diminished as a human being."
Sinclair Gauldie (1969, p. 182)

My first experience as a teacher came in 1967, in a summer all day Head Start classroom located in (where else?) a church basement. I waited for my 18 four year olds to come in off the bus, putting the finishing touches on my classroom: tables with assorted activities, block corner, dress-up area, and bookshelf with colorful books. In they came, some shy, most excited. Then in came Carlos, two feet tall, with a foot high Afro, and a look and bearing about him that proclaimed: here was a man among men.

The other children clearly looked up to him (figuratively speaking). Carlos coolly surveyed the room where he was to spend eight hours a day, five days a week, for the next twelve weeks. A sinister uneasiness hung in the air. I began to get nervous, because it was clear that the children were waiting for Carlos' judgment on my efforts. It soon came. "This place is dooky," Carlos pronounced. (Carlos always pronounced; he never spoke.) Soon all the children began chanting, "This place is dooky," and I saw my summer rapidly deteriorating.

Well, I survived that trial by making Carlos my main man, planning some great experiences and establishing a good rapport with the children. But it took me over ten years to learn all the implications of the lesson Carlos taught me. Carlos recognized at a glance that the church basement was a crummy place to spend a summer. My cheery presence and imaginative activities helped only a little. Carlos knew that places are not containers for experience nor simply stages for interactions between people, large and small. They are, in Elizabeth Prescott's words, "regulators of our experience" (1979, p. 1).

An environment is a living, changing system. More than the physical space, it includes the way time is structured and the roles we are expected to play. It conditions how we feel, think, and behave; and it dramatically affects the quality of our lives. The environment either works for us or against us as we conduct our lives. In the Head Start setting, it worked against the children and me and placed a burden on our talents, patience, good will, and energy. The environment at a given moment in time is either a pleasing place to be or it isn't. The basement wasn't that day in June and all the other summer days, for the children or for the adults.

This book is written for teachers, directors, parents, and children—all those who have a stake in having settings work for them and be reasonable places to be. The all too ubiquitous church basement is a symptom of the lack of resources this society routinely allocates to its youngest members. Programs become used to working with minimal space, minimal adult-child ratios, minimal equipment, and so on and so on. Licensing regulations designed to be floors below which programs cannot fall, in fact, become ceilings which set the standard for the child care industry. The effect is the same as being in a trash compactor—one gets squeezed. Developing knowledge and skills on how to creatively maximize scarce resources and adapt settings is essential to creating livable learning and caring places for children and their caregivers. This volume draws on the ideas of many others who have coped with squeezing for a long time.

Much of the focus of this book is on all day child care settings. These settings encompass nearly all the environmental issues and needs of other early childhood settings: nursery and preschool programs, playgrounds, playrooms. Further, the focus on child care settings is important, because the stakes are much higher in terms of the impact on children and families. These are places where childhoods are being spent, where childrearing is shared. A central tenet of this book is that we need to view these settings as places where children and adults live together—places for childhoods and adult lives.

What kind of place are child care centers to be? What sort of stage? Child care centers are a relatively new social form, compared to homes, schools, prisons, hospitals. Hardly any of us grew up with them. We *know* what school is, but child care? The history of child care is short and has usually taken place in borrowed or invented spaces. Only in the last 10 or 15 years has the advent of the age of building for child care begun; it is time to conceptualize what child care should be. We may be at a crossroads. The adapted nature of the space and the pell mell growth until now have allowed us to sidestep some fundamental questions. Like Winnie-the-Pooh, we have not had time for perspective:

"Here is Edward Bear, coming downstairs now, bump, bump, bump, on the back of his head, behind Christopher Robin. It is, as far as he knows, the only way of coming downstairs, but sometimes he feels that there really is another way, if only he could stop bumping for a moment and think of it."
A. A. Milne (1954, p. 3)

Questions need to be asked now because these buldings are where children will be growing up. Our society tolerates very little institutional variety. Whether they are good, bad, or mediocre, they will be **child care centers**—the form we will have to live with for years to come.

Buckminster Fuller has said that designers don't invent, they discover patterns that already exist and apply them. But for all of us, even the true originals like Fuller, the richest discovery that unlocks the most patterns is coming upon others, creative discoverers who open our eyes.

This book is unabashedly derivative. One of its primary goals is to spread the insights and visions of people, some not as well known (or read) as they should be: architects like Richard

---

Barter
by Sara Teasdale

Life has loveliness to sell,
  All beautiful and splendid things,
Blue waves whitened on a cliff,
  Soaring fire that sways and sings,
And children's faces looking up
Holding wonder like a cup.

Life has loveliness to sell,
  Music like a curve of gold,
Scent of pine trees in the rain,
  Eyes that love you, arms that hold,
And for your spirit's still delight,
Holy thoughts that star the night.

Spend all you have for loveliness,
  Buy it and never count the cost;
For one white singing hour of peace
  Count many a year of strife well lost,
And for a breath of ecstasy
Give all you have been, or could be.

Dattner, Fred Osmon (and others at the Educational Facilities Laboratory), and Gary Moore and his colleagues at the University of Wisconsin at Milwaukee; designers like Jay Beckwith, Paul Hogan, and Anita Olds; educators like Susan Issacs and Milly Almy; and most of all, Elizabeth Prescott and many of her past and present colleagues at Pacific Oaks College in Pasadena, California. All of these people have watched children with respect and sensitivity, and they have thought about the settings within which children deserve to flourish.

Twenty years ago, the movement for *open education* was the source of a storm of ideas and

---

experiments. In the course of researching and writing this volume, I ended up rereading much of the theoretical and practical material on open education in the 1960's and early 1970's—the works of John Holt, George Dennison, Herbert Kohl, Ivan Illich, and others. This period marked the professional rediscovery of Dewey and Susan Issacs, and a growing interest in Piaget.

Their ideas on an education based on an understanding of how children learn and their use of the richness of life as a basis for learning have not lost relevance or power. It is profoundly disturbing that not only is open education out of fashion for elementary school children, but it is necessary now to make the case for open education in settings for children under six.

Some of the beliefs central to this volume are:

1. Good settings respect children's abilities to learn and believe in active hands-on learning.

2. Good settings recognize and respect children as individuals and understand their needs for care.

3. Good settings are established and maintained by adults who learn by observing children, drawing from their own experiences as children *and* as adults.

4. Good settings respect adults' abilities to learn and adults' needs for comfort.

5. Good settings know and feel that "life has loveliness to sell" and work hard to provide it.

Hard Cheese
by Justin St John

The grownups are all safe,
Tucked up inside,
Where they belong.

They doze into the telly,
Bustle through the washing-up,
Snore into the fire,
Rustle through the paper.

They're all there
Out of harm's way.

Now it's our street:
All the back yards,
All the gardens,
All the shadows,
All the dark corners,
All the privet-hedges,
All the lampposts,
All the doorways.

Here is an important announce-
*   ment:*
The army of occupation
Is confined to barracks.
Hooray.

We're the natives.
We creep out at night,
Play everywhere,
Swing on all the lampposts,
Slit your gizzard?

Then, about nine o'clock,
They send out search parties.

We can hear them coming.
And we crouch

In the garden-sheds,
Behind the dustbins,
Up the alleyways,
Inside the dustbins,
Or stand stock-still,
And pull ourselves in,
As thin as a pin,
Behind the lampposts.

And they stand still,
And peer into the dark.
They take a deep breath—
You can hear it for miles—
And, then, they bawl,
They shout, they caterwaul:
'J-i-i-i-i-mmeeee!'
'Timeforbed. D'youhearme?'
'M-a-a-a-a-reeee!'
'J-o-o-o-o-hnneeee!'
'S-a-a-a-a-mmeeee!'
'Mary!' 'Jimmy!'
'Johnny!' 'Sammy!'
Like cats. With very big mouths.

Then we give ourselves up,
Prisoners—of—war.
Till tomorrow night.

But just you wait.
One of these nights
We'll hold out,
We'll lie doggo,
And wait, and wait,
Till they just give up
And mumble
And go to bed.
You just wait.
They'll see!

Photograph by Nancy P. Alexander

Caring Spaces/Learning Places is intended as a resource for those who create, adapt, and cope with settings for young children. Part One explores the power of the environment, the *landscape* of children's lives today—the array of settings they inhabit—and analyzes the dimensions and qualities of children's environments. Part Two looks at how quality settings can be created.

Learning is neither for children nor *adults* something to be poured into them and spit out in practice. It is an active, intellectual, and often hands-on process. Education is not *what* to think, and this is *not* a how-to book, dispensing wisdom and answers and a few inspiring anecdotes. There are very few, if any, *right ways* to do things; and the solutions to most problems have to start with "It depends on this and that. . . ." and end with "Here are the trade-offs if we do it this way. . . ."

Caring Spaces/Learning Places is a book of ideas and observations, problems and solutions that seem to represent the best of current thinking. There are thoughts here to play with, to sort and twist and store in the back of one's mind. Most adults, immersed in practicality, are unable to capture the mood and tone of their childhoods. Scattered throughout the volume are the feelings and thoughts of poets and artists to help us recapture childhood's wonder. There are also the thoughts of professionals from other fields whose perspectives may help to stimulate or, perhaps, jar our thinking.

I lost track of Carlos when he was a three foot high fourth grader who had formed his own corporation on the street and sold candy and fireworks (Carlos Ltd.). But the "Carlos Test" lives on. When I walk into a children's setting, devoid of children and adults, I look around and imagine I'm Carlos at the age of the children in the program and ask myself, "Is this a good place for me to spend my time?" Then I ask myself, "Is this a good place for me as a

teacher to spend my days with Carlos and all the others?" If I can't answer "yes" to both of those questions, there is work to be done.

James Greenman
December 23, 1987

— Table of Contents —

Builders
Licensers, Inspectors, and Fire Marshals
A Goal Based Process
A Creative Process
Problem Solving/Design Tools
Creative Implementation
Hustling, Scrounging, and Doing It Yourself
Making It Work
Conclusions

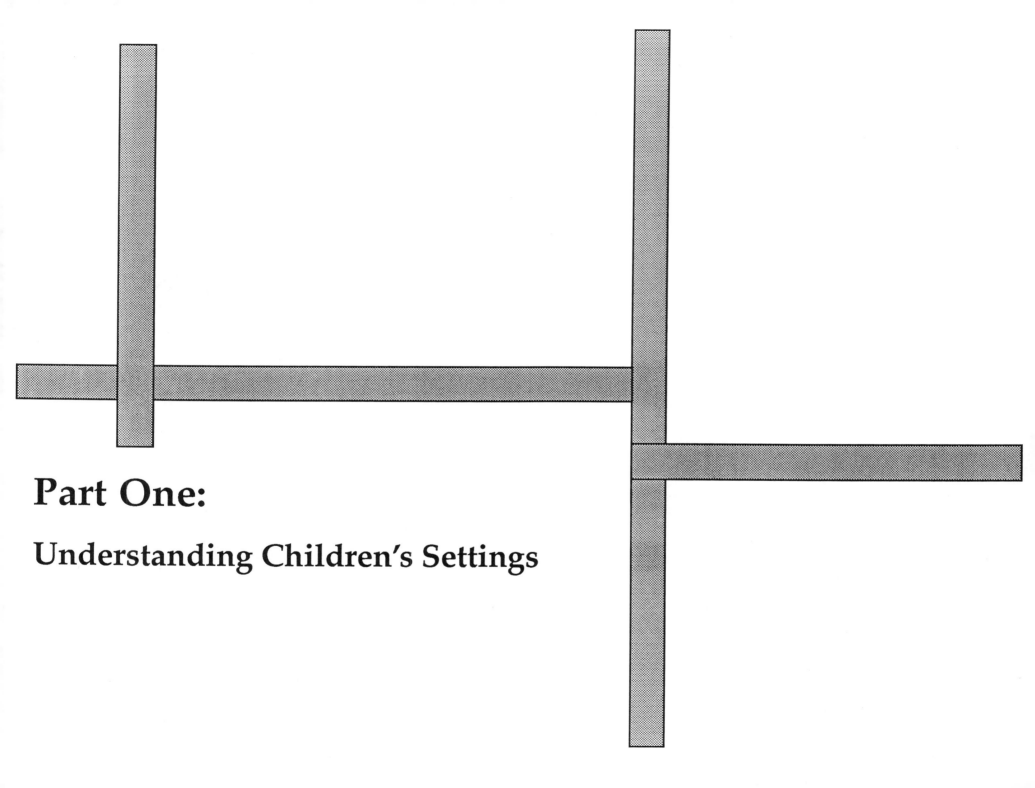

Part One:

Understanding Children's Settings

— Chapter One —

Why Do I Feel This Way?

"How hard it is to escape from places. However carefully one goes they hold you—you leave little bits of yourself fluttering on the fences—little rags and shreds of your very life."
Katherine Mansfield

Entering a cathedral is a humbling experience. The height of the ceilings, the massiveness of the structure, the richness of the wood and the weight of the stone, the deep organ tones, the shards of light from stained glass on high, and the sense of timelessness overwhelm us. Inside a Capitol or an old courthouse, we may experience similar feelings (particularly if we are before the bench). Here the immensity and massiveness emphasize the power of the state and the law of the land. In the cathedral, it is before God and the church that we are meant to feel small. In both, the weight of justice and mercy are embued in the surroundings, just as the architects intended.

A one-story Quaker meeting house, with its simple benches and austere, whitewashed walls, is often humbling; only now we are face to face with ourselves, bare, devoid of any pomp and circumstance. A modern courthouse often has some very human-scale chambers without heavy oak, raised benches, and railings. Here occur the intense, intimate attempts to repair and bring together families torn with conflict. The state is a human presence. These are dramatic examples of the scores of settings that

we, as adults, inhabit; most of which (or all, depending on our religious leanings) are designed with specific goals in mind to influence how we feel, think, and behave—to facilitate the particular piece of living that is to take place within. Architects and designers attempt to give sensible form to the feelings, the moods,

Photograph by Nancy P. Alexander

and the rhythms of the life imagined within the setting.

Our culture excels at environments designed for selling. Consider a discount department store. One enters into well-lit aisle upon aisle of merchandise. Most of the aisles are narrow; and the merchandise seems to jump out at us and spill into our carts, while we navigate around other shoppers. Our senses are assaulted by blue light specials proclaimed over invisible speakers, accompanied by the smell of popcorn and take-out food. The messages we receive: "Everything in the world is here, on sale, and may be sold out soon!" "Aren't you hungry?" "BUY!" "BUY!" "BUY!"

Contrast that setting with a small, fashionable boutique—carpeted, soft accent lighting, a discrete salesperson, and select merchandise very carefully displayed. Here we feel almost like a guest in someone's home. We no longer have the anonymity of the department store, where all but the homeless are welcome. Here our comfort level depends on whether we and the store personnel deem us to have the *right stuff*.

Airports are places almost devoid of any sense of time or space. They are *nowhere* stops on the way to and from *somewheres* in different time zones, with different climates, where people live who speak different languages and have different ways of doing things. They are designed as way stations for all of humanity and are meant to be as familiar and understandable as the international signs that denote their restrooms. What an airport lacks in character increases its comforting comprehensibility.

"But I like airports." The very blandness of airports is attractive to many, who draw security from familiarity and anonymity. Campaigning for the presidency, a resurrected, yet to be disgraced, Richard Nixon explained that he liked Holiday Inns because he knew they would be the same wherever he was. Setting aside the possibility that he was paid to promote Holiday Inns, Nixon (the ultimate placeless man) expressed a feeling shared by many. Some seek

adventure, some do not. We experience settings individually. To some, the quiet, personal experience of the small shop is uncomfortable and intimidating; to others, a welcome relief from the pinball machine frenzy and excitement of dollar days sales that impel flight from the discount store.

These are all adult settings and are not even oriented toward education. Why begin a book on children's environments with a discussion of adult settings? For two reasons: First, if we understand how the environment influences us, we will be in a better position to understand the impact of settings on children. Second, the examples above were chosen deliberately because they have parallels in the settings children inhabit. Many of us spent our childhoods in school buildings no less intimidating to us than cathedrals. Many large open schools or child care centers resemble discount department

Photograph by Jim Greenman

stores in their whirling, kaleidoscopic assault on our senses. In other child care centers, we come close to feeling the same anonymity and impersonal lack of place found in airports and interstate highway restaurants ("Hello, my name is Barbara. Can I take your child today?"). In all these sorts of settings, adults and children grapple with fundamental feelings—of personal power or insignificance, of security, of fear.

Space Speaks

Space speaks to each of us. Long corridors whisper "run" to a child; picket fences invite us to trail our hands along the slats. Physical objects have emotional messages of warmth, pleasure, solemnity, fear; action messages of come close, touch me, stay away; "I'm strong," "I'm fragile." Consider museums with long corridors and modern sculpture, sculptures with dynamic tension that call out for testing, intricate paintings that beckon us to come close and examine, and textured weavings and soft sculptures that cry out to be touched. It is no wonder that children, and some adults, have trouble obeying museum rules.

Hot colors like reds and oranges stimulate; they are used in restaurants because they stimulate our appetites and speed up our eating. Thus, we eat more and leave sooner, making room for others to gulp down more food. Sounds and smells deliver their own messages. The smell of frying onions triggers a physiological response that stimulates our appetites. Rhythmic sounds affect heart rates. At a gambling casino, a state fair, or in a meadow, all of our senses come into play and influence our mood and our choice of behavior.

Space speaks to our emotions. We build images of *places*, meaningful spaces, out of fragments of experiences, experiences significant

Placemakers

"There is a spectre haunting America. It is not the spectre Karl Marx wished upon us in the opening of his manifesto. It is a spectre created of our own design. It is the spectre of placelessness. We have created a banal samelessness everywhere in America. It haunts the old commercial strip on the road to the airport as well as the sparkling new development downtown. . . . Many of us live, and move, and have our being in spaces that never become places.

Of course, there is no anchor for our sensibilities in the twirling franchise signs that mark the widening gyre of commercial detrius at the city's edge. But neither is there much to remember in the phalanx of concrete slab and mirrored glass reflecting the anonymity of newly rebuilt downtowns. . . . We travel through so many of the barren public plazas in the downtown and the sterile shopping centers in suburbia, but we cannot inhabit them with any meaning, any connection to our roots and aspirations. They remain dead spaces that tell no tales. . . .

It is into such a world that the placemakers and place making actions should be welcomed . . . objects that help to define, reveal, enrich, reinforce, expand, or otherwise make accessible place meaning . . . sculptures and objects, fountains and fragments, reliefs and pavement inserts, benches and bollards, murals and wall makers.

The placemakers lay claim to our memories and, as is often the case, to our affection. They offer an anecdote to humanize the face of much new development, and they can build a sense of future value for neglected older environments. It is a value based on associations and images which convey strongly enough that they imprint themselves on the landscape of the mind. This creation of a mental context can transform environments that were previously anonymous or forlorn. By populating the mind with images of the community, its history, characters, stages of development, often with a decorative richness, whimsy, and even humor, placemakers help us to restore a feeling of belonging, and with it perhaps a sort of inner harmony."

from **Placemakers**, by Ronald Flemming and Renata von Tscharner (1981, pp. 7-8)

later, when adult sensibilities merged with the ten year old's fantasy, was disappointing and sad. It was, after all, just an amusement park.

Objects lay claim to our feelings because of associations and qualities of the objects. Wood, leather, and some natural stone and brick objects beckon to be touched. Objects made of these materials tend to *wear with grace* (Educational Facilities Laboratory, 1972). The smoothings and cracks and weathering and nicks often add character. Contrast the wooden school desk, with its history etched in the carvings and nicks, with the metal and formica of modern styles. Peeling paint, chipped formica or concrete block, torn polyester, and broken metal are all evidence of wear that repel us.

Ronald Flemming and Renata von Tscharner, with wonderful photographs, illustrate placemakers that release a particular kind of energy in people, "an energy that is invested in feelings of care and propriety for a place" (1981, pp. 110-111). Placemakers invest meaning in a variety of ways. Some placemakers transform the character of a place, but most of the placemakers have a more modest objective. "They add a layer of decorative richness which embellishes and sometimes commemorates." Some provide just a "whimsical bump in the mind." Some border on the cute, "a sort of forced and affected feeling," and some have a capacity to inspire lasting affection that transcends the moment.

The Environment

The environment is more than the physical setting. It includes "all the external conditions and factors potentially capable of influencing an organism" (English and English, 1958, p. 182)— how time is structured and roles assigned, expectations of our behavior, and physical

to us for reasons of our own. Our memories, imaginings, hopes, and dreams transform places and things. The romantic charm of a cottage or airy sun porch, the foreboding danger of a dark alleyway, the excitement or anxiety brought on by the big city, all grow out of our interpretations of the physical realities. In the 1950's, the televised glimpses of Disneyland were embedded in my child mind as a place of eternal bliss. My conception of heaven included Fantasyland, Adventureland, Frontierland, and Tomorrowland. Experiencing the real thing 20 years

surroundings. In a lecture hall, we are expected to present or listen; in a store, to buy or sell— and this behavior occurs within a limited time frame. We are not expected to be parents or children, sleepers or lovers. In homes, community centers, and parks, a much wider range of roles is allowed—and time, for the most part, is much less structured. On an assembly line, the physical setting, the structure of time, and the expectations of our behavior are precisely ordained. The most anxiety-producing settings are usually those with ill-defined roles, those in which we feel we have no control over our part, or those where we have no role at all like a parent in a school that does not encourage visiting. When we are all of a sudden asked to shift from observer to participant in a class, or to sing along, or to make contact with a stranger on a street, many of us want to run for cover.

The environment plays a major role in our social and psychological lives, influencing the stress we experience in accomplishing personal and group goals, the form and nature of our social contacts, and our feelings of identity and self-worth (Deasy, 1974). We all recognize at times how we behave differently in different settings. None of us are the same people in our living rooms and bedrooms as we are on a public bus (thankfully). Yet our recognition is limited and sporadic. We usually do not take into account how powerful the influence is. In Edward Hall's classic look at man's relationship to space, **The Hidden Dimension** (1969), Hall recounts a story in which there had been so many complaints about the chairman of a malfunctioning academic committee that "a replacement was about to be requested. The architect (Hall's colleague) had reason to believe that there was more in the environment than in the chairman to explain the difficulties. . . . The meeting room was next to a busy street whose traffic noises were intensified by reverberations

from the hard walls and the rugless floors inside. When the reduction of the auditory interference made it possible to conduct a meeting without undue strain, complaints about the chairman ceased" (Hall, 1969, p. 44).

Failure to recognize the power of a setting over children often confuses parents and teachers and strains the parent-teacher relationship. They actually see a different child: Jacob-at-home doesn't eat tomatoes, usually takes two naps, and can't put on his clothes. Jacob-at-child care willingly eats tomatoes, never naps, and dresses himself. Emma is never assertive at home with playmates; at nursery school she has begun biting. Parents and teachers often react with disbelief: "Are we talking about the same kid?" For some children, the child care experience is restricting; for others, liberating; for others, perhaps disorienting. Throughout one's life, the sharp contrast between the person at home and the person in some other setting may continue—at college, in the military, or at the office.

Why do we underestimate the power of the environment to influence us? Most of the time we attribute behavior to personality: the child is ornery, the woman is aloof, that man is crazy. We rarely take into account, first, that each of us has "learned *situational* personalities" (Hall, 1969, p. 115)—we respond differently across settings; and, second, that the environment is always influencing us, working for us or against us to some degree. Children trying to restrain themselves in narrow supermarket corridors lined with shelves face a setting as maladaptive as that of Hall's department chairman; they must learn a non-inquisitive personality, unlike the curious child at home.

Hall's theory is that we have two mistaken notions: (1) "that for every effect there is a single and identifiable cause," and (2) "that

man's boundary begins and ends with his skin" (Hall, 1969, p. 115).

Roger Barker, one of the founders of ecological psychology, explains that part of the problem is that when we attempt to study and explain behavior, "prevailing methods of research shatter whatever pattern and organization may exist within the natural environment; and the conclusion is reached, on the basis of the resulting evidence, that the environment is not a source of the order and organization observed in behavior. This leads to further study of the mysterious mechanism of the black box that appears to bring order out of chaos; and this is done via ever more theory-determined and ever less setting-determined environmental variables" (Barker, 1969, p. 117). The search for the "black box" residing in the psychology of the person historically monopolized research.

The need to simplify and make things comprehensible is understandable. Simplification makes life manageable. As a teacher, it is no easy task to develop a coherent usable picture of Jenny, if Jenny acts differently across settings and if there are 20 other children to understand. We form a stable picture of Jenny and assume it fits across environments. This generally works because we are more like ourselves across settings than we are different. We adjust our picture of Jenny if we happen to notice a side to her we hadn't seen before. It is when we are having a problem with her that we may eventually apply an environmental context. "Why is she acting this way? Is she overstimulated, bored? Is the pace too fast or too slow?" After we have exhausted explanations internal to the child, or at least external to our setting (e.g., "something must be going on at home"), something very interesting happens. Although we persist in identifying the child as the problem, we begin to tinker with the context: changing

Photograph by Francis Wardle

Jenny's schedule, clarifying our expectations or making sure our behavior is consistent, altering transitions, and so on. In our determined search for solutions, we implicitly acknowledge that the problem is not Jenny, but Jenny-in-the-context, and that altering the context may eliminate the problem.

The Experience of Space Is Individual and Cultural

"Some men go through a forest and see no firewood. Others see only firewood."
Old English Proverb

Our experience of space and time is individual, but it occurs in a cultural context. People

The Hidden Dimension of Space

Edward T. Hall is an anthropologist whose two classic works—**The Silent Language** (1959) and **The Hidden Dimension** (1969)—examine the relationship of human beings to time and space. Hall provides countless examples of how behavior is regulated by the language of time and the hidden dimension of space and how cultural conditioning mediates our perceptions. Some illustrations on space from **The Hidden Dimension**:

"In the United States we use space as a way of classifying people and activities, whereas in England it is the social system that determines who you are. . . . In the United States, your address is an important clue to status. . . . The Englishman, however, is born and brought up in the social system. . . . He is still Lord—no matter where you find him, even if it is behind the counter in a fishmonger's stall . . . . In England, propinquity means nothing. The fact that you live next door to a family does not entitle you to visit, borrow from, or socialize with them, or your children to play with theirs" (p. 141).

"When the American wants to be alone he goes into a room and shuts the door—he depends on the architectural features for screening. . . . The English, on the other hand, lacking rooms of their own since childhood, never developed the practice of using space as a refuge from others. They have in effect internalized a set of barriers, which they erect and which others are supposed to recognize" (pp. 138-140).

"Arab spaces inside their upper middle class homes are tremendous by our standards. They avoid partitions because they do not like to be alone. . . . Since there is no physical privacy as we know it in the Arab family, not even a word for privacy, one could expect that the Arabs might use some other means to be alone. Their way to be alone is to stop talking. Like the English, an Arab who shuts himself off in this way is not indicating that anything is wrong or that he is withdrawing" (pp. 158-159).

Hall describes two contrasting ways of handling time, monochronic and polychronic. Monochronic people compartmentalize time; "they schedule one thing at a time and become disoriented if they have to deal with too many things at once. Polychronic people . . . tend to keep several operations going at once, like jugglers. . . . Therefore, the monochronic person often finds it easier to function if he can separate activities in space, whereas the polychronic person tends to collect activities" (p. 173). Plazas and markets suit polychronic people, in contrast to strung out main streets and supermarket check-out lines. While Hall did not undertake the task, certainly classrooms could be analyzed as hospitable to one or the other orientation.

can only act or interact in a meaningful way through the medium of culture (Massad, 1979). Culture becomes part of our nervous system; it influences our fundamental physical perception of the world—"The perceptual world of the Eskimo is quite different than our own . . . and an important feature of this difference is the Eskimo's use of his own senses to orient himself in space. . . . The direction and the smell of the wind, together with the feel of ice and snow under his feet, provide the cues that enable an Eskimo to travel a hundred or more miles across *visually undifferentiated waste*" (Hall, 1969, p. 79).

From birth, Eskimo children, like all children, learn to attend to some perceptual stimuli and ignore others. In rural cultures where distinctions between vegetation or weather conditions may mean the difference between prosperity and famine or life and death, children learn the subtle nuances of the natural world. In Thailand, where there are over 100 words to describe kinds of rice, children don't just see *rice*; they see the many variations. American children just see rice.

Children also learn a set of cultural values about how space is to be arranged, inhabited, and shared. "For example, in the United States no one direction generally takes precedence over another unless it is for technical or utilitarian reasons. However, in other cultures some directions are sacred or preferred: Navajo doors must face east, Moslem mosques are oriented toward Mecca, and in India the sacred rivers flow south" (Massad, 1979, p. 17). Because direction means little to Americans (except *keep to the right*), the idea of behaving with direction as a factor, like placing doors or objects a certain way, seems odd or quaint. But for us, "positional value or ranking is of great importance in our lives, to such an extent that children will fight over who will be *first*. Furthermore, we have a tendency to emphasize equality and standardization. That is, when space is divided, we insist on units being equal and uniform" (Massad, 1979, p. 17).

Perceptions of time are as equally culturally bound as perceptions of space. The United States is more time conscious than nearly all other societies. *Time is money* and is apportioned accordingly. To keep someone waiting is an act which signifies power, disdain, or irresponsibility. Lives and work are scheduled to utilize every minute. Contrast this orientation with the Sioux, who had no understanding of what it was to be *late*—or in rural areas, where promptness does not mean a strict allocation of time, but "the promptness of milking cows at the appropriate time, planting to take full advantage of the season, or dropping the fishing nets at a time and place to maximize the catch" (Massad, 1979, p. 14). A four year old in a child care program trying to build a block castle will experience the attitude of her culture toward time. She will be learning whether the effort must fit the time span or the time span shapes the effort.

There are cultural differences in how the duration of time feels, and different meanings are attached when personal interactions are involved. In many societies a 60 *minute* wait assumes the same significance (or irritation) as a 60 *second* wait in the United States. Children and low income people often learn to wait and speed up on command; time is almost always a commodity controlled by others.

It is important to point out that people are more like each other than they are different.

Photograph by Nancy P. Alexander

Our physical equipment is similar, and our lives are marked by many of the same functions, joys, and struggles. All people face the spatial issues of shelter, overcoming distance, and orienting objects in space. All lives are bounded by time. The translation of Shakespeare and Sesame Street into nearly every language illustrates our common humanity.

There is a paradoxical tendency to underestimate both cultural differences and similarities, particularly when we are trying to get along with others. We assume that people should be the same everywhere (the same as us), which makes some of their behavior odd or offensive to us, such as talking differently or having different sanitary habits. The behavioral differences allow us then to categorize them as so different that they are perhaps inferior (particularly if they look different). In the nineteenth century, the Japanese viewed Westerners as inferior, in part because their standards of cleanliness were far higher than Europeans. At the same time, Europeans perceived Japanese food, feudal society, and religion to be signs of inferiority.

Children Are Not Adults

"Childhood has its own way of seeing, thinking, and feeling and nothing is more foolish than to try and substitute ours for theirs."
Jean Jacques Rousseau

"I most vividly and longingly recall the sight of my grandson and his little sunburnt sister returning to their kitchen door from an excursion, with trophies of the meadows clutched in their hands—she with a couple of violets, and smiling, he serious and holding dandelions, strangling them in a responsible grip. Children hold spring so tightly in their brown fists—just as grownups, who are less sure of it, hold it in their hearts."
E. B. White (**Letters of E. B. White**, 1977)

Children and adults inhabit different sensory worlds. Imagine a young infant's world of touch and taste—a world where you see and hear more than you look and listen—where you, in effect, think with your body and actions, and your whole body is your only means of reacting. Consider the way that young children run from place to place. Children respond to the sensory and motor messages of space, while adults are more utilitarian: "Adults notice whether an environment is clean or attractive to an adult eye" (Prescott, 1984, p. 45).

What we often don't notice are the elements that a child will zoom in on: the right place with the right shape, like a tight angular corner between the wall and a couch or the excitement of a perch; the right sight and sound, like a vantage point from which to watch and hear the torrential rain pouring out of the gutter and splashing to the ground below; or the right feel. We, who don't inhabit the floor, undervalue the hot, sunny spot on the floor that draws cats and babies. We are not drawn to the pile of dirt or the hole, to the puddle or dew, or to the rough spot where the plaster is chipping away that beckons small fingers. Our cold, utilitarian eyes assess for order and function, cleanliness and safety. We assess how the space will bend to our will. Adults appraise, admire, search for connecting memories; they use the environment as their instrument. Children with no such worthy sensibilities are free to simply absorb experience. To their eyes, there is beauty in both flowers and weeds.

Aside from using the shower and our cars to become momentary singing stars and feeling hushed in libraries and churches, adults rarely assess spaces in terms of their potential for noise-making or movement. To children, forever being shushed and stilled, that dimension is no small matter: "Exercise of the body, of the voice, of the whole person in the production of the maximum possible commotion is an absolute necessity at some time or other to every healthy child. Noise is necessary, movement is necessary, and to be healthy these must be allowed to be exactly what they are—shapeless explosions of an over-plus of energy" (Lowenfeld, in Osmon, 1971, pp. 36-37).

It is easy for adults to forget how different the psychological atmosphere of childhood is that children carry to every setting: "How overwhelmingly frightening, devastatingly disappointing, and crushingly frustrating life can be, and is, for young children. As their bliss appears to see no ceiling, so their despair seems to know no floor" (Yamamoto, 1979, p. 64).

Please
by John Ciardi

*Someone about
As big as a mouse
Runs in and out
Of this house
TOO MUCH!*

*Someone about
As loud as a yell,
A bark, a shout,
A drum, and a bell—
CLANG! CLANG!*

*Yes, it might be you.
It just might be.
And if that's true,
Take a tip from me—
STOP IT!*

Photograph by Nancy P. Alexander

The behavior of young children illustrates the complexity of the environment. It takes them awhile to understand (operationally) the relationship between space, time, and roles. A child's (or an adult's) social indiscretion is often behavior not appropriate in a particular time and place: proudly waving to parents while performing in a play, playing in a busy corridor, talking loudly in church, being social in an elevator, or expecting life at child care to mirror life at home (e.g., a three year old's nap time

bottle or toleration of finger feeding). This incomplete understanding of or ability to follow the rules of the context is, of course, also a problem for any of us trying to maneuver within an unfamiliar culture or setting.

The speed with which children develop has implications for the environment. A *new* child can hatch at any moment, suddenly interested in something never before compelling—light switches, climbers, friends, demolition.

Children's environments are accommodations to individual and cultural differences and trade-offs of adults' needs and children's needs; trade-offs of safety and risk, challenge and convenience; and, most important, trade-offs between individual needs and desires and those of the group. As early childhood professionals who design or adapt settings, it is our job to make evident the trade-offs and come up with what seem to be the most workable alternatives. What prepares us for this role?

Who Am I to Judge?

All of us inhabit settings, and much can be learned through observing and analyzing our own reactions to built spaces. How do we feel approaching this building or inside this waiting room? What objects call out to us and lodge in our memory? In carrying out the business of daily life, how do spatial arrangements assist or get in the way? Confusing corridors, unmarked intersections, windows that refuse to open, being left-handed in a right-handed world—one can easily assemble an Andy Rooneyish list of environmental obstacles.

Moreover, all of us, to a degree, are designers and environmental engineers. We design our bedrooms, our kitchens, our work spaces, and our classrooms based on a set of conscious or unconscious, sometimes contradictory, goals. The living room can be a place to entertain, to show off our wealth, or to crash after a hard day. In some homes the television occupies a shrine-like presence and is the central focus of all available seating. In others the living room is a showplace—the lighting, the walls, the location of furniture are selected to focus attention on knickknacks or trophies, photographs of grandchildren, erudite books, or art objects.

Kitchens can be both workrooms and rooms to live and, perhaps, to entertain as well. The layout of appliances and storage, the organization of materials and utensils, and the traffic

---

Spaces for Children: The Built Environment and Child Development by Carol Weinstein and Thomas David (New York: Plenum Press, 1987) is an invaluable source of information to complement the contents of this volume. In chapters by the major scholars and researchers in the field, nearly all aspects of the issues related to children and environment are addressed based on all of the available research. Included are concrete ideas and case studies about design of home, center, and playground spaces for able-bodied children and children with disabilities.

patterns will determine whether it is a good work space. Active cooks tend to arrange kitchens to minimize the effort; the kitchen resembles a workshop, the tools of the trade visible and accessible. If the kitchen is used to entertain, some convenience may be sacrificed, either to display copper cookware or trendy appliances (the Cuisinart is visible, the vegematic is not) or to keep utensils out of sight.

In designing or adapting our settings, we constantly have to make the trade-offs any designer encounters—cost, limited space, convenience versus display, safety codes, and balancing the requirements of different users. In our homes, we, in some fashion, ask ourselves how it feels to live here: to cook, to eat, to rest, to play, to love, to grow older. We begin with what we want, the lives we want to lead, and apply our resources as best we can. The *we* includes all who live within or, more likely, all who have a say in the matter.

Everyone has experienced a home. Homes are places for living. **Child care programs are also places where people live**—people eat, sleep, use the bathroom, work, play, and do everything that is done in a home, except reproduce.

Less understood is that homes can be models for children's learning: "Our most effective mothers do not devote the bulk of their day to rearing their young children. Most of them are far too busy to do so; several of them, in fact, have part-time jobs. What they seem to do, often without knowing exactly why, is to perform excellently the functions of designer and consultant. By that I mean they design a physical world, mainly in the home, that is beautifully suited to nurturing the burgeoning curiosity of the one to three year old. It is full of small, manipulatable, visually detailed objects—

some of which were originally designed for young children (toys), others normally used for other purposes (plastic refrigerator containers, bottle caps, baby food jars and covers, shoes). It contains things to climb, such as chairs, benches, sofas, and stairs. It includes a rich variety of interesting things to look at, such as television, people, and the aforementioned types of physical objects" (White and Watts, 1973, pp. 242-243).

The value of the home as a natural laboratory for learning is not true just for very young children. White's observations are supported by the research of Elizabeth Prescott (1978) and Moncrief Cochran (in Bronfenbrenner, 1979) on family child care. Homes, in general, probably tend to be richer in opportunities for exploration and discovery than child care centers. However, this may be changing. As Francis Wardle has noted, the extent to which the recurring cultural ideal (promulgated by Proctor and Gamble et al.) of a spotlessly clean and tidy home is realized, and the trend toward smaller, more efficient homes both reduce the value of the home as a learning environment. (Television, of course, can negate either home or center as a place for discovery.)

Good space for children (and adults) is the result of asking the right questions to establish goals and thinking through the important feelings and behaviors that are to be supported. Good space doesn't force behavior contrary to goals, such as dependency, or overemphasize unimportant goals, such as a tolerance for waiting (Prescott, Jones, and Kritchevsky, 1972).

A child care setting faces some of the same tasks faced at home, and inhabitants should ask a question asked at home: "How does it feel to live and work here all day, day after day?" That

question is often shunted aside by "What do we do here?" and "What should we accomplish?" These are critical questions; but without asking the former, we have lost sight of the primacy of the day-to-day quality of life.

Exercises

1. List settings where you feel relaxed and relatively at home and settings where you feel awkward. Look for elements that seem to affect your feelings.

2. Pick a child you know well. In what ways does he or she behave differently across settings? Do you know an adult who behaves very differently across settings?

3. Select a work setting, a living setting, and another setting. Analyze the message of the space, and look for elements that seem to work for or against you or the other inhabitants in realizing the goals of the setting.

— Chapter Two —

The Lives of Children

"We wove a web in childhood, a web of sunny air."
Emily Bronte

Monday morning, 7:00 AM. Three year old Jenny and her mother are on the bus to child care. The ride holds few surprises; they have made the 20 minute expedition every day for two years. Jenny's day begins at 6:15 AM and usually ends around 8:00 PM. Sometimes her mom has to attend a meeting, and then she doesn't get to sleep before 9:30 or 10:00. Jenny typically spends about ten hours a day at the center.

Just about the time Jenny is having breakfast at the center, four year old Denise is tumbling out of bed. Three days a week she attends a morning preschool; most other times she is home with her mother and baby brother. She has attended programs at the YWCA and the library, but generally she plays around the house and goes along on errands. Denise is rarely up past 8:00 (a situation she finds deplorable), unless her father is home and lets her stay up later.

Seven year old Felipe is plucked out of bed at 6:00 to make the 7:20 school bus. Three times a week after school he meanders the seven blocks to his Aunt Rosie's. The other days he has soccer or Cub Scouts. His 9:00 bedtime is sometimes extended, which he can easily live with, unless the reason is to finish homework (a

recent intrusion into his comfortable life). There are nights he stays at Aunt Rosie's, if both his mother and father have to work.

More children's days could be added: seven year old Julie is home alone from 8:00 to 8:30 AM and 3:00 to 4:30 PM; three year old Jamal spends the entire day with his mother; four year old Latonia and Barry attend the family day care home down the street; eight week old Jesse attends an infant center for nine hours a day. Widen the scope to a week or a year—summer programs, weekends, and vacations at Dad's, music lessons, babysitters, and so on. Some children need a "Week at a Glance" calendar more than their parents do.

To critics like David Elkind (**The Hurried Child**, 1984), and Valerie Suransky (**The Erosion of Childhood**, 1982) "the landscape of child-hood" (Suransky, 1982), today for many children is bleak. Many children are in a world of organized experiences in managed groups almost from birth—child care, preschool, after-school programs, camps, swim/gym , sports teams, and various classes. Children are organized, scheduled, and programmed according to parental needs for care and social forces encouraging ever earlier schooling. Perhaps in many small towns and close knit neighborhoods, children today still go everywhere and see everything: the world of work and commerce and vacant lots. But, for the most part, we have

institutionalized our children—"Why do we continue to remove children from the center of our lives and relegate them to the confines of age-segregated institutions?" (Suransky, p. 189).

We have done it for admirable reasons: to keep them safe while we work and go to school, to give them opportunities for learning and new experiences. Like it or not, trends in housing, work, leisure, crimes against children, and nearly all aspects of contemporary life seem to make institutionalization inevitable in all modern societies. It is hard to quarrel with any of the children's programs individually, but the net effect is disturbing and warrants attention.

We are a society perhaps more attentive to children than any other; but it is a limited and narcissistic attention—most often directed toward parents and children as consumers. Organized around children's *needs* and desires and parents' desires for their children, goods and experiences are packaged, bought, and sold: Cabbage Patch dolls; Suzuki violins; parent-child classes; sports, computer, and language camps. Needs are defined or created and marketed; goods and services rushed in to fill the gap. Sylvia Ashton-Warner's lament about New Zealand 25 years ago, a society only a mile down a road now much further traveled, speaks to the results:

"The noticeable thing in New Zealand society is the body of people with their inner resources atrophied. Seldom have they had to reach inward to grasp the thing that they wanted. Everything, from material requirements to ideas, is available ready-made. . . . They can buy life itself from the film and radio-canned life. . . . They've dried up. From babyhood they had shiny toys put in their hands, and in the kindergarten and infant rooms bright pictures and gay materials. Why conceive of anything of their own? There has not been the need. . . . The vast expanses of mind that could

Photograph by Francis Wardle

have been alive with creative activity are now no more than empty vaults that must, for comfort's sake, be filled with non-stop radio, and their conversation consists of a list of platitudes and cliches" (Ashton-Warner, 1963, pp. 85-86).

Adults and children no longer share the same world. We have fenced children off from our world. Rita Liljestrom, speaking of Swedish prechools, lays bare the issue: "Let's admit there is something dubious about setting up special sanctuaries for children, about putting children in special preserves with adults who are specialized in looking after youngsters in a segregated child milieu with special furniture and toys for children . . . in a very real sense the preschool can be seen as expressing a hostility to children in the social development" (Liljestrom, 1977). While we may be in an "age of childhood," Ivan Illich points out, "if society were to outgrow its age of childhood, it would have to become livable for the young" (Illich, 1970, p. 41).

What is missing? For many children, it is a sense of the variety of life: the real world of people and nature and machines and an opportunity to explore that world and be a part of it. In the past, children did not need special places for play. They had more free time in houses, backyards, vacant lots, fields, and streets. They lived amidst shops and tradespeople and mothers and fathers working in and around the home. In the past, many children not only saw what their parents did for a living, but often played some role in it (for some, a major, sometimes overwhelming role). And many children had much more time and freedom in their lives to "mess about," captured beautifully by Kenneth Grahame in **The Wind in the Willows** (1980, p. 5):

"Nice? It's the only thing," said the Water Rat solemnly, as he leaned forward for his stroke. "Be-

Photograph by John Gehan

lieve me, my young friend, there is nothing—absolutely nothing—half so worth doing as simply messing about in boats. Simply messing," he went on dreamily: "messing—about—in—boats; messing—"

"Look ahead, Rat! " cried the Mole suddenly.

It was too late. The boat struck the bank full tilt. The dreamer, the joyous oarsman, lay on his back at the bottom of the boat, his heels in the air.

"—about in boats—or with boats," the rat went on composedly, picking himself up with a pleasant laugh. "In or out of 'em, it doesn't matter. Nothing seems to really matter, that's the charm of it. Whether you get away, or whether you don't; whether you arrive at your destination or whether you reach someplace else, or whether you never get anywhere at all, you're always busy, and you never

Dreams

"You don't get far without a dream to lure. A dream keeps you looking forward, whereas the dreamless are inclined to look backward on some former dream defused. Dreams are a living picture in the mind generating energy. They are at once direction finders and sources of power. A dream makes a life worthwhile. Life takes its quality from the glow of a dream. You can lie awake at night beneath the weight of a thousand atmospheres if there is no dream to lure; to look ahead to, plan for, fill your mind with, pretend to be real. To dream what you will do tomorrow, next week, next year and of what you hope the future brings, something that sings. You cannot sleep without the arms of a dream enclosing you between the sheets; you get out of bed and make tea wondering whence the universe, why there is life without the comfort of a dream.

But where do you find the capacity to dream: is it something to be bought in a shop; is it a jewel to be stolen, a prize in a lottery to be won? . . . Dreams are a blast from the living imagery exploding with profligacy. There are no limits to the dreams a mind can conceive, but only the whole mind has the mechanism to dream. We need to dream. . . . Man does not live by bread alone but by dreams also. Yet no dreams combust from imagery which is sedated or dead; not the kind with the power to lure you. Man does not die from breadlessness but dreamlessness also. Only the smell of decomposition haunts the house where once dreams were born. Boredom is the occupier now who swallows up life with a yawn."

from **Spearpoint**, by Sylvia Ashton-Warner (1972, p. 87)

In **Teacher** (1963) and **Spearpoint** (1972), Sylvia Ashton-Warner writes passionately of the minds and souls of children. Her concern and her talent lies in drawing on the child's inner resources to teach—his hope, his fear, his joy, his untamed energy.

"Yes I'm a disciplinarian. It's just that I like the lid off. I like seeing what's there. I like the unpredictability and gaity and interesting people, however small, and funny things happening and wild things happening and sweet, and everything that life is, uncovered. . . . I like the true form of *living, even in school* " (**Teacher**, 1963, p. 93).

Photograph by Nancy P. Alexander

and discover what it is made of and how it works.

Kenneth Eble, in **A Perfect Education** (1966), describes a perfect education as one that "proceeds by surprises and the promise of other surprises, one that offers most opportunity for discovery" (p. 17). He observes that nature is the area in which our urban society is most lacking. "Even though our tremendously rich, tremendously mobile society gives far more people access to the more spectacular areas of nature than ever before, nature is not an important part of daily experience" (p. 21).

He laments this loss because "it was nature, and it, above all, was to be discovered, bounteous, mysterious, unmindful, neither judging nor cautioning nor limiting, but mostly, for children at least, infinitely inviting. . . . Zoos and public parks are wonderful as museums . . . . Yet for discovery one needs some things unmanaged,

do anything in particular; and when you've done it there's always something else to do, and you can do it if you like, but you'd much better not."

It is not just that aspects of children's quality of life has changed, but their education has

changed as well. Mark Twain said, "I never let schooling interfere with my education." What if there is only schooling? What education is lost? It is in messing about that children dream dreams and discover what they might be. Messing about is when children act on the world

undesigned until a child's eye imposes a pattern" (Eble, 1966, p. 21).

"Unmanaged, undesigned until a child imposes a pattern by his or her actions"—here is precisely what is shrinking in the modern child's experience with both the physical and social world. *Everything* is managed and patterned and scheduled and governed by the patterns imposed by the sensible dictates of regulation, insurance, the bottom line, and the compromises of group living. Cut off from the real world of society—a world of work and machines and production, unmanaged nature, social relationships with a wide variety of adults and children in different settings—and fewer and fewer opportunities to simply *mess about*, follow one's own inclinations and dream, more and more children of each successive generation are losing opportunities for delight and wonder.

The Nature of Schooling

One piece of the institutionalization of childhood is the downward extension of schooling. It is not early learning that draws fire but early schooling, that is the downward extension of School (with a capital S), the formal institution of education with all the trappings—instruction, testing, and regimentation. As both the need for child care and the pressure for a head start (either to catch up or to get out ahead) increases, the concern about institutionalization grows.

Criticisms of School in society are constant, and the nature of the criticism tends to be cyclical. Currently, the concerns of the Progressives in the early part of the century, restated in the 1960's by the open school movement, are out of fashion, but still compelling. Unlike much of early education, schools focus on teaching, not learning, and are out of step with the insights of

Piaget, Bruner, Dewey, and numerous others. There is all too much truth to Jonathon Kozol's scathing observation that "school is the ether of our lives," a place where submission and containment are dominant concerns, where mind and body, talking and doing, thinking and feeling, facts and ideas are too often kept separate.

Charles Silberman, in **Crisis in the Classroom** (1970), a report of a three year study of American public schools for the Carnegie Corporation conducted while open education was supposedly sweeping the schools, said that, on the contrary, most schools are mindless, joyless, rigid, and petty, and that they destroy the hearts and minds of many of the children in them. As Illich points out, "School initiates young people into a world where everything can be measured, including their imaginations, and, indeed, man himself" (Illich, 1970, p. 57). What Elkind calls the industrialization of school is, in fact, he points out, out of step with the needs of modern society: "Schools in ostrichlike fashion, are responding to the challenge of poor school performance by regression. *Back to basics*. Back to old methods and old materials. Back to a factory emphasis on worker (teacher) productivity and quality control (pupil competency) that is at odds with the major thrust of modern industry" (Elkind, 1984, p. 48).

Like it or not, most schools are large institutions, enclosed within larger bureaucracies. Michael Katz points out in **Class, Bureaucracy, and Schools** (1971), this bureaucratization was not an inevitable development, a point very much worth noting because child care and early education programs may be at the same crossroads. Bureaucracies value order, efficiency, and uniformity, not responsiveness, variety, flexibility, or creativity—values which seem paramount in institutions of care and learning.

Early childhood education historically for the most part has avoided becoming School. The lack of large bureaucratic structures, the tradition of Froebel, Montessori, the progressive nursery school movement, and the influence of Piaget resulted in the early education mainstream espousing child centered, active learning, experientially rich programs. But the advent of Head Start and the child care explosion, the growing size of child care centers, and the heightened concern for early learning has not only brought into early childhood programs people whose training or lack of training results in elementary schools as the common reference point, but a new concern for early academics.

A further downward extension of School is an increasing reality. A study of 100 child care programs in Los Angeles concluded that at least a quarter of the programs fall into a category described as sit down, shut up, and count to 100. **The Los Angeles Times** (Olenick, 1986) reported that children as young as two years old were spending entire mornings seated at tables or desks reciting the alphabet, counting to 200, and drawing letters with pencils.

It should be noted that many see nothing wrong with this and other trends and view modern childhood as a movement toward full realization of the potential of children and adults. Childhood learning can be greatly expanded using new knowledge of early learning potential and new technology. A vision of Doman's (1984) superbabies has replaced early reading as the new "it's never too early to begin instruction" phenomenon. Montessori's popularity as *serious* preschool is extended downward and homeward. In **Teaching Montessori in the Home**, Elizabeth Hainstock exhorts: "Too often the precious fertile years from birth to six years of age are wasted by parents and teachers who feel that the child is too young to learn. In many cases it is actually *they* who are too lazy to teach. . . . A child must not be allowed to spend the most formative years of his life sitting like a nonentity in his sandbox. By the age of two he has progressed far beyond the stage for idle play and baby talk" (Hainstock, 1968, p. 12).

It is not hard to look back at the childhoods of Tom Sawyer, Laura Ingalls Wilder, and Beaver Cleaver and regret the loss of connections to the community young and old, the world of work, experience with the natural world, and the languid unscheduled days of summer. We, of course, don't fondly remember the ten hour a day child labor, the neglect, the mortality, the back-breaking daily work, or ask the questions Ibsen might have asked about the underside of June Cleaver's placid existence. For many children, childhood has always been, and still is, an immersion in a very grey, grim real world of toil, hunger, and indifference. But that sad reality doesn't change the fact that, as the Buffalo Springfield sang, "There is something happening here, what it is ain't exactly clear" (Stills, 1969).

When we think of our own early childhoods—happy or unhappy, chaotic or relaxed—or perhaps even more powerful, the imagined childhoods we might have had or wish for our children, what images surface—what places, experiences with people, moments of pure pleasure or wonder? For most of us, images of fluorescently lit group times, worksheets, Legos, magic circles, easel time, and so on cannot hold their own with memories of secret places in the home or yard or alley, intoxicatingly serious or silly moments with our friends unwatched (we thought) by adults, real conversations and physical intimacy with adults important to us—times when we were not a small pebble on a

---

"They Told Me I Could Sit In That Chair"

To some, school is a comforting source of security. In **Migrants, Sharecroppers, and Mountaineers** (1972, p. 67), Robert Coles writes about Peter, a seven year old child of migrant workers, whose parents travel up and down the East Coast. He rarely has a place he can claim as his own for any length of time:

"To a boy like Peter a school building, even an old and not very attractively furnished one, is a new world—of large windows and solid floors and doors and plastered ceilings and walls with pictures on them, and a seat that one has, that one is given, that one is supposed to own, or virtually own, for day after day, almost as a right of some sort. After his first week in the first grade Peter said this: 'They told me I could sit in that chair and they said the desk, it was for me, and that every day I should come to the same place, to the chair she said was mine for as long as I'm there in that school—that's what they say, the teachers, anyway.'"

---

large beach. Children are getting cut off from a world of experience much more widely available to them in the past, experience that may be crucial to development, that also represents a quality of life.

Criticisms like the above do not lend themselves to easy solutions. Society is what it is, and social and economic forces move it in directions difficult to arrest. What can be done is to consider what we feel is important in a childhood, *what really matters*, and in the piece of childhood that we affect—homes, centers, camps—look to establishing settings of space, time, and people that provide those experiences to children.

How Children Learn

Beyond all doubt, young children learn from action. Whether children *construct* their world as Piaget maintains, or *actively absorb* it, in Montessori terms, it is action and interaction with people and things that count.

"To know an object, to know an event, is not simply to look at it and make a mental copy or an image of it. To know an object is to act on it. To know is to modify, to transform the object and to understand the process of this transformation and as a consequence to understand the way the object is constructed . . ." (Piaget, in Jones, 1978, p. 6).

In **To Understand Is to Invent** (1974), Piaget wrote, "To understand is to discover, or reconstruct by discovering . . ." (p. 20) and "every new truth to be learned [is to] be rediscovered or at least reconstructed by the student, and not simply imparted to him" (p. 15).

"If you watch a child of three, you will see that he is always playing with something. This means that he is working out, and making conscious, something that his unconscious mind had earlier absorbed. Through this outward experience, in the guise of a game, he examines those things and impressions that he has taken in unconsciously. He becomes fully conscious

> *"Life is either a daring adventure or it is nothing."*
> Helen Keller

The continuing value in the writings of John Holt, George Dennison, Jonathan Kozol, Herbert Kohl, James Herndon, and others of the open school movement of the 1960's and 1970's lies in their passionate focus on what matters.

"Each of us has a mental model of the world as we know it. That model INCLUDES OURSELVES. We are in our own model. We remember what we have done, how we felt about it, how we felt about it afterward. We have a sense of who we are and what we can do.

We have feelings about ourselves, the world we know, and the world we know about. These feelings depend on and very powerfully affect each other.... It is impossible to draw a line between what I know about the world and how I feel about it....

The person who is not afraid of the world wants understanding, competence, mastery. He wants to make his mental model better, both more complete, in the sense of having more in it, and more accurate, in being more like the world out there, a better guide to what is happening and may happen. He wants to know the score ... he wants answers. Even if they are not the answers he expected, or hoped for, even if they are the answers he dislikes, they advance him into the world. He can use any experience, however surprising or unpleasant, to adjust his mental model of the world. And so he is willing, and eager, to expose himself to the reality of things as they are. The more he tries, the more he learns, however his trials come out.

This is the spirit of the very young child, and the reason he learns so well.

The fearful person, on the other hand, does not care whether his model is accurate. What he wants is to feel safe. He wants a model that is reassuring, simple, unchanging. Many people spend their lives building such a model, rejecting all experiences, ideas, and information that do not fit. The trouble with such models is that they don't do what a good model should do—tell us what to expect. The people who live in a dream world are always being rudely awakened. They cannot see life's surprises as sources of useful information. They must see them as attacks" (Holt, 1970, pp. 32-35).

from **What Do I Do Monday**, by John Holt

As children's lives become increasingly institutionalized, it helps to keep in mind that what happens to the spirit of the young child has far more consequences than the specific content of the schooling.

and constructs the future man, by means of his activities.... He does it through his hands, by experience, first in play, then through work" (Montessori, 1967, p. 27).

The child is wonderfully prepared for active learning from birth. Children approach the world with all senses open, all motors running— the world is an invitation to experience. Their job is to develop and test all their equipment, make sense of the confusing world of people and things and unseen mysterious forces and relationships like gravity, number, and love.

Childhoods for Children

"Childhood is the world of miracle and wonder: as if creation rose and bathed in light, out of the darkness, utterly new and fresh and astonishing. The end of childhood is when things cease to astonish us. When the world seems familiar, when we have got used to existence, one has become an adult."
Eugene Ionesco

Early childhood professionals think a lot about children in making particular programs work. The focus is on children's needs, development, and curriculum. But suppose the preoccupation with these and like notions were suspended for a while, long enough to simply think about childhoods—children's lives in a broad context. Of course, childhood is made up of elements that fit into all of these notions; but perhaps by shifting the focus, new insight may be gained into what it is like to be a child today and what our part is in improving children's lives.

In every culture, childhood is a special time. It is perhaps the most powerful period of our lives. Our experiences form the foundation of what we become, the core of our being—our ability to learn, our sense of ourselves in relation

Photograph by Shawn Connell

to the world of nature, of people, of things. It is a time for powerful experiences that forever fuel the scientist, the poet, the artist, and the imagination within us. Recapturing now and then childhood's wonder secures a driving force for grownup thoughts. It is a time that most of us draw on forever for moments of warmth and security. And some of us can trace the doubt, sadness, or nagging fear that underlies our lives to emptiness or hurts in our childhood.

Rainbow In The Sky
by William Wordsworth

*My heart leaps up when I behold
A rainbow in the sky:
So was it when my life began;
So is it now I am a man;
So be it when I shall grow old,
Or let me die!*

"I do not know what I may appear to the world; but to myself I seem to have been only like a boy playing on the seashore, and diverting myself in now and then finding a smoother pebble or a prettier shell than ordinary, while the great ocean of truth lay all undiscovered before me."
Issac Newton

• **Children need an environment rich in experience**

"The child's mode of being in the world is such that the world becomes an invitation. It is things in the beckoning world that invite the child, that awaken his curiosity, that invoke . . . him to make sense of that multitude of experiences lying beyond; in short to become, through his play, both an actor and a meaning maker."
Suransky (1982, p. 39)

Photograph by John Gehan

There is a world of things for every child to interact with if permitted: some living, some hard and cold, some tiny, some shiny. Even the poorest environment is rich with the stuff of experience if made safe.

• **Children need a childhood rich in play**

"The world confronting the child is, as William James called it, a 'great blooming confusion' which the child has to organize by putting into it some orderliness and meaning. . . . The big adult world, the macrocosm, is too large, too complicated, and often threatening to the child who cannot cope with it; and so he focuses on the microcosmic world of play, as Erik Erikson stated some years ago, a world that . . . he can encompass through toys and play materials. To these he imputes his often childish beliefs and expectations and also his feelings, but by repeated explorations he gradually relinquishes some of his more fantastic beliefs. . . . When he tries to make the world conform to his childish beliefs and expectations, he is repeatedly confronted with the actuality of situations and events, and ever-present . . . threats and sometimes painful consequences. But he can do this restructuring of the world only if he is permitted and encouraged to try, to persist until he learns what can and cannot be done; and play provides a minimum of risks and . . . penalties for mistakes. Play . . . is a way of learning by trial and error to cope with the actual world."
Frank (quoted in Caplan and Caplan, 1973, pp. 107-108)

As widely observed by Montessori and others, play is children's work; it is their *job*. But as David Elkind pointed out: "Children need to be given an opportunity for pure play as well as for work" (1984, p. 197). For Elkind, play is the antidote for the "hurried child"; play is nature's way of dealing with stress for children, as well as adults.

Play is self-initiated, spontaneous, and voluntary; the child must remain in control because the play is building upon her understandings, her cognitive structures, her stress. Play can be facilitated and encouraged, but it can't be forced. That is work, which is also necessary in childhood.

Photograph by Jean Wallech

• **Children need a childhood rich in teaching**

Play does not teach children how to cross the street safely, the ins and outs of written language, or how to multiply fractions or bake a cake. Children need teaching. The most effective teaching accompanies active learning. Nathan issues:

"Direct learning—always through exploration, experimentation and the striving for fresh achievement—must in fact be steadily re-stimulated and aided to advance further and . . . further, until the help of planned teaching becomes its own next need and active demand."
(quoted in Weber, 1971, p. 188)

Play And Work

In **The Hurried Child** (1984), David Elkind looks at the consequences of the ideology that play is a child's work. In the process, he illustrates the sensitivity demanded of good teachers:

"Over the last ten years in America, the Montessori idea that play is the child's work has replaced the Freud/Piaget view that play and work are separate but complementary activities. . . . The following example illustrates how the dictum 'play is the child's work' gets translated into teaching practice: While observing in one of my favorite nursery schools, I watched a group of four and five-year-olds playing with some plastic dinosaurs. 'I am going to eat you up,' said one boy, moving his menacing looking beast close to his neighbor's. 'You will have to catch me first, I'm faster than you,' said the other boy as he ducked his smaller animal behind a wall of blocks. At this moment the teacher came over and decided to capitalize upon the children's interest (the so-called teaching moment) and to instruct them in some size concepts with the aid of the dinousaurs. 'Which one is larger?,' she asked. But the boys, clearly sniffing a teaching situation, quickly ended their dinosaur play and went on to other projects.

For young children dinosaurs have a great deal of symbolic significance—they are big and powerful . . . (they) provide children with a symbolic and safe way of dealing with the giants in their world, namely adults. Young children are constantly being told 'no' or 'don't do that' or 'leave that alone' or 'get away from there . . .' so children fight back indirectly and dinosaurs are stand-ins for controlling the world of giants . . . .

Certainly, children need to learn size comparisons and their spontaneous interests can be a cue to teaching topics. . . . At every turn they are learning social rules—how to behave in a restaurant, on a plane, at a friend's house, how to put clothes on. . . . Children are also learning basic concepts about space, time, number, color, and so on.

All of this, and much more social learning . . . is the real work of childhood. But children need to be given an opportunity for pure play as well as for work. If adults feel that each spontaneous interest of a child is an opportunity for a lesson, the child's opportunities for pure play are foreclosed. At all levels of development, whether at home or at school, children need the opportunity to play for play's sake" (pp. 195-196).

Piaget observed that many times experiments are performed in front of the child, but the child is not the experimenter. The teacher has to present children with materials and experiences that allow them to move ahead, not just allowing them to do anything. Children need experiences which offer new problems and subsequently lead to other problems.

Children need a mixture of direction and freedom.

There is one truth about every educational setting: teachers talk too much and listen too little. Children need teachers who know that what motivates children is to have *their* questions answered, not the teacher's. Teachers who stimulate more questions than they directly provide are truly teaching.

Photograph by Nancy P. Alexander

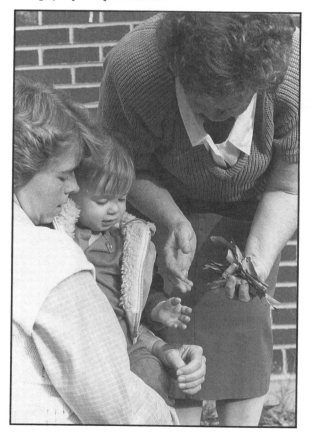

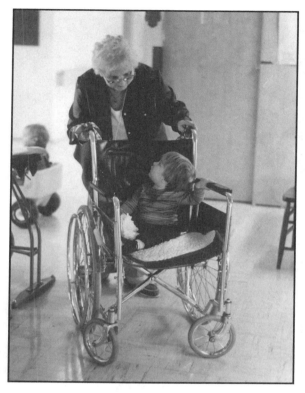

Photograph by Jean Wallech

• Children need a childhood rich with people

"A child is privileged, I think, to have different people moving in and out of the family circle: different in ages, occupations, places of residence, temperament, even in morality."
Eble (1966, p. 24)

It is through people that children become fully human members of society and discover how the social world works and their place in it.

A diversity of people both enriches childhood and prepares children for a widening world.

The Chinese Checker Players
by Richard Brautigan

When I was six years old
I played Chinese checkers
*   with a woman*
who was ninety-three years old.
She lived by herself
in an apartment down the hall
*   from ours.*
We played Chinese checkers
every Monday and Thursday nights.
While we played she usually talked
about her husband
who had been dead for seventy years,
and we drank tea and ate cookies
*   and cheated.*

• Children need a childhood where they are significant

"If he has the chance to develop manipulative and creative skills, to share in the social and practical life of his home, to be active in learning at school, he gradually comes . . . to believe that he can contribute to others as well as take from them, can make a real return for what has been done for him when he was weak and helpless. . . . Only active *learning, however, and active social participation and . . . interchange with those who love him and give him . . . responsibility can build up in him a confidence in his own future."*
Issacs (1948, p. 234)

"Every human being, whether child or adult, seems to require significance, that is "place in another's world. . . . The slightest sign of recognition from another at least confirms one's presence in his world."
Laing (**Self And Others**, 1969)

Photograph by Nancy P. Alexander

Children need *somewheres* to belong to, somewheres with familiar people and objects made substantial with the weight of meaningful past experiences of love, learning, laughter, and care. A child who attends a child care program from infancy through young school-age years will spend more time in child care than all the hours of schooling, and may spend more waking hours in child care than at home. Child care centers and homes are places where childhoods happen.

A child feels significant when his or her concerns are paid attention to and he or she is given some responsibility for something that matters.

Young children have increasingly few responsibilities in our society. They rarely experience caring for someone or something, or performing real work that is more than an exercise for their own development. In homes or in programs, children benefit from responsibilities as participating members of the setting.

• **Children need a childhood with places to call their own**

"It is utterly part of our nature to want roots, to need roots, to struggle for roots, for a sense of belonging, for some place that is recognized as MINE, as YOURS, as OURS."
Coles (1970, pp. 120-121)

"An authentic sense of place is above all that of being inside and belonging to YOUR place both as an individual and as a member of the community, and to know this without reflecting upon it."
Relph (1976, p. 65)

Automobile Mechanics
by Dorothy Baruch

Sometimes
 I help my dad
 Work on our automobile.
  We unscrew
  The radiator cap
   And we let some water run—
   Swish—from a hose
   Into the tank.

  And then we open up the hood
  And feed in oil
  From a can with a long spout.
  And then we take a lot of rags
  And clean all about.
   We clean the top
   And the doors
   And the fenders and the wheels
   And the windows and floors. . .

   We work **hard**
   My dad
   And I.

Photograph by Jean Wallech

Exercises

1. Search your memories of childhood for magical moments. What made them magical?

2. Compare your childhood to that of a child that you know. What experiences do they have that you didn't? What are they missing out on?

3. List feelings and behaviors that you associate with the words *school, play, learning.*

4. Can you remember the experience of "imposing a pattern on something undesigned or unmanaged"?

5. Search your memory for the rewarding moments you have had caring for or teaching children. What made them rewarding?

— Chapter Three —

Programs for Children

"I used to go to nursery school but now I go to day care 'cause my mom works. Everything's the same 'cept I get to eat and go to the bathroom a lot more now and we don't line up any more. And the hamster had babies."
Julie, age 4

Children go to child care homes and centers, nursery schools, before- and after-school programs, and summer programs, often in combinations. While the differences are not always clear to children like Julie, programs vary in terms of purpose (what they exist for), philosophy (how they view the child), objectives (what they want to do with children), and program structure. Some programs have a precise set of objectives or curriculum—children reading at a certain level, obtaining certain motor or social skills; others simply strive for parent satisfaction and happy, active days.

Schools, from nursery through college, exist to provide education. Because children always need some care and because school provides a place for children during some of the work day, acknowledged or not, school serves a child care function. Child care programs, homes and centers, exist to provide care for the children of absent parents. Because children's settings are learning environments, again whether acknowledged or not, education is an important element of care.

The length of time spent in the setting is obviously a factor in whether the unacknowledged elements are particularly important. If a child spends all day in a setting where little attention is given to his needs for care and nurturing in one instance, or learning in another, it is of different consequence than his spending just a few hours a day in either situation.

In a 1985 forum on play, Millie Almy raised the question: "Should the nursery school, or educational institution, assume responsibility for an activity (play) that healthy children are going to initiate and carry on regardless of whether or not they happen to be enrolled in a nursery school?" She (and I) answered the question "yes." But in an all day setting (if the child spends little time at home) the question is not even appropriate; if not in the child care setting, then where and when? The need for play in the educational setting may also be growing as television watching replaces play time for many children.

Another important question that ought to be asked more often is how much can children take? Children, like adults, vary in their capacity to withstand stress. From birth, infants manifest differences in energy levels and these differences persist throughout life. Hans Selye in **The Stress of Life** (1978) discusses "adaptation energy" that enables us to cope with daily life. We each have a reservoir of energy that we call into play periodically to get through each day, making it until that *last straw*. When it is gone, we come apart—we lose our ability to hold together our physical and psychological resources to maintain our good humor, competence, and physical well-being. The result may be a tantrum, a headache, a blue funk, or an exhausted sleep. If a child spends the day in a program (or programs) and has to accommodate to routines, stimulation, and expectations with inadequate opportunities to recharge, the child's parents experience the consequences of the child's depleted resources, at a time when their own reservoirs of adaptation energy may well be low. Considering the loud concern for developing strong parent-child bonds for children in child care, a relaxed day, in and of itself, should be given a much higher priority.

In this book, the emphasis is on creating settings for children and adults where children are cared for in a way that allows them to be lifelong learners, lovers, and responsible, thoughtful human beings. It does no good to lament the loss of the past. What we can do is think critically about our places, our programs, and our roles in terms of the contexts of the lives that today's children are leading. Putting our piece of the child's childhood into context is critical. A program that occupies two or three hours of a child's day faces far fewer issues of institutionalization—regimentation, autonomy, privacy, and comfort—than all-day programs

Life at the Mall

The downtown or main street formed the core of a city. As suburbs grew farther away from the core of the city, they seemed to lose their sense of place. The shopping mall gave suburbs a core, a center, a sense of place—but a far different sense of place than the downtown.

The mall is a carefully measured life represented by trees and shrubs without dirt, or falling leaves, or animal life. Bird sounds may be piped in, amidst the safe cheery music bearing no chords of ethnicity or individual style. There is food to be consumed, magically produced through invisible deliveries and garbage pickup. There are no shadows, no discordant noises, no signs of age or wear.

People are measured, too. There is the entry requirement of an automobile. *The streets and lanes* of the mall are private property, not bound by strict requirements of free speech, or the hapless acceptance of the homeless, or those in pain engaged in dialogues with their tormented inner selves. Unlike city streets, nobody has a right to be there, least of all those who may assert their struggling or divergent reality upon us.

It is a *cool* setting, teeming with neutrality. It is smooth, lacking edges or ideas that delight us or jar us. Life outside the mall is an adventure because of chance encounters of sight, sound, smells, and people. In a mall, adventure is restricted to the buffet of abundant goods and services to be consumed.

The deadening lack of adventure in the suburban mall has led in different directions as malls have evolved. The *restoration* malls—usually in cities—that restore factories and decaying market areas have retained some sensory delights through the use of original building facades, skylights, brick, water and wood, and the fearless toleration of sidewalk dining and ethnic foods. Another direction increasingly found in malls is to add to the number of consumable amusements at the mall. Far beyond more movies, game rooms, and restaurants, malls are adding amusement parks and zoos.

Epcot Center in Florida is the ultimate extension of the mall; a *malled* community with housing, work, amusement all included. As Relph (1976, p. 97) points out:

"These fantasy lands are in part places of escaping from drab, corrupt, inefficient reality; they are also places of inspiration in which everyone is nice and everyone smiles. But in addition they appear to be to some extent utopias made real which provide *guaranteed* excitement, amusement, or interest, while eliminating the effort and chance of travel or imagination."

So what does this have to do with child care? Shopping malls are cities turned outside in. Child care settings are homes turned inside out. The issues in our common spaces of how to balance life—with its joyful, but frequently messy and disturbing, realities—and our desires for a safe existence—with its seductively numbing sterility—are played out in both malls and child care programs. We can learn from malls and other public places. Critics have called shopping malls *canned life*. Can we afford to have *canned childhoods*?

Photograph by Shawn Connell

(unless a child's day is spent in a series of short programs). Children, like adults, can and need to conform to group life some of the time, but not all of the time.

If professionals take cues from both an understanding of child development and our knowledge of the lives that children are leading, the environments professionals provide can enhance childhoods. Perhaps some programs would look less like schools and more like homes and children's museums or like fields and parks. We might develop (or adapt) varied places that resonate with a genuine sense of place—of beauty, variety, with elements of surprise and mystery—places where adults and children delight at times in simply being together, messing about, and working at the tasks that daily living requires. The Jennys and Denises and Felipes and all the others will neither be hurried or forced to accommodate to early institutional living nor lose out on opportunities for early learning and socialization.

Program Structure

Elizabeth Prescott's research (see page 40) makes clear that the physical environment and

experiences offered to children tend to be associated with program structure. Closed centers offer the hardest setting and the fewest opportunities for sensory play, exploration, discovery, and experiences with a range of materials and people. Open structure* centers are significantly higher in these dimensions, but family day care homes are rated the highest.

This book is written with a bias towards open structured programs. An open structure represents an ideology that views the child as a responsible, active participant in his own learning. An organized, planned environment and clear, consistent expectations provide the greatest likelihood that the program will have the flexibility to respond to individual differences for care and learning. In addition, an open structure is more likely to encourage multi-age and peer relationships.

This is not to say that teacher-directed activities are inappropriate in open settings, or that open structures are appropriate for all programs. Program structures grow out of the space, the staffing resources, and the philosophy of staff and parents. Poorly run open structures can become warehouses with huge cracks for children to fall through, places of entertainment not education, or permissive places where children run riot. Further, some children (and some excellent teachers and caregivers) thrive in closed structures.

On balance, an open structure is more likely to allow the opportunity for adults to **be with**

---

*Open structure programs are not the same as open *space* plan programs. Programs with self-contained classrooms may, within each classroom, use an open-structure forum.

children, to care, teach, and converse rather than to manage and instruct. Children need what Rollo May called the "full human presence" of others to overcome the feelings of insignificance that can come from being small, in a crowd, and new to the world. In addition, in an open structure, multi-aging, bringing in other adults, and going out of the program to take advantage of the real world tend to be more likely. An open structure is a step toward deinstitutionalizing the institution and regaining pieces of childhoods lost.

The Adult Role

"Be what you would have your pupils become. All else is mockery and sham."
Thomas Carlyle

Settings can easily be designed to reduce people to dense and boring functionaries, warm blooded laps, or teaching machines who *do* without much need to think. There can be fine lines between settings that work for the inhabitants and build in support, and settings that are *teacher-proof* (designed to work a certain way no

Photograph by Jean Wallech

Open and Closed Program Structures

The most extensive body of reseach on child care settings has been done by Elizabeth Prescott, Elizabeth Jones, and their colleagues at Pacific Oaks in Pasadena. They have spent over 20 years studying how programs structure children's experience in early childhood environments and "who thrives in group day care" (Prescott, 1978, 1979, 1984; Prescott and Jones, 1972; Prescott, Jones, and Kritchevsky, 1972; Prescott, Jones, Millich, and Haselhorf, 1975). They found that "you could classify the arrangement of people-doing-things-in-places in child care settings in one of five ways" (Prescott, 1984, pp. 59-61):

Teacher-directed group activity: The teacher leads an activity in which the children engage as a group, such as story time, music, or rhythm games. Children are expected or required . . . to participate.

Teacher-directed individual activity: The teacher has planned an activity in which all the children are again expected to participate but that is carried out individually by each . . . child, such as pasting, doing puzzles, or drawing.

Free play: Children are free to choose among all activities available in the room or yard. . . . The teacher has not made prior preparations but uses the play area as it exists.

Free choice: Children are free to choose among all the activities available; however, the teacher has made prior preparation and has set up one or more activities especially for this play period. . . .

Official transitions: These periods provide a spacer between activities required by the adult.

Prescott found that "center programs appear to jell around the selection of certain activity formats. In centers where staff feel it is important for children to be engaged in activities of their own choosing, free choice will be the most frequently used format. In centers where adults feel that they should make most of the decisions around how children spend their time, teacher-directed activity formats are frequently used, usually alternating with free play; free choice is seldom used. We have called these alternate types of program structure 'open' and 'closed'. The decision about the use of particular types of activity formats turns out to be a powerful predictor of the use of the physical environment, the behavior of teachers, and the experiences that are made available to children. . . . Centers that use an open program format look very different along a variety of dimensions than centers that use a closed program format. Either format, if thoughtfully developed, can produce a rich experience for the children" (1984, pp. 59-60).

Neither format, in and of itself, is good or bad. "The advantages of effective closed structure lie in its clarity of expectations, its opportunities for a child to experience him- or herself as an important part of a group, and the practice involved in attending to adult input. Its hazards stem from the restrictions necessary to maintain the structure: requirements to maintain specific body positions, limits on mobility, absence of opportunities for tactile sensory stimulation, and performance demands that may undermine self-esteem (for example: 'All right children, sit up straight, don't wiggle, don't touch your neighbor, and be ready for my question!'). In addition, structured transitions tend to consume large amounts of time. . . .

The advantages of open structure lie in its ability to foster initiative and reward child-child relationships and in the opportunities for mobility and tactile sensory stimulation. Its hazards lie in the difficulties of maintaining focus for individual children, in providing sufficient complexity for meaningful choice, and the tendency toward diluted adult input" (1984, pp. 59-60).

The physical environment and experiences offered to children tended to be associated with program structure. Closed centers offered the hardest setting and the fewest opportunities for sensory play, exploration, discovery, and experiences with a range of materials and people. Open structure centers were significantly higher in these dimensions, but family day care homes again were rated the highest.

Prescott (1984, p. 60) concluded that closed structure settings need softness, some open activity settings, and a relaxed attitude toward conversation and playfulness during periods of waiting to avoid being oppressive. "Closed structure is probably easier to handle if the physical setting is inadequately developed and staff are inexperienced." Open structured settings "can easily become disorganized and boring, for both adults and children . . . and must have well developed space and adults who know how to facilitate, problem solve, and keep track of children." After working with numerous programs, Prescott and her colleagues believe: "In our experience, it is not easy to produce a switch from one format to another; it is possible, however, to improve the overall functioning within a given format, and this approach is preferable to an attempt to make an immediate and drastic change in format."

Prescott (1978) and her colleagues also examined home based settings. There they found many similarities and some significant differences with open structured centers. Even more than in open structured programs, children, not adults, initiated and terminated activities; structured transitions occupied little time, very unlike the dynamics in closed structured programs. Home based settings offered more adult input which was more facilitative than in either type of center. There were more informal conversations between adults and children and more engagement with the environment. In homes she found there were great differences in opportunities for tactile sensory exploration, the availability of materials which could be incorporated into children's play, and the variety of settings and people that children were exposed to. Further, "Conversations were not formal discussions of what the little rabbit did, but whether the photograph on the bureau was taken before or after the family day care mother was married, and if her son was born then, or whether 'the post office where my daddy works is the same one where the mail carrier gets the mail'" (p. 17).

The research of both Cochran and Gunnarsson (reported in Bronfenbrenner, 1979, pp. 184-185), looking at Swedish children in their own homes, in family day care, and in centers, support Prescott's research. They found that not only were there far more opportunities for adult child interactions, but that opportunities for exploration were more numerous in homes than centers "where the single role of the adult is child care and the setting is single purpose in design. . . . Caregivers are wives and neighbors as well as mothers at home, and the environment is organized accordingly. Friends and relatives are received in the home. It may be a display area for prized possessions. Plants and flowers are often within reach. The child has access to the dishwashing detergent, the backstairs, the cat."

Following her research, Prescott (1978) posed the question: Should we look to the home as an environmental model for child care centers? Much of the thinking in this book stems from a "yes" to Prescott's question.

Photograph by Jean Wallech

Photograph by Francis Wardle

matter who is the teacher). Because people vary in skills and experience, it is always tempting for experts—architects, educators, directors—to make their visions complete and tamper-proof. (Some architects build in furniture to ensure that people live in the settings the way they are supposed to.). But this has two drawbacks.

First, creative space is a creative attitude, an ever growing sense of what is possible for oneself, for things. The environment can and should be geared for its participants, adjusting space and tempo as change and learning occur. Good teachers know when to develop structure and when to discard it. There is no more a right environment for children than there is a right home, no model room or building layout, no all purpose list of equipment. *It all depends* on the resources, the children, the group, the adults, the climate, and the culture. *Good* space is relative to its inhabitants who grow and change, and it is relative to changing goals and purposes.

Like clothing, settings need to change to fit. *One size fits all* inevitably leaves somebody constricted or something hanging out. It is true that many programs have the same programmatic

skeletons: breakfast, lunch, and snacks; bathroom stops; nap; indoor and outdoor play; movement to different rooms—days woven together with similar transitions. Many programs have similar ailments. Adapting the environment to replace herding with more individualized transitions is a typical one. But each setting is a unique blend of elements that change over time. As the children develop, or the group jells, or new equipment is produced, the structure of space, time, and routines can and should be altered to extend learning or make life easier. The adults, by their relationship to the environment, are teaching children that reality is constructed, that one simultaneously shapes and adapts to the environment.

Maria Montessori, the archtypical designer of children's environments, spent a lifetime observing children, turning ideas into materials and principles, preparing settings to accomplish her ends. Her model as a scientist and designer exceeds the value of her wonderful materials, because she continued to develop and tinker with her ideas of a "prepared environment." Montessori teachers who emulate her approach to the world, but do not accept her insights as undigested truth and themselves as only *the*

keepers of Montessori's prepared environment, have put together some of the most interesting environments for children.

The other drawback to *finished* or teacher proof environments is that adults, like children, invest in the objects they make or transform. Settings reduce involvement unless people can put something of themselves into the setting. Institutions diminish people by reducing their involvement to mere presence or labor, restricting much sense of intellectual or emotional engagement.

Adults play three possible roles in all children's programs:

1. **Environmental Planner:** organizer, provisioner, arranger, and planner of day-to-day activities

2. **Environmental Participant:** caregiver, teacher, cook, role model, and co-worker

3. **Environmental Evaluator:** observer, analyzer, problem-solver, experimenter, and evaluator of the environment

The effectiveness of environmental planning and evaluation determines the quality of the environment to sustain the other roles. A well planned, supportive environment liberates caregivers to care and teach; to ask the right question at the right time; to provide the smile, the lap, or the diaper when needed.

In a book on learning environments, it is possible to lose sight of the importance of teaching and teachers because the topics at hand are designing, planning, and evaluating environments. But teachers are important in the richest of environments. A study by Tizard describes "how some English nursery school

Photograph by Nancy P. Alexander

teachers, drawing on the theories of Issacs, Gesell, and Piaget, have evolved an ideology of play that says that teachers must not initiate or take a major role in play lest they interfere with the child's creative impulses. Such an ideology seems a travesty of the views of education held by Issacs, Gesell, and Piaget" (Almy et al., 1984, p. 19). This is the opposite of the situation lamented by Elkind where teachers intruded into valuable play. Teachers walk a tightrope. The good teacher sets up the environment, sometimes proposing a specific activity for a child, and observes how the child reacts before deciding what to focus on to extend the child's

thinking. The teacher's skills at understanding what goes on in the child's head at each moment determines whether his way of thinking is elaborated or disrupted. As the Elkind **Play and Work** box in Chapter Two illustrated, figuring out the teaching moment is not easy. Taking the dilemma a bit too seriously can lead to what Lillian Katz has called "Analysis Paralysis"— freezing over indecision, fearing disruption, or missing a teaching moment.

When teachers are not always *on stage* teaching, they have the opportunity to enter fully into the children's environment, also to observe the lower depths and to sense how its individual denizens actually experience the day. These observations better inform their caregiving and teaching. They have a chance to talk **with** children, the importance of which is often underestimated. According to Susan Issacs, "A child has little power for sustaining conversation as such, and needs other opportunity to talk with people who talk well. Grownups or older children who will listen to what he has to say and respond appropriately are of far more value to him than specific lessons in clear speech" (Weber, 1971, p. 179).

What Do We Want?

Most of what has been written so far has considered the question of what kind of childhood we wish for our children. But there are three other questions to keep in mind while planning children's environments:

• **What kind of people do we want children to become?**

What kind of adults do we want our children to be? Children are our hope; they embody our dreams. We seek for them a life

better than our own. We all have a vision for our children; mine is that they become resourceful, loving, powerful human beings—powerful in the sense of having the personal strength and confidence to cope with and master all sorts of situations, continually learning, and drawing on inner resources.

More than self-esteem, a sense of personal power is an active sense of self-esteem that will not need a steady consumption of advice on how to *pack your own parachute, pull your own strings, lose weight quickly,* or *dress to intimidate.* It is a power that neither needs guns, great wealth, or subservience to a strong someone to sustain it; a power that allows one to give of oneself, to love, to win and lose; a sense of power and mastery and competence that allows one to not only accept responsibility, but to seek it out.

With each generation we are becoming more fully a society of consumers. We consume education, relying on classes and helpful books for any new ideas. We purchase care for our children and our parents, entertainment, politics, relationships. Many of us are losing the power to create, to produce, to learn by ourselves. It is a revolutionary discovery, as Ivan Illich points out, that **much learning requires no teaching**. He tells a story about talking to a very old Mexican peasant who was giving him an in-depth analysis of the biology, geology, psychology and all the *ologies* of the area. Illich asked the peasant how he knew so much. The peasant replied apologetically, "I have to use my brain a lot since I have no education."

• **What kind of life do we want for the adults in children's programs?**

Are adults to be tenders, managers, low paid babysitters or higher paid nannies, crisp

Photograph by Francis Wardle

professional educators or caregivers, or full human beings who teach and tend and love and learn themselves? Whether the setting considers their needs, their adult size, their wishes, and their potential will determine their lives in child care and that of the children. If they are tired, harried, victims of minimum ratios, minimum materials, minimum space, minimum training, minimum pay, and minimum status, what kind of nurturing can they provide? If they are little more than warm bodies with pleasant smiles and purveyors of teaching materials, rather than active constructors and learners and problem solvers, what are the children learning—faced with these role models?

• What kind of society do we want to be?

As places and as institutions, child care programs shape future visions of what society is and should be. Children reared in fortresses barricaded against the world outside, or in dingy basements, or in worlds of fluorescently-lit plastic and tile will have different aesthetic sensibilities than those raised in light, airy, open places with plants and easy access to the out-side. If "in two straight lines we break our bread, brush our teeth, and go to bed" like Madeline (**Madeline** by L. Bemelmans, 1939), we will be different people than if we arrive at a place and go our own way. These things ought to be considered when issues of program struc-tures, square footage, windows, sinks, and furniture (and staff salaries and staffing) are considered.

"The most beautiful thing we can experience is the mysterious. It is the source of all true art and science. He to whom this emotion is a stranger, who can no longer pause to wonder and stand rapt in awe is as good as dead; his eyes are closed."
Albert Einstein (in **I Believe: A Personal Philosophy**)

Can we design children's places that generate or at least tolerate the mysterious, where descriptive terms like *wonder* and *adventure* seem apt, where there is awe to be had and each day reminds us why life is worth living? This world, after all our scientific analysis, is still a miracle: wonderful, inscrutable, magical to all of us who will experience it. Understanding the sun, the atmosphere (Unit 3—Your Friend the Atmosphere), the rotation of the earth, or how to develop a good tan does not guarantee appreciating the beauty of the sunrise.

Exercises

1. Search your memory for the rewarding moments you have had caring for or teaching children. What made them rewarding?

2. Analyze a child care program for its open and closed attributes.

3. Choose a home with children and an early childhood setting and compare them for opportunities for play and discovery.

4. Analyze a child care program from the standpoint of the teachers' roles. How much autonomy is allowed in environmental planning or provisioning? What supports are there for the teachers?

— Chapter Four —

New Kids on the Block: Infants and Toddlers in Groups

"Babies are not like us."
Jean Jacques Rousseau

With the swiftness of sprinters, babies have crawled and toddled onto the child care scene. Any doubts of their presence or permanence disappears after surveying the burgeoning number of pages in equipment and materials catalogues devoted to the care and education of babies. The number of babies* in center care has mushroomed, as family day care supply has been outstripped by demand. For example, in Minnesota in 1970, there were fewer than a dozen programs caring for babies. In 1985, there were over a hundred. This pell mell increase evident throughout the country shows no sign of abating as we grope unsuccessfully for ways to increase the supply of home-based care.

A New Ball Game

The care of babies in groups in a center context represents a significant departure from other early childhood programs. It presents some particular problems and it crystallizes many of the issues equally relevant to child care for older children. Rarely are human babies found in groups in the wild (a bunch? a gang? a gaggle of babies?) or in society's formal institutional settings, excepting hospital wards, orphanages, some day nurseries, and European creches. The all day care of infants and toddlers in a group setting requires a thorough rethink-

Photograph by Jean Wallech

ing of the appropriateness of most of the assumptions and ensuing practices that characterize programs for older children.

But because of the relatively sudden and unceasing demand, child care programs began caring for babies with precious little time to think it through. A director explained:

"When we started, we assumed the setting should be like child care for preschool, but we needed cribs, a changing table, and a rocker. We all believed babies really belonged at home. We felt that if they were here, we should really have

---

*I like the term *babies*. It is out of fashion, but using it reinforces the point that infants **and** toddlers are indeed babies. Toddlers sometimes suffer because we forget this. *Babies* is used where the point applies to both infants and toddlers—children under two.

a one-to-one staff/child ratio, but we settled for a one-to-four. We knew we had to have activities that were developmentally appropriate for babies and more of them because of babies' attention spans. It all seemed to make sense.

What we didn't ask was: Is a one-to-one or one-to-two ratio desirable in group care or does that make everything adult centered? Those times we had those ratios, the talking, bickering, and crowding seemed to overwhelm the program. We never asked ourselves whether it was useful to think in terms of an activity-based structure for babies. Picking up lint, tearing, letting go, dumping are all activities. Did we want *2:00 - 2:20—Reaching and Pinching*? It took us a pretty long time to stop simply trying to do what we were doing better and instead question some of our assumptions. Without the luxury of time to examine assumptions, programs naturally drew from what they knew about child care for older children, preschools, schools and homes."

Before some of the differences are explored, it is useful to consider the long term stakes involved with the incorporation of infant care into

Photograph by Jean Wallech

the landscape of children's programs. Looking back at the history of the development of kindergarten and early education, it is clear that when attention shifts to a new, younger group of children there is much discussion of both the promise and peril of the new development— promise because perhaps not only will the new group of children be well served, but through them we can make changes that will filter up.

The argument goes as follows: These programs for the younger children (kindergarten, Head Start, preschools in the schools, and now infants) can be based on how children **really** learn (actively), the care that children need (individual), and a relationship with families that is truly a supportive partnership. The new programs will help break through the traditions that have established School as a formal institution with a capital S, characterized by large institutions with an emphasis on teaching rather than learning, with no recognition of the *whole child*, the individual child, and with perceptions of parents as distant and less than equal partners.

The peril is, of course, that the reverse will happen and the institution of School will be further extended downward. This has been the usual result. School is, after all, everyone's common reference point when designing programs for children.

The prospect of School shaping the nature of programs for babies is frightening. Even worse would be its extension to our view of good home learning environments. The curriculum of an infant and toddler program in child care should be everything that happens to the baby, everything that goes into good care. Sensitively helping a toddler through his rage-ridden frustration dance is curriculum. So is responding to the persistent ache of separation that at

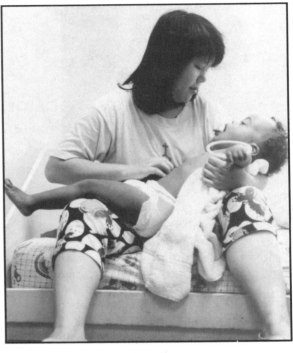

Photograph by Shawn Connell

times resonates throughout a room of babies like a melancholy foghorn.

Care is precisely what has been shrugged aside by schools and defined out of the school teacher role. **Curriculum** is *what happens*; care *happens*. Care and learning together are the curriculum; this is true for all programs and schools for **all** children. (As Aldous Huxly pointed out, "Facts don't cease to exist because they are ignored.") With babies, it seems even more absurd to think of curriculum in any other way, given the contortions needed to separate care and learning. Yet stranger things have, are, and will happen. To avoid creating programs that we may have cause to look back on with horror or regret necessitates our clearly understanding the idiosyncrasies of infant and toddler care.

Babies

Babies are not only not much like us, as Rousseau observed; if one considers the phenomenal changes in all facets of development occurring in the first two and a half years of life, they aren't much like each other either or even themselves from day to day . As Jerry Ferguson put it (Jones, 1979, p. 13): "Children go all the way from complete helplessness to autonomy and assertiveness without any moral responsibility."

If infant/toddler programs were to begin at the beginning, they would start here: What do babies do? They cry, eat, sleep, create not inconsiderable bodily wastes, and bond to others. They also learn by thoroughly investigating the world and themselves.

Beginning at this point may lead to programs with similar features to preschools, plus cribs, but it also very well may not. The result may be a design similar to homes or a new synthesis of home and school. Before they plan, it is useful for program developers or staff to just sit down and list in clear behavioral terms

Photograph by Jean Wallech

what these little creatures known as babies actually do in a space.

What Do Babies Do?

Among other things, young babies:

see	squeeze	sit up
watch	pinch	pull up
look	drop	crawl to, in, out,
inspect	transfer - hand	over
hear	to hand	creep around,
listen	shake	in, and under
smell	bang	swing
taste	tear	rock
feel	clap together	coo, babble
touch	put in	imitate sounds
mouth	take out	react to others
eat	find	accommodate to
reach out	look for	others
reach for	kick	solicit from
knock away	turn	others
grasp	roll	experiment
hold	lift their heads	endlessly

In addition to doing many of the above, older babies:

walk in, out,	stack	order
up, down,	pile	carry
over, under,	nest	rearrange
around,	set up	put in
through	knock over	take out
climb in, up,	collect	hide
over, on top	gather	discover
slide	fill	investigate by
swing	dump	trial and error
hang	inspect	explore with
jump	examine	each sense
tumble	select	imitate
take apart	sort	try adult
put together	match	behavior

doll play	splash	hug
paint	make sounds and	kiss
smear	words	test others
draw	label	accommodate to
mix	read symbols	others
separate	converse	help themselves
pour	follow directions	wash, erat,
sift	cuddle	and dress

What Do Babies Need?

If the above is what babies do, what settings do they need in order to thrive? According to Jerome Bruner (1973), a baby needs a safe world where he or she is "encouraged to venture, rewarded for venturing his own acts, and sustained against distraction or premature interferences in carrying them out" (p. 8). She needs a world rich with opportunities to see, hear, feel, touch, and move—to undertake all the actions listed above. The child needs a setting where, in the words of Frank and Theresa Caplan in **The Power of Play** (1974, p. 107) he will "feel that the world is at his fingertips, that it is his to explore and enjoy."

Movement is essential. Moving around gives babies the different perspectives and vantage points which they need to move from an entirely egocentric view of space to develop a more sophisticated sense of the relations between self and space and other people. We know that objects are the same regardless of the angle or the distance from which we observe them, whether bathed by sunlight or blanketed by shadows, but an infant does not.

There is a tension between the need for safety and security on the one hand and the need for a rich world a fingertip away on the other. Among other things, infants explore each other, not always with tact and delicacy. They also occasionally find each other as obstacles to overcome. These strange others are sometimes the sources of unwanted stimulation, like noise or motion—that distract or overstimulate. Often this tension increases the staff's tendency to restrain rather than facilitate motor exploration and exuberance. Playpens, infant seats, and automatic swings receive more use than slides, ramps, stairs, and riding toys (and, sometimes, the human stimulation of being held, rocked, and walked).

This seems to be a mission impossible: Provide a safe enriched world for a **group** of tiny explorers and scientists devoid of any manners or sense of moral responsibility, a rich world to explore that sustains each child against distraction and learning interruptus. This is no mean achievement for child care staff. And yet, this is not enough; in fact, it is even secondary to a more fundamental concern: the critical nature of the adult-child relationship. This relationship provides the security and encouragement to

Photograph by Jean Wallech

Baby's World
by Rabindranath Tagore

I wish I could take a quiet corner in the heart of my baby's very own world.

I know it has stars that talk to him, and a sky that stoops down to his face to amuse him with its silly clouds and rainbows.

Those who make believe to be dumb, and look as if they never could move, come creeping to his window with their stories and with trays crowded with bright toys.

I wish I could travel by the road that crosses baby's mind, and out beyond all bounds;

Where messengers run errands for no cause between the kingdoms of kings of no history;

Where Reason makes kites of her laws and flies them, and Truth sets Fact free from its fetters.

Photograph by Jean Wallech

Photographs by Jean Wallech (below) and Shawn Connell (above)

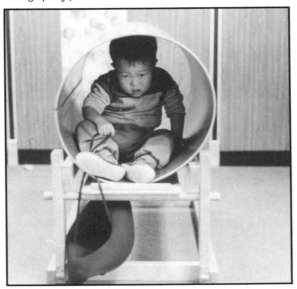

venture out into the world. Consider Mary Ainsworth's description of "the sensitive mother" (McCall, 1980, p. 118):

"The sensitive mother is able to see things from her baby's point of view. She is tuned-in to receive her baby's signals: she interprets them correctly, and she responds appropriately. Although she nearly always gives the baby what he seems to want, when she does not she is tactful in acknowledging his communication and in offering an acceptable alternative. She makes her responses temporally contingent upon the baby's signals and communications. The sensitive mother, by definition, cannot be rejecting, interfering, or ignoring.

The insensitive mother, on the other hand, gears her interventions and initiations of interactions almost exclusively in terms of her own wishes, moods, and activities. She tends either to distort the implications of her baby's communications, interpreting them in the light of her own wishes or defenses, or not to respond to them at all."

Bruno Bettelheim, in discussing child-rearing in another group context, the kibbutz, suggests that "the inner experience of the infant leading to trust is that of security, whatever the outer experience that creates such a feeling, and whether or not it is based on any sameness in the person of the provider. And security derives from the feeling that we can safely relax, that we need not worry—provided this feeling is not delusional, but is based on a correct estimate of reality" (Bettelheim, 1969, p. 83).

To "safely relax," an infant literally needs to feel "at home." What does this mean? In the words of a hypothetical baby: "This is my place. I know these people. They know me and they like me; despite my crying and diarrhea and difficulty going to sleep. I can count on them to take care of me, to respond to me. I can be **ME** here with all my quirks and still be accepted. I will be safe here." What makes a feeling of home is that sense of familiarity, acceptance, and safety.

If Ainsworth's characterizations of *insensitive* behavior are applied to the workings of an infant center, instead of one-to-one mother-child interactions, and if we consider Bettelheim's standard of security, the magnitude of the task of providing quality in a group setting is laid bare. Even using primary caregivers systems and assuming a stable staff (a very brittle assumption), responses to the baby may often be contingent upon the program's routines, sched-

Photograph by Shawn Connell

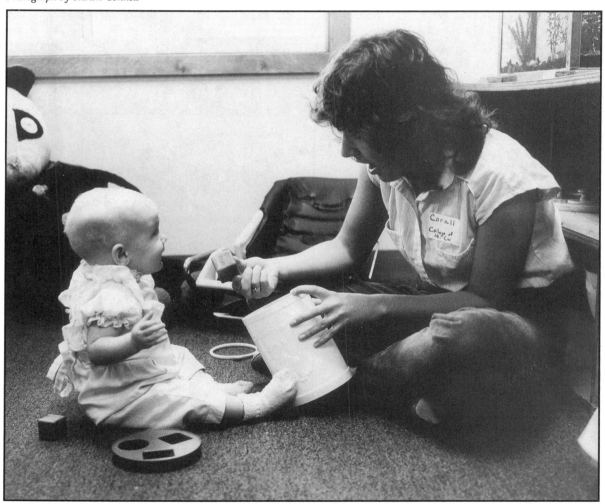

from **Like a Rolling Stone**
by Bob Dylan

How does it feel?
How does it feel?
To be without a home
To be on your own
no direction home
like a complete unknown
like a rolling stone.

Photograph by Nancy P. Alexander

ules, and priorities, or the competing demands of the other children. In addition, the caregiver's need or desire to teach, or appear busy, or take a break enters into play. How in group institutional settings can *sensitive mothering* be the rule and not the exception? How can the setting allow the child to relax and feel at home? These are the difficult critical questions infant and toddler programs must address.

Toddlers: A Breed Apart

Toddlers* are child care's equivalent to junior high school students. They often appear

Photograph by Jean Wallech

Photograph by Jean Wallech

to be more mature than they are, and the frequent result in toddler programs is the tendency to treat them as proto-preschoolers—smaller and less competent. (The label *terrible twos* speaks to the lack of appreciation for the toddler mode of being.) What Bettelheim calls their "collective monologues," their parallel play, and their sometimes remarkable compliance mask the differences between the two year old and the four year old. Neither infants nor preschoolers, toddlers are furiously becoming: increasingly mobile, autonomous, social, thoughtful creatures with language and insatiable urges to test and experiment. They embody contradictions: anarchist with an instinct to herd and cluster, assertive and independent now, passive and completely depend-

---

*In child care the term *toddlers* often applies to children from 12 months to preschool age, 30 months.

ent moments later. These restless mobile characters have a drive to take apart the existing order and rearrange it, by force if necessary, to suit their own whimsically logical view of the universe.

How do you develop an environment that allows collecting, hauling, dumping, and painting (with the requisite tasting of the paint and experimenting with the logical primary canvas—themselves)? How do you allow the necessary robust, explosive, and occasionally clumsy motor learning with a group of amoral beings who are largely oblivious to the safety of others—a group, however, that often hums with a current of collective energy. In a group setting, how do you accommodate to and support the wonderful, albeit erratic, *do it myself* desire and the equally developmentally important but often less wonderful assertion of "No!" and still accomplish anything in a reasonable time frame? Finally, how do you muster up the time, let alone the patience and sensitivity, to help **each** child through the agony and ecstasy of toilet training? Perhaps mission impossible may understate the situation.

Environments for Babies

The key to providing a good program for infants and toddlers is understanding two paradoxes, the first of which is relevant here:

Paradox Number 1

A. The most important ingredient in good care for babies is the child's caregiver.

B. What separates high quality programs from others (adult-child ratios and group size being relatively equal) is often not the caregivers but the environment.

Photograph by Jean Wallech

Because of the obvious truth of statement A, the importance of the environment is misunderstood in many programs. Support for adult-child ratios of one-to-two, even one-to-one, stems from this misunderstanding. One often encounters a caregiver with three or more babies clustered around her (more rarely, him) while she struggles to diaper a child. Diapering is hurried to get back to the needy cluster. The image of a mother bird returning to a nest of chirping baby birds is often realized. The ratio is visible before our eyes. Or a group of 13 toddlers must function as a large group with one teacher while the other caregiver sets up for lunch. Because one baby always seems to need personal attention, caregivers are left feeling they never have enough time, arms and legs, and smiles to give. The caregiver is nearly always the focus: she is the teaching machine, the toy, the care dispenser, and the referee.

---

*I don't think that it is necessary to always separate infants and toddlers, which seems to be the prevailing trend outside family day care. Multi-age settings work well when the environment is appropriate and staff are well trained and believe in multi-aging.

What if we begin thinking about infant care with two assumptions? First, infant care will for all practical (read *economic*) purposes have ratios of one-to-three, more likely one-to-four, and unfortunately worse in some areas. Toddler ratios will range from one-to-four to hopefully no worse than one-to-seven.* Because of the staggering amount of set up, clean up, and one-to-one care, on the floor ratios with children will be much worse.

Second, assume that the most important times for the child are those one-to-one moments of real nurturing and communication, where the baby has the caregiver's full human presence. These are the times that need to be relaxed and even extended *prime times*: diaper-

Photograph by Nancy P. Alexander

Photograph by Shawn Connell

With Care and Respect:
Magda Gerber and the RIE Approach

Magda Gerber and Tom Forrest established Resources for Infant Educaters (RIE) to help support parents and professionals with an approach to infant and toddlers based on the work of Dr. Emmi Pikler of Hungary. The approach stresses the importance of respectful, responsive, reciprocal adult-infant interactions. In **Infancy and Caregiving** (1980), Janet Gonzalez-Mena and Dianne Widmeyer Eyer detail the approach for caregivers and students. The principle of relating to an infant or toddler with respect permeates the book.

The implementation of the approach is based on the understanding that curriculum consists of **interactions** with people and things. The point is not to stimulate babies: "If you are concerned only with stimulating, with doing something **to** the baby, you ignore a vital requirement for learning and development: that babies need to discover that they can influence the people around them. Yes they need stimulation, which they get from objects, and more importantly from people. But they need to perceive their own involvement in these stimulating experiences. . . . When stimulation is provided without regard to the baby's response, the baby is being treated as an object" (p. 45). Unlike some infant stimulation programs, RIE believes that education results when, in T. Barry Brazelton's words, "a baby finds 'the pleasure of being the cause'—of learning how to act in order to produce the results he wants, of learning about things that are the results of his own actions" (p. 45). When adults respond to a baby's language or gestures, or participate in her exploration of the space, the baby develops a sense of power.

The RIE approach to curriculum emphasizes the primacy of caregiving moments for reciprocal interactions and developing trust. A key adult role is to prepare the environment for free play, replete with choices. "Learning occurs when there is maximum incongruity between what is already known and a new situation. . . . The question is how can we set up an environment so that it has elements of "optimum incongruence?. . . All we can do is provide a number of choices of appropriate toys, objects and activities, and let the child play. Given the chance, children will naturally move to novel situations and novel uses of materials" (pp. 70-71).

Sooner or later a child with an interesting, challenging environment is bound to find a problem that he wants to solve but can't. Magda Gerber calls this situation "getting stuck. A child is stuck when he cannot figure out his next move. The adult can then step in and provide the smallest possible bit of help—the tiny link that allows the child to move forward again. This help is the selective intervention mentioned earlier" (p. 71). It is these times that require the adult's full presence.

ing and toilet training, putting a child to sleep, feeding a child, responding to a child's distress or the excitement of discovery. What if a major goal were to have all the time in the world to diaper a child—to touch, to talk, to listen, to play all the call-response games the baby sets in motion?

These premises lead to two conclusions about the environment: First, the environment needs to be furnished, equipped, and organized to maximize the caregivers' time and ease of providing care: no sinks down the hall; no looking for bottles, training pants, or materials; no constant relaying of messages or on the spot substitute orientations.

Ideally, a substitute (or parent) should be able to walk into a room and quickly function effectively. The order is visible and logical: a well designed diapering area, shelves and cabinets labeled inside and out, adequate storage close to the point of use, and clear communication systems located sensibly. Many

Photograph by Shawn Connell

parent coops, Montessori programs, and health clinics provide good models for order, as will be discussed later.

Second, the play environment should be developed as a wonderful, interesting place that continually captures a child's attention and is laid out to ensure individual and small group experiences, **without the continual presence of many watchful adults.** Neither in homes nor centers will it work to assume continual visual contact. One should be able to enter the room in the evening with no staff present and marvel at the learning environment, *the world at the child's fingertips*—the built-in opportunities for motor and sensory experiences, the ranges of places to be with different visual and auditory stimulation, the number of protected spaces for young babies, and the problem solving opportunities for small detectives of varying interests and skills. Lying on the floor you should see pathways and small divided spaces—opportunities to go in and out, up and over, and so on; to be alone, to be enclosed on three sides, and to peer over thirty inch walls. You should be able to

imagine adults helping children get unstuck from the challenge they have set out for themselves.

If, instead, you only find a couch, a rocker, and some toys, you can guess the heavy burden placed on those missing caregivers to make it all work. They not only have to provide the language, patience and sensitivity, but all the challenge and excitement. If the learning environment is planned to work with few adults ever present, a *yes* environment free from temptations and the need for verbal restrictions, then many more of those one-to-one interactions are possible where babies develop trust and security knowing that they are loved, and powerful, and worthy of undivided attention.

Is the above learning environment possible? After all, babies are a pretty disorderly bunch.

Photograph by Jean Wallech

How can one keep the floor from becoming a mine field of scattered nesting cups, dolls, and other playthings left in the wake of active babies? A carefully arranged space where materials are understood by both adults and children to have a particular place, a room arrangement that confines materials to smaller bounded areas, and built in learning will all reduce disorder (as will be emphasized in greater detail throughout this book).

The Adults in Infant/Toddler Programs

Paradox Number 2

A) The caregiver's knowledge and sensitivity to children is the single most important quality to consider.

B) In centers the adult relationships are central to good infant and toddler care.

As with the other paradox, the validity of the first premise masks the reality of the second. Adult relationships provide the context that may or may not allow children the benefits of adult sensitivity. In an infant center, the child's experience is dependent on teamwork between caregiver and parent and among the three to six adults that staff the ten hour plus day. How that work group plans, behaves, and communicates will determine whether each baby experiences a relaxed, individualized day or standardized care and assorted mayhem. The individual caregiver's skills are only a part of the equation. The level of communication and organization necessary to simply get children fed, diapered, and put to sleep (let alone individualize care); to maintain rigorous sanitation procedures; and to record the essentials of a child's day for parents is mind boggling. Add to this maintaining the learning environment and keeping track of the clothing and paraphernalia for each baby, and the dimensions of the task become clear.

If this *team* functions as independent operators, each caregiver with his or her *own* children, how then can the planned environment described above come to pass? And what happens to the caregiver's children those hours/days when that caregiver is not present?

Parents and Caregivers

Parents of babies are likely to be the most insecure of all child care parents. Most are new to parenting; some new to marriage; some single parents; almost all experiencing some stress and fatigue due to recovery from childbirth, return to work, and late night caregiving. Simply leaving the house with the baby and all the necessary paraphernalia may seem to require a major effort. All are experiencing the pain of separation, child care guilt or ambivalence, and

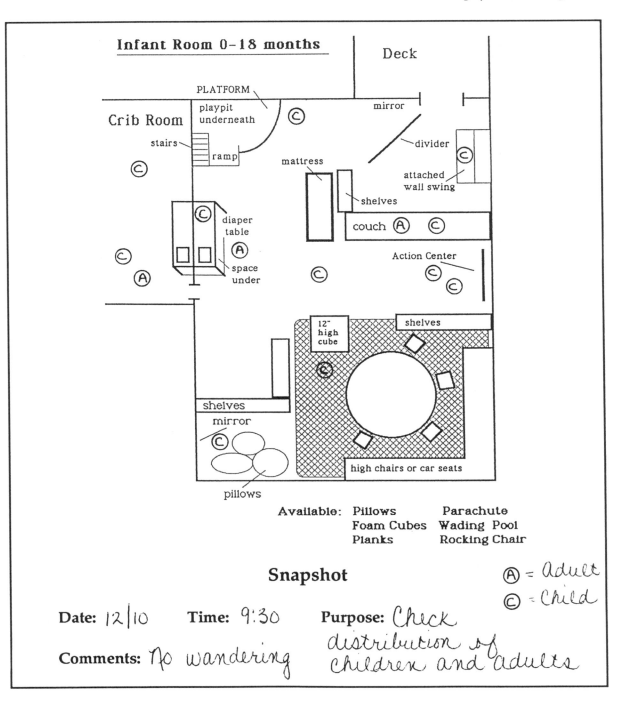

Infant Room 0–18 months

Deck

PLATFORM

Crib Room

playpit underneath

stairs

ramp

mirror

divider

mattress

attached wall swing

shelves

diaper table

space under

couch Ⓐ Ⓒ

Action Center

12" high cube

shelves

shelves

mirror

high chairs or car seats

pillows

Available: Pillows   Parachute
           Foam Cubes   Wading Pool
           Planks   Rocking Chair

Snapshot

Ⓐ = Adult
Ⓒ = Child

Date: 12|10   Time: 9:30   Purpose: Check distribution of children and adults

Comments: No wandering

the insecurity that comes from placing their trust in others to care for a child who seems very small and vulnerable and who is unable to tell them what he or she is experiencing. Parents usually approach child care uncertain about what to expect, particularly about what role their knowledge and wishes will play in the whole scheme of things.

So the parent arrives at the program and is met by whom? Infant caregivers are likely to be the most insecure of child care staff, who are not a very secure group (professionally) as a whole (Pettygrove and Greenman, 1984; Joffe, 1977). Status is derived in early childhood programs from teaching, not caregiving. Although there is probably no greater physical and **intellectual** challenge than trying to provide good care to babies in groups (which to be good must include a good learning environment), this is not generally recognized. Infant care seems most like babysitting. There is no agreed upon body of knowledge and expertise recognized by parents and staff, no *right way*. Further, another source of insecurity is that staff are constantly aware of the hopeful, tenuous trust placed in them for the care of the family's most precious possession.

Caregivers of babies need to be people who can develop a personal, intimate relationship with a child, and at the same time have the sensitivity and skills to maneuver through a delicate relationship with parents—one that is free from competition over the child's affection and over primary claim to knowledge of the child's needs and child care in general. In addition, unlike most children's settings, caregivers must moderate their territorial instincts and extend their boundaries to include parents who visit to nurse their babies or to spend time with their children. This is no small matter. All of the above call for good adult

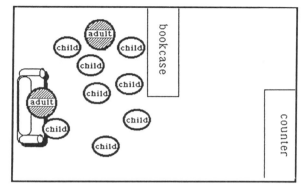

Diagram A

communication skills from caregivers, some of whom are working with children precisely because they are more comfortable working with children than with other adults.

Planning the Environment for Adults

Good environmental planning facilitates adult relationships. The infant-toddler setting has to be a good place for adults to be with children and with other adults—a place where adults are physically comfortable and have the equipment and tools to work with, and where social relations are friendly and relaxed. In short, the setting must be a place where the caregiver also feels at home—at home enough to make dopey faces, coo and babble with a baby, wrestle with a toddler, or lie on the floor or couch without having to explain herself to an office-bound administrator.

Bunching Up

There is a complication. The caregiver needs to feel at home enough to also be able to readily ignore another adult sitting three feet away and to face away from that other person. There is a phenomenon endemic to infant centers: **bunching up**, a condition where the

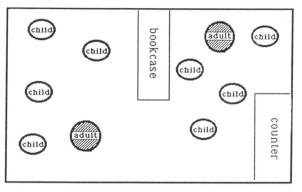

Diagram B

majority of adults and babies end up packing together and using only a limited amount of the available space, whatever the overall size of the space. Understanding this phenomenon is critical to good care. All too often, infant settings become adult centered (which is why one-to-two ratios may not be a good idea, regardless of cost) and crowded, regardless of the size of the overall space.

Unlike preschoolers, many babies seem to stay within close proximity of their caregivers, creating a field of action portrayed in Diagram A. Whether this is due to the child's or the caregiver's need to be close and retain face to face contact or a mixture of both child and adult need has not been studied. (Little relating to the behavior of babies and adults in groups has been studied.)

A second tendency is for the adults to sit in close proximity to each other, thus increasing the number of children in the bunch. Layout of furniture often encourages this as adults draw from their experience of home settings in arranging the furniture. The couch and chair arrangement pictured in Diagram A seems comfortably homey but often results in two or more adults sitting on the couch and chairs and five to ten children in a tiny area—a decidedly un-homey condition. In living rooms and lounges we want to draw adults together to socialize; but in infant settings we want to separate them and spread the children out, increasing the field of action and reducing the chances of conflict and collision.

Unfortunately, this is easier said than done. Nearly all adults' behavioral predispositions are to face each other and to face the action. It feels alien to turn our backs and focus away from the center of a space and other adults. There is also the desire to talk to another verbal human being, particularly in a charming but non-verbal crowd.

Avoiding bunching up requires a room ar-rangement and daily planning that consciously draws staff and children toward the far reaches of the room or to secondary rooms. The furni-ture arrangement in Diagram B will help to accomplish a better distribution of adults and

children, but it is so foreign to the eye that there will be a constant urge to rearrange back to the familiar. Self-monitoring and super-vision that recognizes the tendency to bunch up and the need to spread out is always essen-tial.

Incorporating Parents

How can the environment help to foster the staff-parent relationship? This can best be done by incorporating parents into the setting. For parents to feel welcome in the infant toddler setting, they too need to feel at home. There is a place to hang coats and purses and a place to sit. There is knowledge of where not to sit and what to do and not to do (diaper procedures, for instance). That visible order discussed above helps to make parents feel comfortable in the space.

There is again a complication: If parents truly feel at home, won't the environment

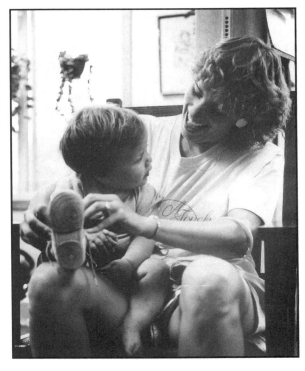

Photograph by Jean Wallech

become crowded and adult centered? Yes, but this is a rather nice problem to have. (It is largely unrecognized that infant and toddler programs require more space per child than pro-grams for larger children because of the adults in the room.) In a close relationship with parents and a staff that works as a team, the complication can be resolved by fostering a high degree of awareness. When the environment is adult heavy, it can be changed. Staff can take some babies outside or on a trip through the center. The problem can be discussed with parents to heighten everyone's awareness.

Conclusion

The routines, the interactions, the pace, the ambience, even (perhaps especially) the smells

---

FIRST DAY NOTE

CONGRATULATIONS

Your child made it through his/her first day—and so did you! The first day is always the hardest. Separation and adjustment should get easier as time goes on. I want to do what is necessary for your piece of mind. We are in this together and a sense of partnership should develop between you and I. Don't hesitate to let me know about anything that may be bothering you about your child's care.

are different in classrooms for babies. At a given moment, babies are waking up or winding down, eating, or needing diaper changes. A parent may be coming in to nurse, another to drop off or pick up a child. Staff schedules are staggered so staff come and go as well. When a child needs undivided attention to be consoled or to be put to sleep, he needs it now or the whole room is affected. Rapidity of change in children as they grow in the first two years, turnover of children as parents battle the cost of care, turnover of staff as they battle living on substandard wages—the potential for chaos is great. The order necessary to make life reasonable for babies, parents, and staff does not come easily.

Exercises

1. From a baby's perspective, list all the things in a child care setting that might make you feel insecure or not *at home*. What things would increase your security?

2. List some problem-solving situations for babies at 3, 6, 9, 12, 15, 18, and 24 months.

3. Observe a *wild* (unsupervised) infant and a *wild* toddler in the home or yard. What problems do they solve?

4. Give five examples of how babies in play situations can influence and direct adults.

5. What changes in an infant/toddler setting would make parents feel more at home?

— Chapter Five —

Some Characteristics of Space

All spaces have size and scale, aesthetic qualities, entries and pathways, and a degree of spatial variety. These characteristics together give a space its *feel* and its sense of worka-bility.

Size and Scale

"In the United States today a great need exists for inner quiet and stillness, for things perceived at a comprehensible scale, and for meaningful human relationships."
Robert Sommer (1972, p. 32)

Scale is the proportion of an object relative to its surroundings. The most significant objects to consider as reference points are people. Scale is an aspect of size, numbers, even time. It is an important dimension in children's programs where inhabitants may range from 18 inches tall and 10 pounds to 6 feet and, well, let's just say very large.

Space and Objects

Scale affects how we feel. The cathedral mentioned earlier puts adults in a position that children are often in; we feel small and not very powerful. In a sports arena we feel part of a mass or, if we are down on the field, we feel the focus of mass attention. These feelings, of course, can be exhilarating or frightening. The double edged nature of scale is important to take into account. In an open field or at sea, we can feel *out in the open*— intoxicatingly free and unconfined. Or, we can feel *out in the open*— painfully exposed and vulnerable. In a tent we can feel snug and secure or closely shrouded. Children, who operate most of the time in

outsized surroundings, gravitate to the tiny in spaces, objects, and living things. But children

Photograph by Jean Wallech

also grow big before they grow well coordinated, and their need to move and exercise makes larger spaces desirable as well.

Scale affects our behavior and our ability to act competently. A dramatic example occurs when adults try to climb the stairway of an infant loft where the stairs have only a two inch rise and four inch depth. Everyone stumbles and inevitably feels gargantuan and foolish. Bodies, in this case, feet, *have memories*. When people outside children's programs sit on preschool chairs, they usually feel awkward and behave in a parallel fashion. Bottoms have memories also.

The scale of objects relative to the surroundings affects our experience of the space. When a piece of furniture is disproportionately large, like a climber or heavy storage unit, it can dominate the space and alter its feel, much as

Photograph by Nancy P. Alexander

mountains or skyscrapers dominate the landscape. An object out of proportion exerts an almost gravitational force. Of course, people of inordinate size have the same effect, such as adults relative to children.

The absolute size of a space is often less important than the perception of it. Some spaces appear larger or smaller because of the aesthetics, or because the layout creates pockets of dead space and compacted use, or because space is maximized by efficient use.

Objects and People

Maria Montessori pioneered "child scaling." Familiar to us now, one can imagine the astonishment she evoked in her time. Child scaled furnishings, equipment, and toys allow children to behave competently and feel powerful. But Montessori would have had trouble visualizing

our present child centered age in the United States; the child is no longer the "forgotten" in an adult world. Now it is the opposite; children are a market—sold to, deprived of reality and communion with the real world.

One could argue that a program environment where everything is child scaled may be appropriate for children who spend most of their time in homes (homes that make no concessions to child scale). But for children in all day settings and their caregivers, it can be stifling and oppressive. A mixture of adult and child scale is valuable for both caring and learning and minimizes the teacher as an outsized Gulliver in a Liliputian world.

Child scale is critical where we expect children to become independent and competent. How neatly do adults eat when the table is at chest level? How secure do we feel when chairs are too high for our feet to touch the floor or when we have to reach on tiptoes for essential materials? Utensils, sinks, toilets, water fountains, and storage units should be scaled to maximize independence.

How does the room look at eye level, all the eye levels—the teacher or parent, the baby in a back carrier, the child on the floor, and the five year old standing. If a visitor cannot guess the age of the children in the room by the location of the wall displays, there is work to be done. The world we see depends on our size.

Social Density

Social density refers to how many people inhabit the space. If there are too many people in a given space, we usually react negatively. Children react both by withdrawing, physically and socially, and by acting aggressively. The

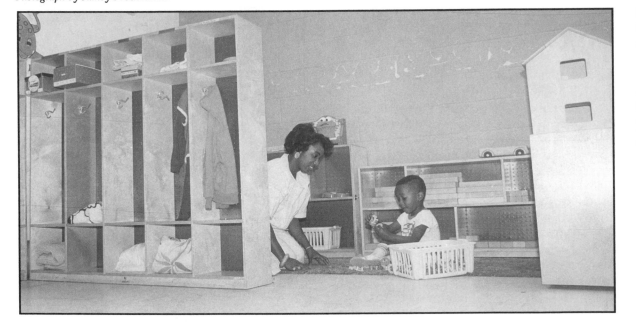

number of people affects the size and quantity of the objects possible in a working space. The more people, the more empty space is necessary for people to feel comfortable. The feeling of being crowded is the feeling of being observed, of being in the continual presence of others. Visual separation in space reduces the sense of crowding.

But there is both an individual and cultural dimension to density. Kritchevsky and Prescott (1969), echoing Hall, have found that children of certain ethnic groups, Mexican Americans for one, function well in what to most middle class Americans is relatively crowded and congested space. Kritchevsky and Prescott suspected the settings they observed resembled those which the children had experienced at home as affectionate, warm, and comfortable.

Our perception of crowding is affected not only by space but by smell and sound, and, even more importantly, temperature and humidity. A crowded, hot room is much less bearable than the same number of people in the same size cool room.

There is a time element as well to social density. Spending a large part of the day in a large group is wearing, whether in a school room or a family gathering.

Time

Why did summer seem so long when we were children and so short now? Why do farmers and corporate executives and people from other cultures respond to the passage of time differently? How does an infant experience time? There is no way for us to know, although we can suspect that a period of time seems much longer to a baby than to an adult. Time is a dimension to be taken into account in children's

environments. Anyone who remembers school is aware of the feelings of oppression when time is controlled by others.

Infants and Toddlers

Scaling for infants and toddlers is extremely difficult for architects, builders, and teachers. Babies are so small and operate so close to the ground. To paraphrase Randy Newman from his song, "Short People" (1977), they "have tiny little hands and tiny little feet." They are so different from us that we inevitably have problems. For example, for years I had recommended that programs purchase the four or six ounce juice glass scaled for toddlers' hands. The small narrow circumference fits a small hand. Some programs use dixie cups for the same reason. The problem is that, because of the small circumference, these glasses tip over at the drop of a pin. Also, given the carefree one-handed holding style of your average toddler,

Photograph by Jean Wallech

adults are constantly urging the children to use two hands. Far better are the eight ounce squat cups that are hard to tip over. These cups physically require children to use two hands.

Finding tables and chairs that allow older babies to both have their feet on the ground and the table at waist level and arranging to have sinks at toddler level are two common problems. The world of standard size sinks and cabinets and plumbing fixtures is not made for putting things 14 to 16 inches off the floor.

We also get fooled. We forget that young babies experience a range of sight lines and physical proximity because they are held so much.

Aesthetics

Imagine a room where there are bright splashes of color, often attached to moving bodies, and warm muted hues on carpet and walls. Sunshine catches the light of a prism in one corner, and there is a small patch of sunlight so bright you have to squint. There are soft indirect lights, shadows, and cool dark corners.

There are hanging baskets of trailing green plants, flowers, pussy willows and cattails, angel hair and dried grasses. The beauty of life is captured by Monet and Wyeth and assorted four year olds.

There are the smells of fresh dirt, lilacs and eucalyptus, garlic and baking bread.

One hears laughter and singing, animated conversation, soft classical music and the back beat of reggae from somewhere in the corridor. There is a ticking of clocks, chirping of birds, and the squeaking and rustling of a guinea pig.

There is a breeze from an open window as one walks around feeling heavy dark wood and silky fabric; hard cold metal and warm fur; complex textures; and watery, slippery, gooey things.

Everything somehow seems to fit together in a comprehensible way. The elements are not random. These are the aesthetic elements of life, of what makes the world a rich experience. They stimulate and nurture our many moods. Through them we glimpse the soul of nature and of humanity. They are the elements we hope to have in and around the places where we live, settings where children and adults spend days together.

The aesthetics in a children's setting are, as is everything else, a trade-off of cost, convenience, and health concerns. Plants and animals require tending. Fluorescent lighting is cost effective; uniform lighting coverage results in maximum flexibility. Washable surfaces are healthier and more functional; water, earth, and clay are messy, and so on. Too often the trade-offs don't take into account equally important concerns—appreciation for the rich sensual nature of children and the importance of beauty in our lives.

If a children's program is a *work* or *school* site geared to accomplishing narrow objectives in a constricted time frame, then aesthetic appeal may be secondary. All we ask of lecture halls is reasonably comfortable seating, good lighting, and a clear view of the teacher and the blackboard or screen. In a room with no highlights, the teacher is the highlight. For a child or adult in a setting for a few hours a day, beauty and character are nice, but not essential; we have that in our other settings. But as Golan et al. (Prescott and David, 1976, p. 131) found, we often lose the "essential totality" and continuity

in a child's life. Children who live in crowded, dingy apartments are likely to go to crowded, dingy schools; walk on congested, dingy streets; and use crowded, dingy transportation.

For babies, the importance of the perceptual environment, particularly the visual environment, cannot be underestimated. The more an infant sees and recognizes, the more an infant wants to see. Vision is the means the baby uses to make the world familiar. It is not simply a matter of quantity. Visual environments that are dull and sterile, or random and chaotic, or that contain busy murals that appeal to adults or complex (to a baby) images that appeal to older children are negative learning settings.

Consider the world of care and living: restaurants, motels, apartments, playgrounds, and nursing homes. These settings often lack character and a sense of beauty. Child care programs, with a diversity borne of homes,

The Importance of Beauty

In the 1950s, Dr. Abraham Maslow and Dr. Norbet Mintz conducted a study on the effects that beautiful surroundings have on human mental functioning. In the experiment, the researchers rigged up three rooms—an "ugly" room with a bare light bulb, grey walls, and torn shades; a "beautiful" room with large windows, indirect light, a Navajo rug, works of art, an armchair, bookcase, and a desk. The "average" room, according to the experimenters "gave the appearance of a clean, neat, worked-in office in no way outstanding enough to elicit any comment" (Hiss, 1987, p. 62).

Volunteers in the study were told that they "were studying photographs of people to see whether the faces displayed 'energy' and 'well-being'. The volunteers were supervised by three examiners, two of whom were themselves unaware that the real purpose of the exercise was to look at people's reactions to their surroundings. The results showed that people found energy and well-being in the faces when they looked at them in the beautiful room and found fatigue and sickness in the same faces when they looked at them in the ugly room; setting had a real impact on judgment. The behavior of the two examiners unaware of the project's intent also varied from room to room: they consistently rushed through interviews conducted in the ugly room, and also showed 'gross behavioral changes' when they worked there, and complained of 'monotony, fatigue, headache, sleepiness, discontent, irritability, hostility, and avoidance.' Surprisingly, although their job performance and their job satisfaction were over and over again affected by where they were, neither of the examiners noticed this fact even once. . . . Reactions to the average room more closely resembled the reactions to the ugly room than they did the reactions to the beautiful room" (Hiss, 1987, p. 62).

What do we see in the faces of children and adults in church basements or other resource-poor adapted child care settings? Where does the fatigue and irritability come from?

churches, and storefronts, tend to have character. But as the child care industry has grown and standards rightfully increased, character has sometimes given way to the pleasant and impersonal uniform aesthetic, indistinguishable from that of fast food places or branch banks. It is often an adult aesthetic designed to offer parents the images they associate with young children and their needs: bright colors and Sesame Street characters, furnishings clean as newsprint that appear riveted in place.

It does not have to be that way. Programs for children should take their ideas and inspiration from those places where we experience the world of people and things most fully.

Aspects of Aesthetic Appeal

Lighting: Few of us choose to live in windowless basements or light our homes uniformly with banks of fluorescent lighting. Uniform fluorescent lighting washes out colors and flattens perceptions, there is no focus and all subtlety is lost. Lighting can give space warmth and character and highlight specific areas and features. Light and shadow alter perceptions of things—their volume, shape, color, and texture. A mixture of lighting of different wattages and types as in homes creates a variety of living and learning spaces.

Color: Like light, color creates moods and highlights features. Human beings react physiologically to color. Cool colors like blues can exert a calming effect; warm reds and yellows stimulate us. Preliminary research in a new field of color therapy indicates that a bubble-gum color called passive pink may have an almost immediate effect on aggressive behavior (Hiss, 1987). Color can tie spaces together or create boundaries. Bright accent walls or patterns (visual texture) draw children to spaces.

Particular Places

The preschool programs in the schools in the Commune of Reggio Emilia in Northern Italy embody an appreciation of beauty and a sense of the wholeness of life: "The rooms are simply beautiful. There is attention to detail everywhere: in the color of their walls, the shape of the furniture, the arrangement of the simplest objects on shelves and tables. Light from the windows and doors shines through transparent collages and weavings made by the children. Healthy green plants are everywhere. Behind the shelves displaying shells are mirrors which reflect patterns which children and teachers have created. But the environment is not just beautiful—it is highly personal. For example, in one of the halls, a series of small boxes made of white cardboard create a grid on the wall. On each box the name of a child or teacher is printed with rubber stamp letters. These boxes are used for leaving little surprises or messages for one another.

Walking a little further, you see a display of pine cones placed in order by size, and next to them a series of round, polished pebbles arranged in rows by shades of color from white to dark gray. The natural beauty of these found objects, along with their form and size, is highlighted by the careful attention with which they have been arranged on a lighted shelf just at children's eye level.

Children are encouraged to bring in tokens of their home experience connected with daily or special events. They bring home shells from the seashore in the summer or traditional decorations when they return from winter vacations. Teachers collect these items and build displays where each child's contribution is respected and at the same time becomes part of a larger picture. For example, the children's decorations were each put in a transparent bag; the bags were all put together into a huge transparent hanging which caught light from a nearby window. Children could simply watch the play of light on the hanging, they could play counting games with the objects, they could gather round and compare what each of them had contributed.

The space in the schools of Reggio Emilia is personal in still another way: it is full of the children's own work. Visual expression is so important in the curriculum that an art director . . . works with teachers to help them display children's work. The results literally surround the people in this school. . . . It turns up even in unexpected spaces like the stairways and bathrooms."

from "Not Just Anywhere: Making Child Care Centers Into Particular Places," by Lella Gandini (**Beginnings**, 1984, p. 18)

Whites (and mirrors) make a space feel larger, while dramatic colors and patterns have the opposite effect.

Art and Display: Many programs use pictures that seem to appeal to children to signal that it is a child's place, like figures from children's books and cartoons and cute childish images. It is a signal both adults and children recognize. But cute and commercial does not have to be the dominant image. Images that appeal to children and represent higher artistic standards than mass cartoons can be selected. There are photographs and illustrations from children's books and numerous images from the art world that might compete with Fat Albert and Mickey Mouse.

However, because the children's own artwork should be displayed in abundance, added pictures and murals in the group space often create visual clutter. Bright cheery graphics present the same problem. Some programs seem kaleidoscopic; one is assaulted by colors and shapes—brightly clad children moving around bright primary colored plastic furniture and toys, encircled by bright graphics, murals, and children's art. Pictures, bright colors, and contrasting shapes are targets for attention. Too many targets create a sensory overload and exact their toll in fatigue or dulled senses, no matter how acclimated everyone becomes. Limiting the amount of display and locating display areas carefully improves the program aesthetics.

Texture: Texture is appreciated almost entirely by touch. Even when visually presented, it is the memory of tactile experiences that we appreciate. The skin is the largest organ of the body and provides our most personal sensations. For most people, life's most intimate moments are associated with touching and

Photograph by Nancy P. Alexander

being touched and with the changing texture of the skin. For children this is unquestionably true. If young children were designers, the textural quality of the space would be one of the first orders of business.

Nature: There is a tremendous aesthetic and learning value in living things. Plants and flowers add aesthetic appeal to the setting. Because they are alive, they also add complexity and novelty. Aquariums offer patterns of form, color, and motion, while birds offer color, motion, and sound.

Sounds: Our sense of space is derived from the sounds we hear and the silences. Sounds evoke strong physiological and psychological reactions. Sounds can soothe or jar, help one to focus, or serve as a bridge from one activity to

another. Music can be a stimulant more potent than caffeine. Because adults and children differ in their tolerance for noise and in their drive to make noise, the acoustical properties of settings are extremely important. Making noise is a powerful experience for a child, not being able to is a heavy restriction.

A great need to prevent noise is hard on teachers and children and will color all interactions. Keeping noise down becomes a test of a child's self-control and the teacher's competence in her own eyes and the eyes of other staff. The crowding voices of children close in on adults, and the felt need to control noise can alter both program structure and content. Children and

---

"Mediterranean Beach, Day after Storm" from "Love: Two Vignettes" by Robert Penn Warren

How instant joy, how clang
And whang the sun, how
Whoop the sea, and oh,
Sun, sing, as whiter than
Rage of snow, let sea the spume
Fling.

Let sea the spume, white, fling,
White on blue wild
With wind, let sun
Sing, while the world
Scuds, clouds boom and belly,
Creak like sails, whiter than,
Brighter than,
Spume in sun-song, oho!
The wind is bright.

poets, Robert Penn Warren and others, bring inner sounds with them to spaces, sounds that often must get out. Yet the absence of silence can be equally oppressive to children, silence to hear their inner sounds. Noise is a major cause of stress for both adults and children.

Ideally, spaces in children's settings would allow for silence, the steady hum of play, and the explosive noises that punctuate exuberant living. Sounds from the outer world would neither be absent nor intrusive.

Smell: Researchers take seriously the view that we respond to smell much as we respond to color. Some smells, cooked onions for one, cause us to salivate and feel hungry. Others, like pine, seem to have a calming effect. Certainly the psychological effect of a smell such as baking cookies is obvious.

Entries and Pathways

All space has a way in, a way out, and ways to get from one point to another. Together these features regulate the traffic flow of inhabitants. When well designed, entries and exits and movement between spaces are physically and emotionally smooth, even during emergencies.

Entries

Opening a door brings with it a sense of promise or peril. Who knows what the greeting will be? What will be taking place within? Will my teacher be there or will it be a stranger? Are they doing my favorite thing? Will I feel stupid? Will I be able to leave?

Closing the door ends an experience. It's over. Am I glad? sad? content? ambivalent? Some exits are dramatic, some routine.

The physical space structures the ease of our entry and exit. Doors carry a greater sense of finality than open entry ways. Foyers and open space between the entry and the action allow a more measured entry. I talked with a four year old who was unhappy going to her child care center, a wonderful setting bustling with life and learning opportunities and talented adults. It turned out that what she hated was going in, by mid-morning all was fine. Her entry got her off to a terrible start. She was usually the last child in and the door was shut. She opened the door to an active scene, formidably social, that came right up to the door. There was no measured entry; bang she was in, as if she had stepped into a video game. As I listened, I identified completely. She could have been expressing my feelings about entering a crowded party.

Everyone at times, but perhaps children especially, needs to reconnoiter before acting, to go part way and test the waters. The world is a much less familiar place to children. Each day brings new wonder and unexpected trials. It must appear to many children that their lives can change the way a day changes from sunny

---

Doors
by Carl Sandburg

An open door says, "Come in"
A shut door says, "Who are you?"
Shadows and ghosts go through shut doors.
If a door is shut and you want it shut,
     why open it?
If a door is open and you want it open,
     why shut it?
Doors forget but only doors know what it is
     doors forget.

Photograph by Shawn Connell

to rainy. Their control over themselves is often shaky, and they find themselves in situations that bring on anxiety and fear. How pathways and entries are structured—whether there are staging areas and observation points, for instance—makes a difference. When the physical space does not allow a measured entry or exit, there is an increased responsibility on the part of adults to make greeting and departure a positive experience.

Separation is central to coming and going in children's programs. Whether a source of pain or hard won pride, it is always to some degree an emotional experience. The more abrupt the transition, the more difficult the experience. Yet a seamless transition presents problems. Both adults and children benefit from a transition space or time. A foyer with windows into the room, a cubby area, the ritual act of helping a child with his things, or a spot in the room where there is an implicit exchange of responsibility for the child, between parent and teacher, can each serve this function. With a baby, a literal handover is important for most parents. For older children, it can be a three-way acknowledgement through words, touch, or, minimally, smiles, gestures, and eye contact.

Pathways

A pathway is "the empty space on the floor or ground through which people move from one place to another. Pathways are difficult to describe in words but easy to identify, if well defined. Look at a space and ask yourself the question 'How do children get from one space to another?'" (Prescott, 1984, p. 46). Without clear pathways, it's like being in a huge unmarked parking lot. Either you need traffic police (the teachers) or all present must be continually alert (both tiring and stressful), or you have collisions. A clear path is important whether it's four feet or forty feet long.

Pathways are the routes commonly taken, not necessarily planned. Outside sidewalks are the official paths; dirt paths worn into the grass are unofficial, but no less real. With children under 18 months—where a slight incline or bump, an object, or even a crack may force the novice toddler back to his knees—the clarity of a pathway is not always obvious to the adults. Spillover of materials from one area to another may negate the path. Also, for that age, a pathway is a perfectly respectable place to plop yourself down and investigate whatever catches your fancy. This results in some delicate social maneuvering.

Designed with People in Mind?

In "Mental Health and Urban Design," Bruno Bettelheim (1979) looks at the architecture of schools:

"No more dismal view of man can be imagined than one that seems to inspire our public school buildings. . . . Consider the corridors in most of our schools. The first thing that strikes one is their appalling length. Our big schools, by their very size, rule out any chance of intimacy and defy the human dimension . . . at set intervals several times a day, a few thousand pupils rush in every direction for five minutes. Instead of relaxing and socializing between classes for ten or fifteen minutes in *their* corridor, youngsters in the high schools merely jostle a horde of other youngsters, most of them essentially strangers to each other. . . . Yet corridors could educate and give the feeling that they were built as something for children to enjoy, not to be funnelled through. But these corridors are so structured as to compel us to hurry through them. We cannot tarry to enjoy momentary leisure, to let our thoughts wander as we stroll to develop personal relations. . . .

To make matters worse, most school corridors double as locker rooms. Unfortunately, as far as design is concerned, no thought is given to these lockers, although they figure importantly in the lives of the students. . . . We all know what we mean when we speak of a locker room spirit. Now, it may not be a completely desirable spirit, but it does work—it makes for friendships. Yet in our schools we don't even give our students the locker rooms that might make for this spirit. As a result, the corridor is neither a place for informal encounters, which it could be, nor does it invite companionable walking, which it could do. . . .

If it were not bad enough to herd children through the school corridors, we do the same in the lunchroom. Eating together is the greatest socializing experience in life, beginning with the infant's earliest relations when he is fed by his mother. . . . The cafeteria is the place where the children could and should socialize; this if anywhere, is where they could come to feel attachment for their school and their friends. But compare this with the actual situation: typically, the cafeteria is much too large a room, seating far too many youngsters at one time" (pp. 210-212).

Similar problems exist for visually impaired children. Pathways can be made into avenues of sound and texture to guide children with limited sight.

Pathways structure our experience. "A meandering path between activities will allow the children to look over each potential activity and a bypass route would allow quick movement

Halfway Down
By A. A. Milne

Halfway down the stairs
Is a stair
Where I sit.
There isn't any
Other stair
Quite like
It.
I'm not at the bottom,
I'm not at the top;
So this is the stair
Where
I always
Stop.

Halfway up the stairs
Isn't up,
And it isn't down.
It isn't on the nursery,
It isn't in the town.
And all sorts of funny thoughts
Run round my head:
"It isn't really
Anywhere!
It's somewhere else
Instead!"

from one side of the room to another without disrupting those engaged in an activity or those children 'shopping'" (Osmon,1971, p. 35). A straight line path with forks or intersections defines specific choices. A child's visual scope may change along a path. Inside, different divider heights create different visual access, as do corners; a child has the chance to come across the unexpected. Pathways that narrow and expand create different social experiences or at

least the potential for interchange. Again, a path is a path no matter what the length.

Pathways are in themselves experiences. They can occasion different motor experiences, depending on surfaces, grades, steps, and railings. A path in a Japanese garden is designed so that each step brings forth a new view, a new sequence of muscular actions: lifting the foot onto a step stone, walking over a narrow bridge, peering between branches. A child's path may be designed in the same fashion. Inside, the pathway can involve motor experiences as

Photograph by Jean Wallech

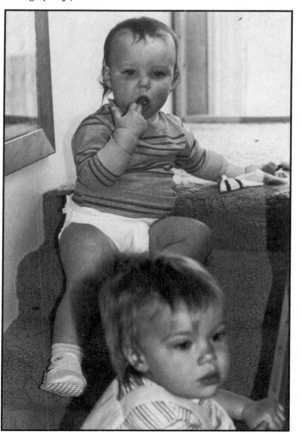

The Stone Frog
Glenn Pritchard

The great stone frog doorstop
watched my passing legs
with sinister eyes. The hop
that never came dared
me to pass; I was twelve
before I knew it never cared.

well—tunnels, balance beams or planks on a rug, and rough or smooth surfaces.

Stops on a pathway may or may not be demarcated. An entry or exit to a space that requires some physical action such as opening a gate, stepping up, down, or over, or even making a sharp turn forces the child to **decide** whether to go in or out and reduces wandering and flitting.

If adults periodically travel the pathways on their knees, or even hands and knees, they can see the child's view from the path—the hidden materials, the imposing entrance and so on.

Spatial Variety

When we look for places to live, we use a number of criteria: Is it big enough? Does it have enough rooms? How is it laid out? How much light does it get? The color, the way it's built, and so on enter into our decision. There is something else we look for—character or charm, those elements that make a space interesting and attractive: an alcove or skylight, high or sloped ceilings, unusual windows or an abundance of windows, fireplaces, different

Photograph by Shawn Connell

the room six inches higher than others. This forever limited the possible grouping arrangements, to say nothing of the endless embarrassing stumbling. Sky lights flooding a room with light is a positive, unless the room is destined to become a nap or crib room.

Many open classrooms are designed to be ultra flexible: large open spaces, movable dividers and furniture. Many church basements are similarly open. Maximum flexibility allows us to accommodate to program changes, but there is a cost. This is a trap that so many proponents of a certain kind of "flexibility make: they leave too much to use. To achieve *flexibility* we are encouraged to sacrifice not only the variety of familiarized features (the defining objects) but also the variety of familiarized places (for our occupation) between them. It should not surprise us that *flexible* buildings are

---

levels, or rooms of different dimensions. Some combination of these factors cause us to **love** a space; it is these aspects we remember long after we have moved. The homes people covet are filled with spaces that can become *our places* as they catch our experiences like dust: sunny bedrooms and airy porches, shady yards and warm kitchens, steep stairs and cool cellars. Of course, some of these elements we remember because we subsequently hated them or found them useless, like the charming little room too small to be a bedroom or the curved windows that cost a fortune to fix.

Potential for a collective sense of *our place* and a number of *my places* is important in

children's programs. Space with character, with placemakers and friendly or defining objects, will enhance those other elements that *make houses homes*: beloved familiar people, daily rituals, and the feeling, in both children and adults, that they can personalize the space.

Good space in a children's setting offers character with flexibility. Small rooms, however charming, are still small rooms; and changing group size, staff-child ratios, or the age group served may negate the value of small rooms. One can always create small spaces within a large space, but the reverse is not possible. The same thing is true with multi-level space. One open center was designed with some areas of

---

The Cellar
by Hilda Conkling

I love my queer cellar
with its dusty smell,
its misty smell,
like smoke fringes from clouds blowing past;
with its shelves and jams and goodies,
with its boxes, barrels, woodpiles here and there.

There is a passageway to an unknown room
where bins hold carrots and things.
There are glass doors that bang
and cob-webbed windows.
I love the quietness of my cellar,
thinking in the dark.
My cellar has apples in its breath, potato's even.
That smell of earth.

inevitably so unrewarding because by removing their landmarks and their features—they lose their potential" (Pragnell, 1969, p. 39).

It doesn't have to be one or the other, flexibility or character. Character can come from furnishings and woodwork, windows and lighting, placemakers and friendly objects. As the day stretches on, the right space for the particular moment becomes important. In an

Photograph by Jean Wallech

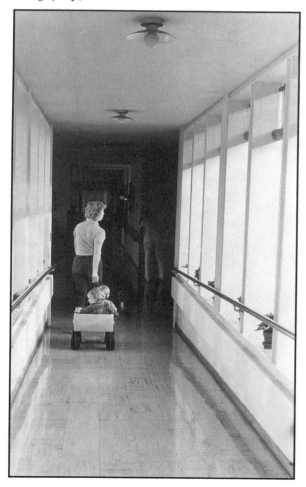

office or factory, we **need** that moment at the water fountain, in the lounge or bathroom, by the window. The child needs that moment, too, whether under a table, on a window seat, or in a secluded corner. For children space is the terrain *from* which they learn, not a site they learn in. Bland or uniform space limits their learning.

As the days turn into weeks and the weeks turn into months, as each child develops, the group develops and the seasons change, space with a potential to change greatly assists staff in their efforts. Some space has more potential than others. Square spaces are the hardest to work with because it is hard to create pathways and distance between activities without creating *dead* space. Dead space is empty space that defies definition as an activity area, often in the center of the room. Narrow rectangular space is equally difficult and almost never escapes a corridor effect. Good outdoor space offers the most opportunity for variety.

Exercises

1. Close your eyes and try to remember settings (gyms, waiting rooms etc.) in terms of smell, sound, touch.

2. Where do you feel the smallest? The largest? The most alone? The most crowded?

3. What are some "lovely things close by" if you look?

4. Think about the pathways and entries that you experience frequently. What behaviors and feelings do they engender?

— Chapter Six —

Dimensions of Children's Settings

"Be not afeared, the isle is full of noises,
Sounds and sweet airs, that give delight, and
hurt not.
Sometimes a thousand twanging instruments
Will hum about mine ears; and sometimes voices,
That, if I then waked after a long sleep,
Will make me sleep again: and then in dreaming,
The clouds methought would open, and show riches
Ready to drop upon me; that, when I waked,
I cried to dream again."
from **The Tempest** by William Shakespeare

"This is a good place for children." "I like working here." "I feel so good about my child's program." These are testimonials to a setting that works. Why does it work? "The staff really care about kids." "The children do a lot of really neat activities and really learn." "The children seem very happy and well behaved."

Yes, but why are the children happy and well behaved, and how are the staff able to care for children and provide wonderful activities? While children's settings vary in purpose and philosophy, and the people in early childhood programs vary in expertise and personalities, there are environmental dimensions that apply to all settings and are useful analytical tools. This section will consider ten important dimensions of children's settings.

1—Comfort and Security

"American education seems to have reduced the senses to nil."
Isadora Duncan

The classroom was spotless as the three year old children entered. Gleaming tile floors, walls, and tables; a tidy, carpeted area; orderly, well stocked shelves; cheerful teachers; cheery murals and bulletin boards—all greeted children as they wandered, exploded, and reluctantly made their way into the room. All day long the children were busy at tables, in the block corner, in the housekeeping area, or in activities with the teachers. The routines were efficient—lunch and snacks were downed, the children slept, noses were wiped, more activities were performed, and the children went home.

It was all very impressive, but I went home feeling terribly sorry for the children. Something was missing, something important. When the children were gone, there was no imprint, none of the general residue or artifacts of lived lives. The image in my mind was the famous picture of Harlow's monkeys, reared in cages and fed by cloth-covered wire monkeys. The care and the education were there, but it was a place devoid of feeling, of character, of real warmth.

Most people demand comfort* from the places where they live and work. They need pliability, a responsiveness in their furnishings and co-inhabitants. The strains and tensions of everyday life may literally be washed away by an evening shower or made manageable by a stretch on a couch, cuddling with a child or lover, or simply a few moments of silence in an easy chair. Young children, more recent womb-dwellers, operate in a world dominated more by sensory impression than by mind and language. The classroom described above, appropriate for a half day nursery school, lacked the essential comforts of home—physical contact with others and soft places to be.

Another setting: Children were sprawled around the room, on the rug, on laps, on and behind the couch. Some children played outside in a sandbox, others whiz-banged around with trucks, others pounded play dough. One little boy gave himself a sponge bath while purportedly washing his hands. As the day went on, children worked at tables while others stretched out with books. Adults were free with hands and laps and legs to lean on (literal pillars of security). During the course of the day, almost all

---

*For a fascinating and witty look at the idea and practice of *comfort*, see **Home: A Short History of an Idea** by Witold Rybczynski (New York: Viking, 1986).

Photograph by Jean Wallech

of the same activities would take place as in the other classroom, but the contrast in warmth and comfort was enormous. Here, children seemed to have full use of their bodies and senses. Life seemed embedded in this setting.

2—Softness

In schools, workplaces, and other institutions, many things are far too hard, edgy, cold, and unrelenting. People like things rounded and cushioned and warm to the touch. A hard physical setting, combined with the inflexibility of institutional or group life, deadens people. They are left with no way to make an imprint—literally, to **make their presence felt** on anything.

Prescott and Jones identified *softness* as a key dimension in their research on day care settings:

"The dimension of *softness* was so named because it appeared to indicate a responsive quality of the environment to the child, especially on a sensual/tactile level. It was based on the presence or absence of 11 components: (1) malleable materials, such as clay or play-doh; (2) sand that children can be in, either in a box or play area; (3) "laps"—teachers holding children; (4) single-sling swings; (5) grass that children can be on; (6) a large rug or carpeting indoors; (7) water as an activity; (8) very messy materials, such as finger paint, clay, or mud; (9) child/adult cozy furniture, such as rockers, couches, or

lawn swings; (10) dirt to dig in; and (11) animals that can be held, such as guinea pigs, dogs, and cats. The softest activity settings are also the most perennially appealing" (Prescott, 1984, p. 52).

A soft, responsive, physical environment reaches out to children. It helps children to feel more secure, enabling them to venture out and explore the world, much like homes provide adults the haven from which they can face an often difficult and heartless world. The moments alone *spaced out* on a swing, rocking in a chair or a rocking horse, or kneading dough allow children to recharge. But softness has an equally significant educational purpose, because so much of young children's learning is sensory-motor based and requires hands-on (more accurately, bodies-on) experience. Pounding on play dough or smearing paint is not only therapeutic and fun but exactly the kind of learning that teaches children how the material world works. Handling animals and plants requires children to be gentle and sensitive to living things. Adult stomachs and laps and arms reassure with the intimacy of touch, smell, and body warmth, and at the same time provide the proximity necessary for quality language interactions and social learning. The younger the child and the longer the day, the more importance softness and comfort assume.

Comfort and softness are adult issues as well. A six to eight hour day with children requires considerable giving of one's physical and emotional self. Adults, no less than children, replenish their reservoirs of energy, patience, and good will through moments of relaxation free from the need to remain upright and erect. Adults also reduce stress by working with pliable sensory materials like clay, bread dough, or water, and by having moments of relaxed physical contact with other human

Photograph by Jean Wallech

beings. The intimacy of snuggling with a young child or rubbing a baby's stomach calms both human beings involved.

To say that comfort and softness are important is not to say that children's settings need to be pleasure domes fit for sultans. Early childhood educational settings are also work settings for children and adults, sites for no-nonsense upright learning and performing. Activities that require concentration of mind and body, such as building, listening, writing, and stacking, benefit from a hard context with minimal distractions. There needs to be a balance. Comfort provides the security for fledgling scholars to tackle the demands of sustained concentration. It masks and mutes the necessary efficiency and order of institutional life. A physical environment that yields compensates somewhat for the imposing demands group living requires of individuals, yielding to the pace, interests, and sensibilities of the group.

3—Security

Probably nothing is more fundamental than ensuring that each child feels secure in a pro-

gram. Earlier, in the discussion on babies, it was mentioned that children feel secure in places where they can "safely relax." They are in a safe, familiar place with people they trust. The world is predictable, manageable, and fits their idiosyncratic concerns. A sense of security is bound up in all the dimensions discussed in this section.

"In smaller, more familiar things," says Freya Stark, "memory weaves her strongest enchantments, holding us at her mercy with some trifle, some echo, a tone of voice, a scent of tar and seaweed on the quay. . . . This surely is the meaning of home—a place where every day is multiplied by all the days before it" (Morris, 1948, pp. 138-139).

Home

Mole's return to his home, Mole's End, after exhilarating experiences in the (upper) world at large, captures the value of a home:

". . . the Mole, his bosom still heaving with the stress of his recent emotion (joy to be home mixed with shame at the humbleness of his home), related [to his friend Rat]—somewhat shyly at first, but with more freedom as he warmed to his subject—how this was planned, and how that was thought out, and how this was got through a windfall from his aunt, and that was a wonderful find and a bargain, and this other thing was bought out of laborious savings and a certain amount of 'going without.' His spirits finally quite restored, he must needs go and caress his possessions, and take a lamp and show off their points to his visitor and expatiate on them, quite forgetful of the supper they both so much needed. . . .

But ere he closed his eyes he let them wander around his old room, mellow in the glow of the firelight that played or rested on familiar and friendly things which had long been unconsciously a part of him, and now smilingly received him back without rancor. He was now in just the frame of mind that the tactful Rat had quietly worked to bring about in him. He saw clearly how plain and simple—how narrow even—it all was; but clearly, too, how much it all meant to him, and the special value of some such anchorage in one's existence. He did not at all want to abandon the new life and its splendid spaces, to turn his back on sun and air and all they offered him and creep home and stay there; the upper world was all too strong, it called to him still, even down there, and he knew he must return to the larger stage. But it was good to think he had this to come back to, this place which was all his own, these things which were so glad to see him again and could always be counted upon for the same simple welcome."

from **The Wind in the Willows**, by Kenneth Grahame (pp. 74-75, 81-82)

Home Two

But homes are not always physical places. For very young children and many adults, home is where needed loved ones are. In Tennessee William's **Night Of The Iguana** (1962, Act 3), two rootless people—Hannah Jelkes, a middle-aged spinster, and her grandfather—are home to each other. Hannah Jelkes describes this to another character:

"Hannah: We make a home for each other, my grandfather and I. Do you know what I mean by a home? I mean I don't mean what other people mean when they speak of a home . . . a place, a building . . . a house of wood, bricks, stone. I think of a home as being a thing that two people have between them in which each can . . . well nest—rest—live in, emotionally speaking. Does that make any sense to you, Mr. Shannon?

Shannon: Yeah, complete. But . . . when a bird builds a nest to rest in and live in, it doesn't build it in a . . . falling down tree.

Hannah: I am not a bird, Mr. Shannon.

Shannon: I was making an analogy, Miss Jelkes.

Hannah: I thought you were making yourself another rum-coco, Mr. Shannon."

4—Safety and Health

3 Facts and a Paradox

Fact Number 1: Children learn by physically doing. People learn how to do things safely by doing them and learning from mistakes. Spills, scrapes, cuts, and bruises are part of a childhood where human beings develop their physical capacities and learn how the world works.

Fact Number 2: Fact Number 1 is easier to swallow, reading it here, than coping with a child's broken leg or worse.

Fact Number 3: Most insurance agents, regulating agencies, and many parents do not want to hear about Fact Number 1.

A Paradox: (1) There is nothing more important than ensuring a healthy, safe setting. (2) There is nothing more important than ensuring a warm, personal, challenging setting.

No one would ever entrust their child to a setting that did not view the child's well-being as the primary concern. Clearly, a safe and healthy environment is at the top of any list of goals. Group care of children poses some particular concerns in the area of infectious

disease control and accident prevention, particularly for infants and toddlers. Yet, important as they are, safety and health are only two of several characteristics of the environment that involve trade-offs with other desirable characteristics, like learning and warmth and security.

Health and safety are relative after all. Everyone does cross busy streets, talk to strangers, eat foods untasted by others, take some risks to health, and so on. Reasonably prudent precautions are taken to ensure continued well-being, although seat belt usage, and tolerance of pollution, toxic waste, and weak arms control policies may somewhat belie this. Unfortunately, in an institutional setting under the purview of various regulating agencies and insurance underwriters with preemptive power, this need for trade-offs may be disregarded.

Health

Warmth and security for a young child comes in part (the non-people part) from a familiar home-like setting and physical contact with other bodies and softness—a relaxed, sensual, and personal experience of the physical and human universe. This sounds inviting. It also sounds germ ridden. Our model for sanitary places is the hospital: hard, clean places of stainless steel and tile, uniforms and plastic gloves, the pervasive smell of disinfectant. *Warm* and *sensual* and *home-like* are seldom used adjectives in bright, gleaming corridors.

In a group setting, the transmission of infectious disease is an ever-present serious threat, as is food poisoning. Sanitation obviously plays a critical role in providing a healthy setting. The personal and environmental hygienics of diapering, toileting, food handling, and washing and bathing are constant causes for concern. The importance of handwashing cannot be overstated. Programs where hand-washing is routine and thorough are far superior in reducing the incidence of infectious disease (Aronson, 1984). The amount of fresh air and the number of children and crowding play a role, as does the amount of stress and strain the setting requires the children and adults to cope with. A growing and frightening concern that applies to any setting is the exposure to unhealthy materials in the environment: lead, asbestos, toxic chemicals, and radiation, to name just a few.

Health issues involve a delicate balance. There have to be policies restricting the attendance of ill children and staff. The setting must be washable. But an excessively overriding concern for health may create antiseptic, sterile places of plastic and stainless steel. Overconcern may make most current child care settings unsuitable and unlicensable without costly change (generally, plumbing), decreasing the supply of child care or at least the **legal** supply. Rigid exclusionary policies for children and staff may make it difficult for parents with illness prone children to work; staff illness may leave the program understaffed. Too much or too little is obviously not good for children, parents, or staff.

There are few aspects of environmental design that do not have some implication for health and safety, from the location of the building to the location of a sink to the selection of furnishings and equipment. This will be considered in Part Two.

5—Safety and Risk

Many of the safety issues in children's settings are identical to those in other settings. Is the environment free of hazards that are likely to cause serious accidents from falls, falling objects, burns, fires, poisoning or choking, cuts, punctures, and so on? The quantity of equipment and material in a group setting and the number of activities occurring during the course of a day can provide the raw material for much bodily harm. Children present special problems because they are less experienced with the world of things and people; their judgment reflects that. They are less experienced with their bodies which are changing so rapidly that they literally grow into them overnight; their movements reflect that. But, as they grow, their physical and social coordination increases, their egocentrism diminishes, and their judgment and impulse control improves.

Children are major instruments in their own protection. From birth on children begin learning how to protect themselves to the limit of their judgment. Infants in a group setting learn how to avoid some threatening social situations and handle new motor learning. As they grow older, most children acquire a sophisticated sense of what they can and cannot do, often through painful trial and error. But children approach the world progressively. They don't climb to the top of a tree and jump from the top branch. When children are doing something they know to be risky, like being up high on a climber, they are usually much more alert. Some children, of course, have poor judgment or are extremely impulsive or are risktakers. They are usually easily identifiable because they are often banged up.

Young children are also instruments of harm and carriers of mayhem. Children under three are usually oblivious to the safety of others and a major potential source of harm to each other.

There is a continuum of thought on the issue of how much a children's setting should factor out the risk of various degrees of harm. This ranges from A. S. Neill's (author of **Summerhill**) observation that we **must** give children rope in order for them to learn **not** to hang themselves (or others) to that of an anonymous day care director who, upon hearing of Neill's conviction, remarked: "Why would I give them rope? I took out the climber and the swings because of accidents. No way am I going to give them rope, shovels, or anything else that they can use on each other." The *things* that do the most damage are other children. (Does that mean solitary confinement as a risk prevention alternative?)

Most programs would agree with the Toronto Ministry of Culture's guideline for playgrounds that the goal is to eliminate the chance of serious accidents that might lead to permanent injury (skull fractures, concussions, and so on) and to minimize minor injuries. Their definition of minor injuries, which includes broken bones as well as cuts and abrasions, would no doubt inspire spirited debate.

There are often serious consequences if a program eliminates opportunities for children to use their bodies and materials in a way that involves some risk and daring. In a sterile, padded world with insufficient stimulation or challenge, humans either turn themselves off or turn to and on each other for stimulation. One sees this repeatedly in some child care programs. It is probably most dramatic with toddler age children in settings devoid of challenge, particularly motor challenges: some children respond through withdrawal and regression, others through biting and other antisocial acts. Or challenge is found illegally: climbing on shelves, escaping to other rooms, knocking about to get a reaction. The net effect is often that the potential for harm is not reduced, only the source of harm is redirected.

The second consequence may be that trial and error learning and risk is simply deferred to another time and place, possibly where the risk is much greater. Children **will**, in fact **must**, experiment with running, throwing, climbing, building treehouses and forts, daring death and destruction and discovering that, in fact, they are not invulnerable Wonderwomen and Supermen. They **will** apply their bodies to equipment in a *scientific test* of the properties and relations between the objects in space: running up the slide, sliding or swinging on stomachs, standing on a chair, and like experiences.

Children should learn to approach all the world has to offer in a safe, competent way.

Photograph by Francis Wardle

Caroline Pratt, a leading educator in the early part of the century and the inventor of unit blocks and other wonderful materials, "believed in teaching children to 'manage danger.' To this end, she removed guard rails on climbers, slides, and platforms (four feet from the ground). She increased the *danger* in each grade. The tens pedaled an automatic jigsaw machine; the elevens operated a printing press, the twelves worked on a motorized wood lathe. A child graduating from the City and Country School usually developed manipulative skills, regard for safety, and self-control that served him well throughout his lifetime" (Caplan and Caplan, 1974, p. 270). Pratt, Neill, Prescott, and other educators with a respect for children's competence and potential for learning believe children are cheated if we sacrifice challenge and experience before the altar of ostensible safety. Educational settings are where the resources and know-how should be available to **safely** offer experiences that challenge and teach children.

Safety issues are complex and not simply a matter of the presence or absence of certain equipment. A common response to an accident is to remove the offending equipment. But safety involves the use and context of the equipment, the expectations of staff and children, and program knowledge, expertise, and staffing. Equipment and materials should be **continuously** monitored for safety and repair and safe use. It is the safe use that is critical; the use should always be considered in the context. Swings are not unsafe in and of themselves, even swings where children can stand or swing on their stomachs. Nor are platforms, ladders, or slides inherently unsafe. However, if there are too many children and/or too few things to do, if crowding is common, if it is too small a space or if the layout is poor so innocent bystanders are in jeopardy, or if there are hard

Photograph by Jean Wallech

surfaces or objects close by that increase the potential for injury, the **use** of active motor equipment does present a threat.

Equipment may work in one context and be unsafe in another. A loft or climber with only one exit may be fine in a context with a small number of children, or with other equally attractive equipment, or in the midst of relatively mannered motor play. But in a different context, the single exit may inspire *king of the mountain* play or traffic jams and subsequent accidents. Some pieces of equipment or settings are appropriate for one age of children and dangerous for another (e.g., older children may scale the roof of a toddler playhouse). Appropriateness for the age group is an important consideration that is often hard to design for settings like playgrounds which are used by children of different ages. The safety implications of design choices is a major concern in Part Two.

It is sad that most outdoor play or indoor active play areas have the minimum amount of space necessary or equipment that offers too few play opportunities. And frequently, a minimum amount of time and effort is spent on maintenance of outdoor play spaces. A consequence is that adults are forced into the role of police, sometimes under the guise of *teaching*, to constrain the natural and necessary play of children. "Don't swing on your stomach." "Slides are for coming down." "Hold on." This doesn't sound like a litany of oppression, but it can be. Depriving children of the chance to experiment with movement is no less oppressive than later trying to deprive them of the chance to experiment with ideas. Too much concern for safety and containment prevents learning autonomy and responsibility.

6—Privacy and Social Space

"Don't get me wrong. I love my family. But at our family reunion in San Francisco, with spouses and children, after three days we were all ready to kill each other (or at least kill Murray). We had done everything together. We went to the museum in a group, ate together, relaxed in a group, argued in a group. We were like some weird middle age gang." Bernie, unwittingly recreating a common childhood experience

Children's settings are social settings. A major appeal of the nursery school movement was the opportunity for young children to have the opportunity to leave the home for structured group social experiences with other children. Companionship with other children mitigates the child's intense intellectual and emotional egocentrism, when the child is forced to accommodate to other perspectives and purposes. However, "it is not the mere presence of other children but active participation with them, doing real things together, an active interchange of feeling and experience, which educates the child" (Issacs, S. 1970, p. 226).

Good design in early childhood settings reflects the need for a congenial active social

Photograph by Jean Wallech

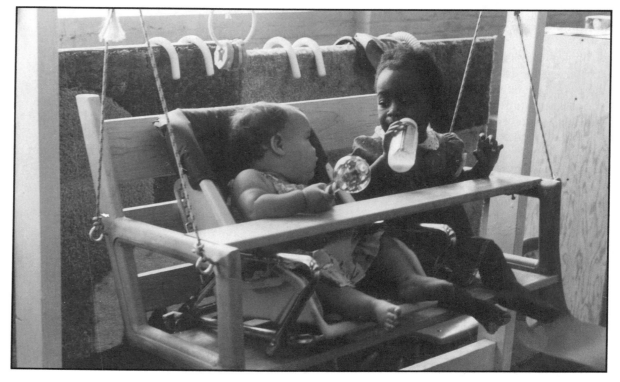

environment, where positive social relationships are fostered. This requires settings that facilitate play and encourage participation at different levels and at the same time allow non-participation. Early childhood programs are usually the first time a child submits himself to the judgment of his peers. This is a serious business.

Prescott observes that not only do activities differ in social structure—large group, small group, individual—but there is another important dimension of activities, "intrusion/seclusion," that the setting must take into account (Prescott, 1984, p. 52). Some activities thrive on the intrusion of people and events, such as "high-energy, fast moving dramatic play. . . . Making social contact and getting something started often require an opportunity for some intrusion. Climbing structures from which a child at the top can call, 'See me! See me!' are appropriately planned for intrusion" (p. 52).

No less necessary is providing for those play experiences that require seclusion—"places where a child can play privately or in a more deliberate, intimate way" (p. 53). Reading a book, trading treasures with a best friend, or concentrating on some difficult task, like doing a stacking toy if you are 18 months or a model if you are 8, all require seclusion. Away from the action and flow, a preschool child can construct and sustain an imaginary world: a manageable world where he or she is at the center, working through the bewildering issues of growing up. School age children can explore what it means to have best friends or exclusive, secret clubs.

Prescott and Jones (1972, p. 47) point out, "Children need a simplified environment when they are feeling little, tired, unhappy, or out of control." Private spaces to retreat to, removed from the stimulating hustle and bustle, allow for

that. In all day settings these feelings are more frequent.

Adults, of course, have similar needs; the oppression of the family reunion scene above stems from the adult's feelings of being unable to leave the pack and seek his own space. Withdrawal can be a healthy and necessary adaptation.

Adults generally break down into groups of manageable sizes if given the chance. At parties or a lunch table, once the group size increases much beyond four to six, people break off into subgroups for conversations, or at least often wish they could. Otherwise, someone may capture and hold the center stage. This is not unlike what occurs in group times with children. The person in the limelight is either the teacher or an attention-seeking child.

It is important to recognize that there are degrees of privacy in a space. Physical boundaries may or may not provide visual or acoustic separation. Our needs for total separation depend on the setting and our state of being.

Photograph by Nancy P. Alexander

Acoustic separation assumes great importance in a noisy setting, particularly if the noise is sharp and irregular or if we want privacy to wail and moan or explode with joy.

Fred Osmon considers these needs when he discusses designing another kind of place: "places to pause for awhile" (Osmon, 1971, pp. 43-45). Trying to pin down the illusive qualities of the spaces that children choose to pause in, Osmon found that "these places can generally be characterized as not obvious, multi-purpose, and having a 'found' quality." They are enclosed, but the "amount of enclosure needed was not absolute—a **sense** of privacy was desired rather than total physical isolation." Children are attracted to "elements within the environment that have a quality of delight and constant change." Places to pause often reflect this—a window to the street, a view to another group, a fish tank, a mobile, or a teacher designed *surprise* space.

Places to pause are not all the same. There is a distinction between enclosed spaces that allow a teacher to see in, enclosed spaces which allow children to see out, and spaces that may not be enclosed but that have a defined sense of place and allow lingering. Children need places to watch from and to hold back in, places in which to hide and seek things, and places which enable them to pause and reflect.

Unfortunately, as Prescott, Harms, and Clifford (1986) and others have found, these private spaces, retreats, and "places to pause" are often absent in centers or limited to a single "cozy corner." The contrast with homes is dramatic. Most homes are rich in private spaces and places to pause, beds and tables to be under, closets and rooms to be in, windows and doors to look out, varied furniture to be behind. Again, observing children in their *natural habitat*

The Secret Cavern
by Margaret Widdemer

Underneath the boardwalk, way, way back,
There's a splendid cavern, big and black—
If you want to get there, you must crawl
Underneath the posts and steps and all
When I've finished paddling, there I go—
None of all the other children know!

There I keep my treasures in a box—
Shells and colored glass and queer-shaped rocks,
In a secret hiding place I've made,
Hollowed out with clamshells and a spade,
Marked with yellow pebbles in a row—
None of all the other children know!

It's a place that makes a splendid lair,
Room for chests and weapons and one chair.
In the farthest corner, by the stones,
I shall have a flag with skulls and bones
And a lamp that casts a lurid glow—
None of all the other children know!

Sometimes, by and by, when I am grown,
I shall go and live there all alone;
I shall dig and paddle til its dark,
Then go out and man my private bark:
I shall fill my cave with captive foe—
None of all the other children know!

can give teachers a wealth of ideas to go beyond the "cozy corner."

When privacy is not available, people do what Robert Sommer, the author of **Personal Space** (1969), calls "cocooning." We simply filter out or ignore unwanted contact; our behavior in elevators or crowded sidewalks

provides a good example. Children do the same. Young babies simply shut down all their systems. Programs, however, don't always recognize or allow children to regulate this need to simplify the environment, and "cocooning" or "spacing out" may be seen as a disciplinary issue or a sign of child pathology.

There are always issues of power and control in the granting of privacy to people deemed dependent, or lower in rank or status, or in institutional settings—schools, hospitals, prisons, and so on. The absence of privacy is always justified in terms of the need for social control and the protection of the institution's inhabitants. Adult institutions may remove the doors to rooms and toilet stalls or showers, place people in wards or only provide common space and restrict access to corridors and rooms. In children's settings, because children are lower rank, dependent, and in an institution, it is no surprise that often the same things happen. In all institutional settings, including those involving young children, the justification for the **absence** of privacy should receive close scrutiny.

7—Order

"Because something is happening here
But you don't know what it is
Do you, Mr. Jones?"
Bob Dylan ("Ballad of a Thin Man")

The new two year old looked into my eyes with a mixture of panic and fear and a hint of excitement, as if to say, "What the hell is happening here?" I recognized the expression. It was almost identical to the look on the face of the new student teacher or the look on my face the first time I set foot in New York City.

Photograph by Jean Wallech

We need a physical order in our spaces to make them tolerable. Our homes are **our** homes because we create within them a physical order that expresses our values, logic, goals, and concerns related to living. Our home is where we feel secure and competent when it reflects us and when it is familiar and predictable.

We (at least Western cultures) need a temporal order. "Our lives, necessarily run by pattern, are regulated by the clock, or, if not that, by the rhythm of physical needs or the outer rhythm of the world. We may measure the necessity of order by the discontent we feel in being wholly deprived of it. A day spent without plan is refreshing, a week possible, a year deadly, a life impossible" (Eble, 1966, p. 34).

We need some routine, welding actions and expectations to the clock. Routine adds clarity and depth to our days. As Sylvia Ashton-Warner put it (1972, p. 75): "Routine has a rhythm and rhyme to it which answers man's immortal need for monotony and symmetry, as well as for surprise."

Children's settings require ordered time and space—space that furthers the program goals while making the program a pleasant place to live and work for all those (large and small) who inhabit the program. What is needed is planned complexity—an environment rich enough to challenge, but not so complex as to frustrate.

Order is always a trade-off. Goals are often in some degree of conflict—children's autonomy and safety, for instance. Differences in the concerns of individual members of groups are always present. There are those who feed and flourish on disorder and other fussy souls who are thrown off balance by anything out off place. Teachers in a single classroom often seem to

span this range. And then, of course, there are toddlers, who seem to have a sense of order based on some vision undecipherable to the adult mind.

Structuring Space

The job of a young child is to make the world sensible, to construct or discover the properties, patterns, relationships that exist in the material world of people and things and figure out where he might fit in. The path of learning and development, as Phillip Jackson has noted, is more like that of a butterfly than that of a bullet. The early childhood professional's job is to provide a setting where a group of energetic, idiosyncratic seekers go about this task and where all, adults and children, thrive amidst the daily rigors of group living. To accomplish this, the setting must have an order that is **comprehensible** and functional to all

occupants. The look of the order is busy and alive. Some guidelines:

• The order should be based on program goals and values (which may well include individualization). Order for order's sake is often mere tidiness and control. If independence is a primary goal, then the materials should be stored and displayed for independent use.

The High Scope cognitive curriculum provides an example of a program where the order is clearly based on developed goals: "We have planned and equipped our preschool rooms in such a way that the environment structures the child's learning and enables him to deal with classification and seriation through the simplest manipulations at the beginning of the year to more complex ones later in the year.... For the first six weeks of school the goal is for the children to learn to classify things that are the *same* and things that are *different*. Therefore all the blocks are kept in one cabinet and all cars in another.... We realize that a similar kind of classroom arrangement is often set up in preschools, but this is done to maintain order rather than to differentiate *same* and *different* so that, while blocks and cars may belong in different places, they are not necessarily separated" (Weikart et al., 1971, p. 37).

Continually analyzing the order using the goals—what matters—as a reference point helps to prevent an order based on an individual's fussiness, territoriality, need for control, or lack of concern; or an order based on historical conditions—the last director's logic—or institutional mindsets. Order begets efficiency, trying to accomplish the goals with maximum productivity and minimum waste. Often, particularly in large institutions, order itself and smooth management—ostensible efficiency—become

---

Disorder Is Confusing

Adults may think disorder is obvious. But is it really?

"Dirt (is) matter out of place.... We can recognize in our own notions of dirt ... all the rejected elements of ordered systems. It is a relative idea. Shoes are not dirty in themselves, but it is dirty to place them on the dining-table; food is not dirty in itself, but it is dirty to leave cooking utensils in the bedroom, or food bespattered on clothing; similarly, bathroom equipment in the drawing room; clothing lying on chairs; out-door things in-doors; up-stairs things downstairs; underclothing appearing where over-clothing should be, and so on."

from **Purity and Danger** by Mary Douglas (1966, p. 35)

There is a lot for children to understand before "What a mess!" signals much beyond adult displeasure.

The Myth of Mess

"Office workers came under the scrutiny of industrial psychologists, efficiency experts, and industrial designers, as industrial workers had suffered similar attentions half a century earlier. Corporations were forced to compete for the supply of knowledge workers and tried to increase their efficiency and the attractiveness of their surroundings.

As a result, work places became hygienic, clean, dry, well lit, safe, temperature controlled, and absolutely sterile. Clutter was eliminated and workers were assigned fixed work positions in relation to their productive importance, as management conceived their importance to be. . . . But office workers did not become more productive. The malaise of office workers, like sabotage on the assembly line, became and remains a management frustration. . . .

Designers seldom live or work in the places they design. The designer who proclaimed the virtue of the precise alignment of office elements, the elimination of superfluous decoration, white immaculate surfaces, bright uniform lighting, in the precise logic of Mondrian, usually lived in a period house and worked in a nondescript office surrounded by clutter.

The workers who process information in offices tend to work just as the designer does in his or her private life. They adjust their work spaces and artifacts to suit their own unique creative processes, and, if allowed, live and work in creative clutter. . . .

The compelling tensions that everyone faces in organizational living is a continuing struggle for identity. Knowledge workers must constantly reassure themselves of who they are and what they are doing. Successful surroundings are those that allow this need to be expressed by conveying identity information.

Work clutter appears despite the designers deliberate effort to suppress it. If the space cannot be personalized and possessed by its occupant, it will be abandoned or the occupant will lose interest in the tasks at hand. Places that stimulate the worker are developed, elaborated, and preserved by appropriate use. Evidence of possession can be concealed or eliminated, but the penalty in efficiency is enormous. . . .

The tendency to *mess up the place* is the occupant's imprint. Working mess is a visual identity of tasks and areas of responsibility. Work artifacts are the feedback notations that remind the occupant of the spaces of their involvements in their tasks. They are the keys to what the occupant knows, rearrangeable signals in the structure of the occupant's thinking process.

The knowledge workers must establish an identity with their surroundings and display their work to reaffirm who they are and what they do in much the same fashion as those housed must establish a personal place using familiar memory objects around them.

The price paid for ignoring or suppressing either human tendency in the office or in the housing project is atrocious. When office workers cannot establish a sense of place in the world they do not destroy or vandalize their surroundings as do the occupants of housing projects, for the conditions of work are rigidly controlled. Overt destruction is rare, but unproductive lethargic behavior is commonplace."

from **The Joy Of Building**, by Forrest Wilson (1979, pp. 131-133)

Photograph by Shawn Connell

the goals, rather than what should be the real goals of learning or better care.

• The order should be understood by children as well as adults. The more turnover in adults and children, the more obvious and predictable the order needs to be. Understanding the developmental abilities of the children is important. An understandable order for babies requires anchoring objects and activities to times and places and using the simplest classification categories for child-access storage, like using duplicates and photographs to identify the object's place.

• The order should be restorable by children and adults. The order should be obvious; labels should use photographs, pictures, symbols, and language depending on the cognitive skills of the children (and the adult reading levels). The storage sites and routines should accommodate child capabilities. If the order is not easily restorable, then the adults will inevitably reduce the potential for disorder, usually barring child access or removing materials, particularly those with many small parts.

• The program order should be functional, working to make life easier, better, and more productive. This is obvious but necessary to keep in mind. Sometimes the order has the opposite effect. A too meticulous order can bring program life to a halt. There is a need for toy bins and chests for quick *dump it in* storage to keep the action flowing.

• The order should reflect changing conditions. This is not always easy as people become accustomed to a familiar order. A telling example of a once logical order, no longer logical, is the standard typewriter. The keyboard's line—Q W E R T Y U I O P—was designed, not to increase the ease and speed of typing, but to **slow** the typist down. In the 1870's, typewriter keys would stick together when the operator went too fast and the QWERTY configuration solved this problem. Now obsolete, the resistance to new learning keeps the old keyboard alive (a situation not unlike the glacial movement to the metric system). When an order is designed to achieve goals, as with the High Scope classroom, change is necessary because the children change. The High Scope classroom only makes sense if the children move on from *same* and *different*. Active intelligence is ordering and reordering, imposing and uncovering patterns.

• The order should contribute to a sense of aesthetic harmony. There is more to life than function. Highlighting contrast might be balanced with harmony in colors and shapes.

Structuring Time

It had been a particularly hectic morning. It seemed like every fifteen or twenty minutes we had to move on to something else—snack, gym, the art room, outside, cleanup. We were always a little behind, and the other teachers and the cook exchanged that *why can't he get his act together look.* At lunch, Carlos, always the helpful critic, looked up at me and said, "Man, you need an alarm clock to carry around, then we wouldn't always be behind." Oh, Carlos, I felt, if you only knew what lies ahead for you the next twelve years.

The structuring of time has an enormous impact on how we feel. Charlie Chaplin or Lucille Ball trying to keep up with an assembly line that speeds up on the one hand, and Vladimir and Estragon waiting for Godot with time an open and terrifying expanse on the other, testify to this. Institutions of social control use the structure of time to discipline, torture, or drive people mad by assuming absolute power over the rhythms of living and applying varying amounts of randomness amidst a rigid order. Having control of our own time and establishing our own patterns can be at once exhilarating and scary.

Yet, a too casual approach to the clock can limit program achievements and deprive children and adults of the security that comes with predictable routines, (to say nothing of a prompt, regular meal and a dry diaper). Sylvia Ashton-Warner describes the need for routine (1972, p. 77):

"So they know what to do, feel where to go, relax in a shape around them. It's a protection and haven for them from their bewilderment—from what they think is freedom if you like. This doesn't happen to be freedom as it is; it's intoxication. They're only children, and need direction finders. Routine, shape, stability."

In early childhood settings, basic time blocks and the day's rhythms are defined by the tasks of living: eating, diapering and toileting, sleeping, and housekeeping; staffing schedules and breaks; and the physical space, particularly the amount of scheduled shared space. Routine weds the tasks and times. In some programs achieving some important goals—staff breaks, a wider range of learning experiences, or use of more space—results in the rigid, assembly line scheduling of time. This is similar to the higher education that David Elkind aptly decries as the "industrialization of childhood" in **The Hurried Child** (1984). If every activity must be completed in a short fixed time period, obviously both children and teachers are severely constricted in what they can do. "I never get to finish anything" is a common complaint of preschoolers and a clear message as to the social value of depth and concentration, as well as to who is in charge.

A Lazy Thought
by Eve Merriman

There go the grown-ups
To the office,
To the store.
Subway rush,
Traffic crush;
Hurry, scurry,
Worry, flurry.

No wonder
Grownups
Don't grow up
Any more.

It takes a lot
of slow
to grow.

Timetables, like space, need flexibility if learning and caring are to take place. Building a cardboard castle, cooking breakfast, visiting a farm, or reading a book may be hard to fit into the schedule. Waking up after napping, diapering two babies, successfully completing the training mission to the potty chair, and other caring elements don't always lend themselves to the clock.

What makes life worth living is the chance, the hope, that wonderful things might just happen—a hope based on experience with random surprises. Children delight when the order wavers, by chance or design. Breakfast outside or waffles for lunch, a change in nap, mixed up space—these are memorable experiences that open up eyes to possibilities.

Avoiding rigid and narrow schedules that choke or loose schedules that frighten or intoxicate generally requires a thoughtful and complete analysis of how all the program structural elements interact—time, space, goals, organization, and people—and creative problem solving to minimize negative side effects.

Ritual

Our individual lives are ordered with daily rites: the first cup of coffee, good-bye kisses, how we enter sleep, the routes taken to work or school. Group life has its own rites: Walton's "goodnights," holiday ceremonies, pregame warm-ups, Pledges of Allegiance. Ritual joins routine and the physical order as the secure skeleton that holds individuals and groups together in times of stress, against the uncertainties of staff and children who come and go and change from mood to mood, day to day.

Adults have rites to help live their lives: rites of beginnings—weddings, baptisms, house-warmings, dedications; of renewal—birthdays, anniversaries, holidays; of endings—funerals, graduations; and of passage—firsts (kisses, job, car, child), coping with aging, responsibility, and loss. These rites are marked by symbolic acts that have great meaning and emotional power—exchanges of words and rings or papers, breaking glasses, dances, chants and songs, and very often eating or drinking.

Ritual serves the same purpose in children's programs. Group daily rites, like sharing the same song or the same story day after day, reassure against the unknown void. Children under three will listen to **Good Night Moon** by Margaret Wise Brown (1947) with delight every rest time. There are acknowledged rights of passage as children give up diapers and bottles, enter older groups, leave for school. Individual rituals between children and caregivers can become pinions of security—a special touch, a shared joke, any regular shared exchange. Groups might experiment, rites of destruction perhaps. Consider this excerpt from the journal of writer Katherine Mansfield:

"Tidied all my papers. Tore up and ruthlessly destroyed much. This is always a great satisfaction."

There is always occasion to restore the order through ruthless destruction.

The word *autonomy* derives from the Greek words *autos* (self) and *neiman* (to hold sway). Autonomy, the power to govern oneself, to be independent, is always a dual struggle for self control and freedom from external restraints. Young children are struggling to gain control over their bodies, their emotions, and their impulses. At the same time they have to learn how to balance their desire to be independent with their adjustment to the demands of the

There'll Be Some Changes Made

When a teacher leaves, children face the loss of a familiar, perhaps loved person. A new teacher arrives and children face all the ins and outs of establishing a relationship with a new powerful person in their lives. Early childhood professionals have long understood that this is a time of trial for children and teachers. Staff turnover is a regrettable and, for the present, inevitable fact of life.

The trauma of turnover can be lessened, however. When new teachers arrive, they often immediately begin the process of making the classroom theirs: changing the space, the routines, adding their own rituals, their own expectations. The need for teachers to put their own stamp on the group for them to feel competent and in control in a new situation is understandable. But, in the process, the children's world may be turned upside down.

Perhaps the best solution to this dilemma is an expectation that teachers assess the environmental impact of their plans for change on the children's sense of security and adjust the extent and pace of change accordingly. A program rich with rituals and low staff turnover may sustain quite a bit of change in the physical environment when a new teacher arrives, provided the rituals remain. A high staff (or child) turnover program may need all the rituals and environmental predictability it can muster.

"Can I get a drink, take off my socks and itch my foot, lie down and rest (or get up and play)?"

• Mobility: to move around, to be still. "Can I hop, climb, or stay and rest on this pillow?"

• Space: to adapt, define, personalize, or protect a space. "Can I *pull up a chair*, turn a light on or off, create my own order or clutter which may look simply like a mess to the unknowing eyes of others?"

• Social life: to choose one's own company. "Can I be alone, choose my lunch date or my loft associates?"

Photograph by Jean Wallech

larger world. The child's environment, in the words of Erik Erickson (1977, p. 50), "must back him up in his desire to stand on his own two feet, lest he be overcome by that sense of having exposed himself prematurely and foolishly which we call shame, or that secondary mistrust, that looking back which we call doubt." To "back him up," the environment must provide the support structure—physical space, time, expectations—that encourages independence in thought and action "but protects him against the potential anarchy of his yet untrained judgement."

Issues of autonomy are present in all aspects of children's environments. How much are children allowed or encouraged to hold sway over their:

• Bodily needs: hunger, thirst, access to the bathroom, sleep, body temperature, and so on?

from **Sometimes Life Is Not a Literary Experience**
by Eugene Lesser

*Tonight I sat on my back porch
and drank a bowl of
Campbell's chicken vegetable soup.
All that time watching the moon
and feeling absolutely great.*

The Fury of Overshoes
by Anne Sexton

Remember when you couldn't
buckle your own
overshoe
or tie your own
shoe
or cut your own meat
and the tears
running down like mud
because you fell off your
tricycle?
Remember, big fish,
when you couldn't swim
and simply slipped under
like a stone frog
The world wasn't
yours.
It belonged to
the big people.

• Time: to set one's own pace, to stop and start. "Can I take a break?"

• Things: to be able to select, determine the use, and put things away. "Can I go get the Legos by myself? Can I use them to make a space gun?"

• Activities: to choose activities and conduct them free from intrusion. "Do I have to listen?"

Children are not adults. For reasons of safety we don't grant children the autonomy that adults often have —to protect them from their own impulses and from failure, and to protect the entire group from the effects of egocentrism run amok. Yet, without sufficient autonomy, how can children develop into independent, resourceful, confident people?

All institutional settings face many of the same issues. Without some standardization, uniformity, and order, there would be a sloppy, unsafe anarchy. Without flexibility and sufficient allowance for individuality and freedom, there would be an oppressive, impersonal, and deadening dullness. One issue is how institutions for group living and working allow individuals to personalize their space. As Margaret Mead, reflecting on childhood, observed (1972, p. 10): "The need to define who you are by the place in which you live remains intact, even when that place is defined by a single object, like the small blue vase that used to mean home to one of my friends, the daughter of a widowed trained nurse who continually moved from one place to another."

In most schools, the student desk is the most personal, friendly object in the classroom; in child care, it is often the cubby. It is often the only thing owned by children. It becomes theirs by location and the marks they make on it.* The ability to make an imprint on a setting where one spends up to ten hours a day for a number of years seems important in the development of self-esteem.

8—Autonomy

Autonomy is an issue in simple enjoyment of life. From an early age, we all pluck our own joys and delights. Nothing can take them away

---

*Yamamoto raises an interesting question (1979, p. 93): Would the children's need to own space be reduced, if all the rest did not belong to the teacher?

Photograph by Jean Wallech

Photograph by Nancy P. Alexander

from our minds. Poet Michael Brownstein said, "Pause before anything ordinary and it becomes important." Yet, without the freedom to pause, to choose our objects of desire and wonder, life is dreary and diminished (from an early age).

Autonomy does more than build children's self-esteem and add to life's quality; it helps the setting work better. Given the freedom and the necessity, **children invent the spaces they need.** They squeeze behind furniture, climb on whatever is available, seclude themselves under blankets, build forts or houses. Creating spaces that allow children to do these things safely regulates behaviors like climbing. But creating all these spaces removes the need for children to invent them. Is that desirable? If children are given the opportunity to remake and adapt spaces, aren't they learning that conditions are not fixed, but subject to their ideas and actions, that they can make things and settings work for them in many different ways?

Of course, autonomy is not only a children's issue. Settings that are teacher proof—finished environments and curriculum that turn teachers into technicians and devalue the idiosyncrasies that make individuals human— reduce work to mindless toil.

9—Mobility

"In schools, it is stillness we have to justify, not movement."
Susan Issacs

In the wilds of homes and yards, how do children usually move? They race pell mell, hop zig zag, and inch along. They rarely move like adults, measured strides from Point A to Point B. The primal urge to climb on, crawl under, squeeze in, and so on often compels action. Children share with bowlers the need to punctu-ate with their whole bodies. But growing up and adjusting to social living requires learning physical restraint. Children learn that crashing around Grandma's condo or Mom's office will not do. For most of us, growing up tightens our physical expressiveness and leashes our actions to the extent that our power to unleash is lost, except perhaps on the dance floor or in the bedroom.

Children's settings can be characterized in terms of mobility in two ways: freedom to move within the setting from place to place or activity to activity, and the amount of mobility allowed or required by the routines and activities. Prescott and her colleagues at Pacific Oaks used "high/low mobility" as a dimension to characterize activity settings in their research (Prescott, 1984). Activities that specify utilizing large muscles like running, climbing, and riding trikes are high mobility. Doing puzzles and listening to stories which require sitting still are low mobility. Indoor block building, dramatic play, and water play allow moderate mobility.

Prescott notes that adults often forget how difficult it is for children to mold their bodies to the demands of some settings. The overall balance between activities requiring high mobility and low mobility is an important characteristic of a program.

Mobility in a program is a function of physical space, staffing, program ideology, and predispositions of the staff which are all, of course, interrelated (Prescott and Jones, 1972). Long corridors, stairways, poor staffing ratios or inexperienced staff, or a teacher-directed program structure will tend to limit mobility. Easy access to the outside or common space, abundant space that is well organized, and good staffing will likely increase mobility.

Children are not all the same in their need for movement. Whether it is due to genetic predisposition or environmental conditioning, some children adapt to low mobility much more readily than others. But why should children have to adapt as much as they often do? For children (and adults) there are few things as oppressive as excessive restriction of movement. Further, for a young child, learning to use his or her body, which is changing at a phenomenal rate, is a major developmental task.

Photograph by Nancy P. Alexander

Their exuberant drive to test their equipment and use all their developing powers results in more than physical learning. As Anita Olds points out, "Sensorial and motoric experiences are the bedrock upon which all intellectual functions are built. Therefore, to deny movement is to halt development at its very source" (Olds, 1982, p. 16). Susan Issacs made the point fifty years ago in **The Nursery Years** (Issacs, 1968, pp. 71-72): "Walking and running are enjoyed not only for the pleasure of actual movement, but also for the new discoveries of space they bring. For the knowledge of space relations grows by the fusion of what is seen and touched with the feelings of one's own movements in stretching or walking through the space seen."

The requirements of a group setting inevitably restrict movement. Children in homes, even apartments, with much more space than 35 feet per child, usually have more opportunities for high mobility activities and freedom of movement. High mobility and the noise that goes with it wear children and adults down and limit the learning that requires concentration and quiet. "To adults, nothing is as aggra-

---

What Is Once Loved
by Elizabeth Coatsworth

What is once loved
You will find
Is always yours
From that day.
Take it home
In your mind
And nothing ever
Can take it away.

---

vating and enervating as the incessant, unpredictable activity of many little bodies, each moving to a separate drummer" (Olds, 1982, p. 16). The result is the severe restriction of movement. A major task for early childhood professionals is to design child care settings that allow more free expression of movement indoors.

10—The Adult Dimension

I must have appeared a pretty sad case after a long, hard, botched day. Carlos, now four year old therapist and teaching assistant, had the bus driver wait (something the driver rarely would do for me) and came over to me for some words of consolation. "I feel sad for you 'cause we all get to leave every day and you have to stay and live here in this dooky basement. Want to come stay at my house some time?"

Staff do have homes to go to, but children's settings are places in which they may spend eight hours a day, 2000 hours a year, living and working with children. It is their place as well as the children's. And to the extent the program's philosophy and goals incorporate them, parents are a second adult population the setting needs to acknowledge. To consider how the environment should reflect the needs of the adult inhabitants, it is useful to begin with analyzing what adults actually do there and the environmental implications of those actions:

Staff Role — Environmental Issues

Think and Plan — Where? When? Work space?

Organize Environment — Storage? Equipment? Materials?

Stock and Re-stock Shelves — Storage: Amount, Accessibility, and Location?

Prepare and Do Activities — Storage? Equipment? Activities?

Clean Up and Maintenance — Sinks? Janitor's closet? Equipment?

Teach and Guide — Time? Environmental support?

Manage Children's Traffic — Layout? Furnishings and equipment?

Lift and Hold Children — Lifting minimized (diaper tables)?

Converse with Children — Acoustics? Furniture? Layout?

Meal Set Up, Serving, Clean Up — Storage? Equipment? Sinks?

Toileting, Diapering — Room size and scale? Storage? Layout?

Work with Adults — Space size and scale? Individual space?

Communicate — Message space? Meeting space? Equipment and materials?

Record Keeping — Materials? Storage space?

Manage Staff and Parent — Space size and scale? Layout? Traffic? Furnishings?

Host for Parents and Visitors — Space size? Layout? Closets? Furniture?

Parent Confidant and Advisor — Private space?

Parent Role — Environmental Issues

Separate from/Reunite with Their Children — Layout? Privacy?

Visitor/Participant Communication — Space size and scale? Closets? Furniture?

Nursing Infant — Privacy?

Observer — Layout? Observation spot?

Consumer/Evaluator — Communication/Display space?

Learner — Communication/Display space? Meeting space?

A Supportive Environment for Adults

Does the setting facilitate and support the desired staff and parent behaviors? If a program aspires to being a *smart program*, then some provision for meeting space is necessary. If the program goals involve much adult—parent or staff—interaction, then confidential space becomes important. In all programs the ease of performing the tasks of set up and clean up, storage, communication with parents, and other standard tasks determines the energy left to teach and care for children. In programs providing care all day, the daily logistics of group living make environmental support critical.

The quality of the work is clearly affected by the work setting. Sanford Hirshen, an architect known for a number of centers, has noted that, given the minimum staff-child ratios and low operating budgets, a large portion of the success of a program has to do with morale and the ability to keep talented staff happy (Cohen et al.,

1978, p. 362). The quality of staff space can directly affect this.

Inevitably, inconvenience, fatigue, and stress take their toll. The greater effort required to use storage because it is inconvenient, the less it will be used. The more lifting required, the less energy available for other things. The less communication space, the less communication. If the only seating available is designed for very young children, if the adult bathroom is one flight up, if the adult private space is that very same bathroom, then the setting works against staff.

The dimensions discussed in the previous pages apply to adults as well as children. Do adults have some sense of autonomy in relation to the environment? Are they able to adjust time and physical space? Architectural designer William Gill discusses equipment:

"I try to supply just enough of a structure so teachers will feel comfortable adding on to it. Often when a structure is too *architectural*, teachers view it as a monument and are afraid to

Photograph by Jean Wallech

So What's the Big Deal?

Is it really that important that everything be just so for arrivals and departures? Why can't parents of infants get along without that handover? Staff are usually busy and parents could just put the child by the caregiver.

The emotional significance of arriving and departing moves behavior beyond rationality. Consider the behavior of mature adults at airports. For many people, any alternative to being left or met at the gate is a poor one. Someone should be there as we enter or leave the umbilical-like tube extending from the plane. However rational and convenient it might be to use the airport entrance or baggage area a few minutes and a few hundred yards away, it is not the same experience.

interfere with it. . . . Architects have to leave room for people to grow into it. Otherwise they'll never think of it as their own" (Ellison, 1974, p.21).

Mobility is an important adult dimension. The program should allow and encourage the staff mobility that accomplishes program goals. This may include a freedom to move to avoid a feeling of confinement, as well as arrangements that allow staff to stay put while accomplishing tasks like diapering, so that appropriate staff/child ratios are not thrown out of whack. In an infant room there may be spatial encouragement to sit and nurture; in toddler and preschool settings, the goal may be to encourage moving around. The amount and location of adult seating will influence adult behavior.

A question sometimes overlooked is: "Does the setting facilitate the socialization of new staff, substitutes, and volunteers?" If there are no clues to the storage scheme, the structure or flow of space and time, then the unfamiliar newcomer will take longer to feel at home.

Parents IN the Program

While parents are often considered important in terms of program philosophy and goals, particularly in Head Start and all day child care, their projected role is less often reflected in the environmental planning. In traditional nursery schools, a design issue was how to structure the entryway as a transition place for parent and child separations, allowing for an unassisted child entry (Osmon, 1971). Separation from home and the parents and a first big step toward the world at large is a major function of nursery school. Yet, in Head Start and most child care

(and many nursery schools today), a major goal is to somehow bring in and incorporate parents *into* the setting, rather than leaving them in the hallway. They are wanted as sources or repositories of information, as volunteers or students themselves, or as active sources of support of one kind or another.

How are they drawn in? If the child does not come on a bus and if the cubbies or sign in sheets are inside the room, parents will enter the space. If a daily information sheet asking for a parent response is right next to the cubby and there is always a pencil there, the likelihood of parent use increases. If the physical space and staff verbal and nonverbal behaviors give off the message *welcome, take off your coat and hang around to chat*, parents with time are more likely to chat. Do they know staff as people, or at least by names and roles? A display with pictures and short biographies of all staff, including substitutes, can help.

Do parents feel in the way or out of place or on someone else's sacred ground the moment they enter? To the extent that there are places to be and to hang up a purse or put a briefcase away from children, and the extent that the activity of the classroom makes sense to them (perhaps accomplished through labels and wall posters, handouts, prior meetings and the like), parents will feel more at ease. Knowing where the adult bathrooms are is an important aspect of feeling at home. Photographs of parents and families can signal that it is their place as well.

The environment cannot overcome all the inevitable tension between parent and caregiver. What a well designed environment can do is reinforce a genuine message of *parents belong here too* and *this is their role within the setting*.

Exercises

1. Consider five people you know well, preferably of different ages and cultures or backgrounds. Characterize them in terms of the way they approach ordering time and space. How do they differ in their need for mobility?

2. List some of the daily rituals that are important to you. What other rituals provide order and security in your life?

3. In what settings do you feel the least autonomous? What are the things you have no control over in these settings?

4. Analyze the space in a children's program allocated to the adult tasks considered above.

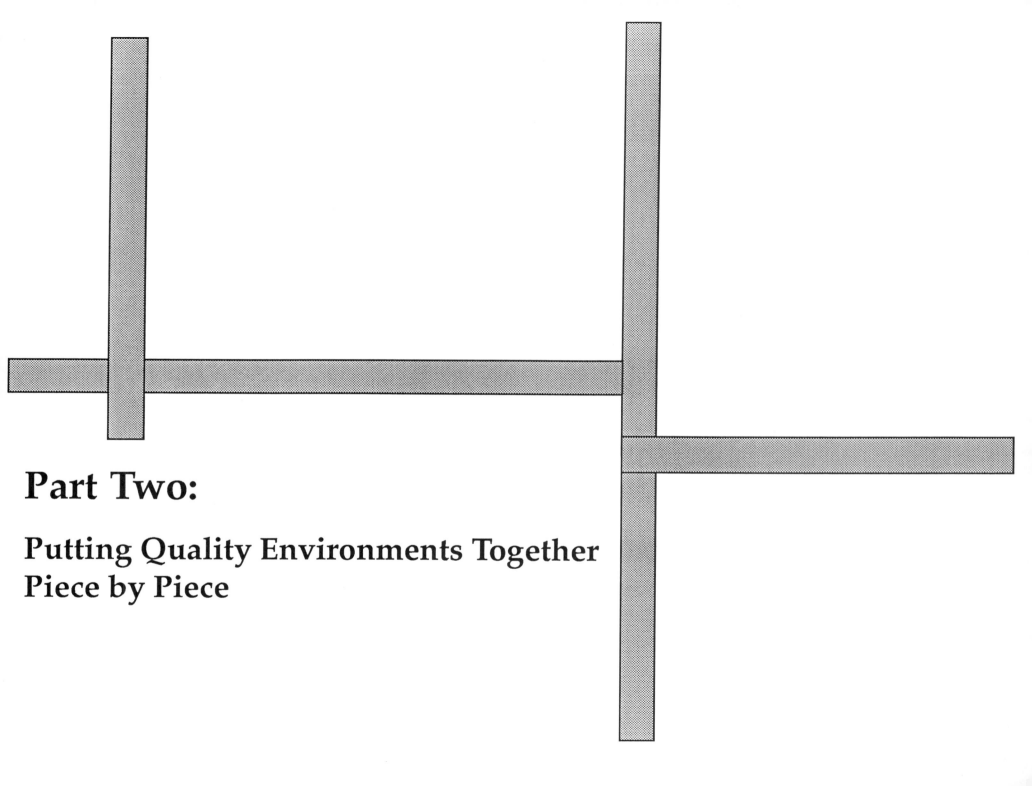

Part Two:

Putting Quality Environments Together Piece by Piece

— Chapter Seven —

The Building and Site

"A construction is a new organization of the world and life."
Mircea Eliade in **The Myth Of The Eternal Return**

"The thesis of organic architecture is simple: the basic idea that an organic building is designed appropriately for the people who will live and work in it, for its site, for its purpose, for the geographic climatic and economic conditions for which it is to exist. As such, the nature of the design must be **individual,** *whether it is a house or a church, a bank or business or department store. It will not have a pleasing appearance merely from one side. . . . It will be well coordinated in all its aspects, taking shape from its inner reality—an entity."*
Frank Lloyd Wright (1966, p. 122)

Photograph by Jean Wallech

During the explosive growth of child care in the 1960's and 1970's, centers sprouted in every conceivable site. Homes, churches, and schools, empty supermarkets or gas stations, warehouses and office buildings, storefronts, and garages were converted for child care use. Increasingly, however, since the early 1970's, buildings are being constructed for child care, albeit frequently with an eye toward conversion to office, warehouse, or multiple use space as a hedge, contrary to Wright's dictum. This chapter will consider some of the factors involved in choosing buildings and sites and in undertaking renovation, with a recognition that some programs have choices in designing or adapting

their settings and some do not. The discussion is not intended to be comprehensive; it is primarily directed to areas that are often not given their due.

The Building Site

Buildings are located on a site. The size, shape, topography, and surroundings shape the

building and its use. In the best of circumstances, there is an "essential fittingness" implied by Wright in the quote above. Architect Bill Rahn expressed the feeling in Tracy Kidder's **House** (1985, p. 13):

"Every little place connotes something. It has a feel to it. . . . A sense of place and how to fit a building into it."

Photograph by Nancy P. Alexander

Topography and Surroundings

Do the immediate surroundings present any significant positives or negatives? Locating close to a meat processing plant may result in interesting though unwelcome odors (although vegetation can be used to mask some odors). A location in a heavy traffic area may result in noise, odors, and long range potential health hazard from lead and other pollutants. A noisy site may be an unremediable problem, depending on the building construction and the kinds of windows.

Are there trees to shade the building, absorb the sound, and provide shade for outdoor activities? Shrubs, hills, and other landscape features enhance outdoor life, and vegetation absorbs sound and odors. Access to the life of the community without crossing busy streets is a large plus—parks, playgrounds, libraries, and shops. A major factor in security is the relationship between the building and the surrounding area.

The Facility

"Why do we think humane learning can go on in buildings that look as if they were designed to hold atomic secrets?"
John Holt

Talking to directors and teachers about their ideal centers uncovers a range of dreams running the gamut from Victorian mansions to the standard design of a large multiple site chain. A *good building* is one that meets Wright's criteria: it is appropriate for the program, the geography and climate, and the economic conditions. It is not uncommon to find buildings designed for one setting (a nursery school in Arizona) reproduced for another context

Site Size

Is the site the right size or too small for the use intended and the projected number of children? Sites are often less than ideal. The need to make the best of inadequate space will haunt a program for years to come in countless moments of irritation, hours of problem-solving, and dollars spent to adapt the space to make it work.

Is there sufficient outdoor space for play, parking, and transition from the street? In an automobile culture, parking warrants special

concern. Five minute drop off space pulls parents back out to their cars. If the program wants parents to enter and linger inside, there should be convenient parking spaces that allow a longer stay. Staff parking is also essential.

It is possible for a site to be too big. If the program is shaped to the site size, there is a danger of unrealistic optimism—either in projecting full enrollment or in the ability to provide quality in a large site. The latter is a problem well documented in the Children's Environment Project's study of military child care programs.

Wildwood

Unfortunately, the sensitivity to place expressed by Bill Rahn is quite rare in practice. Designer George Nelson (1979, p. 114) tells a story that should be required reading for all developers:

"Last week on the way to Fort Wayne's airport, I passed a new housing tract. The land in the area is wooded and rolling, but the development has been bulldozed flat and all the trees, of course, were gone. At the entrance to this instant wasteland there was a sign: Wildwood."

There are now thousands of child care programs in suburban tracts, treeless Wildwoods, a sad commentary on how far we have come from the notion of places for young children as children's gardens—kinder (children) garten (garden).

Photograph by Nancy P. Alexander

(child care in Minnesota) with poor results (snow drifts in front of doors, sealed windows). The location of the building on the site and its relationship to the sun and wind, as well as the nature of the building itself, will shape the program structure and process and the program's future. Governmental regulations will determine the essential parameters guiding

A Proper Place
by Robert Nye

*Outside my window
two tall witch-elms
toss their inspired
green heads in the sun
and lean together
whispering.*

*Trees make the world
a proper place.*

Selecting a Site

If you were opening up or relocating a restaurant, a new store, or most other new businesses and failed to heed the time honored marketing maxim, *location is everything*, your chances of success would plummet. Early childhood programs face the same factors. Rarely will quality and marketing overcome poor location. On the other hand, however desirable from a marketing or service standpoint, quality is impossible at some sites. What considerations are important in site selection besides the size and topography of the site?

Clients/Customers: Who is to be served? Where do they live and work?

Zoning: Is the area zoned for child care? How much off street parking will be required?

Access and Visibility: Visibility may be important for new programs and programs that are seeking to attract new families. Access, the ease of actually using the program, is an important factor for any program.

Ownership: There are advantages and disadvantages to both owning or leasing a facility and site, usually boiling down to cost and control.

Cost: The cost of buying or leasing the site, utility connections, and property taxes have to be within the program's range.

The Children's Environment Project

The Children's Environment Project was funded by the United States Army to develop design guides for military child care sites. In the process, Gary Moore and his colleagues at the Center for Architecture and Urban Planning and the Community Design Center at the University of Wisconsin-Milwaukee conducted the most comprehensive study to date of child care facilities and outdoor play areas. Their five major publications are essential reading on children's environments. They go into great (and very readable) detail on every aspect of building design, from mechanical systems and site selection to laying out children's play space for social interaction. Almost ten years later, there is no better look at what exists and what might exist, if theory and practice were bound together with the necessary resources:

Abstracts on Child Play Areas and Child Support Facilities (1978)
Case Studies of Child Care Play Areas and Support Facilities (1978)
Case Studies of Outdoor Play Areas (1978)
Recommendations for Child Care Centers (1979)
Recommendations for Child Play Areas (1979)

Their publications are available from:

The Center for Architecture and Urban Planning Research
University of Wisconsin-Milwaukee
P.O. Box 413
Milwaukee, WI 53201

choice (e.g., first floor occupancy, handicapped access, number of exits, etc.). The following factors are important to consider:

Size

Average center size is growing, from 49 in 1979 to 80 in 1985. Inevitable, perhaps, this trend is not particularly positive. There is little doubt that quality, as expressed in the preceding pages, is harder to produce in larger programs of over 75 children (Prescott and Jones, 1972; Coelen et al., 1978; Moore et al., 1979). There are some economies of scale in larger programs, but they are slight when stacked against the costs of institutionalization. If large numbers of children are to be served on site, a cluster or campus plan (see Moore et al., 1979) with multiple linked buildings may preserve a semblance of the intimacy and personal relations that follow small scale.

The effects of large center size—both the feelings and the behavior—can be offset by good building design that breaks the building down into recognizable smaller units (wings, multiple entrances) and softens the impression of size and large scale and by programmatic structures that decentralize and personalize. Larger centers can be high quality; it simply takes more thought and savvy.

Whatever the program size, most centers—building and site—are too small for the program planned. It is important to keep in mind that the building needs to accommodate **all** that will take place, in February as well as in June, next year as well as now. Most states require a minimum of 35 square feet per child for children's space and do not have guidelines for support space. This is **minimum**, and may barely be acceptable at that, depending on other factors such as: Are there other common spaces to be used? Do the children nap and eat there? How much of the time is the outdoors available? How long are children (and adults) confined to the space? What is the group size, how many adults, and who are the children? Infants are small, but have more adult retainers. Children with physical disabilities and school-age children need more space. How developed and how **nice** is the space? Are there windows, lofts, etc.? We know a human being can live for years in an 8 by 10 foot cell, but can they live **well** is a better question. In a space that serves for everything—eating, sleeping, and playing—there is a burden on staff to continually alter and restore the space with the children present.

What will take place in the building? If a program depends on intelligence and planning, then places to meet and plan are necessary. Private space to meet with staff and parents, funders, and community people is important in most programs. It is not unusual in some programs for the staff bathroom to be pulled into use as a quick conference room. In a program where supervision is considered important, parent intakes and conferences are frequent, group meetings are regular, and resource professionals are utilized, the competi-

Photograph by Shawn Connell

may lead to creative ways to maximize the use of the space and surrounding area and to the application of more pressure to improve the resources allocated to children.

The Program Perimeter

The central issue for the perimeter of a children's center is clearly defined by Fred Osmon (1971): access versus protection. The perimeter may be the border of the program within a larger structure, such as a public school or office building, or where the program meets the sidewalk or street. The center should at once *welcome* children and parents—present a *friendly face*, welcome the goods and services that supply the program, and welcome the community at large in the sense of being perceived as a dynamic part of the community. Flowers, colorful banners, pleasing graphics, and windows to glimpse the inside life as one approaches attract visitors. Imposing, confusing or hard to find entrances give off the unfriendly message "Keep Out—You are not wanted here." High fences, mirrored glass, and the absence of windows are other good examples of unwelcoming messages.

At the same time, however, the center must protect—keep children in and unwanted intrusions out. The most effective welcome is being able to see the activities within as one approaches, and to enjoy the beauty and charm of a pleasing landscape, display, or an intriguing

tion for space to meet during naptime hours is often heavy, especially if there is only a staff room and the director's office from which to choose.

Is there room for the program to grow, **and maintain quality?** It is usual practice, though regrettable, for programs to grow to their highest possible licensed capacity. Typically, space planned as common space that can be used as a classroom eventually will be, as programs move to meet the demand for expanded services—school-age children, infants and toddlers, drop in, and care for moderately ill children.

Given the cost of construction, renovation, and rental space, making do with minimum space is often the rule. The least we can do is recognize that this is a rather deplorable state of affairs which sets a cap on the quality possible. Recognition, rather than unthinking acceptance,

---

Efficient Buildings

"Buildings can easily be arranged to package people as moronic and tiresome objects who have to be organized in much the same way as material is processed through a factory. These buildings do not encourage any of the seemingly chaotic and haphazard patterns of encounter that distinguish the more civilized buildings of other times. . . .

Today we demand that our buildings be precise in the manner of efficient machines. Conceived as machines they are inevitably unsatisfactory as they do not recognize our imprecise and unpredictable habits. Their organization is generally based on an idea of efficiency that is derived from a simple-minded concept of circulation or time-motion studies. The way an old fashioned kitchen could absorb grandparents, children, and visitors and at the same time produce meals is in contrast to the modern kitchen which reduces the cook to the level of an operative. For the sake of economy we have come to accept minimal spaces because we believe that they are anthropometrically correct and efficient. Nothing is more humiliating than the minimal bathroom capsule. Because of its sophisticated appointments it is not cheap; it is, however, space-saving. I believe that a larger, perhaps less well appointed bathroom with windows and sunlight may be psyche-saving (and allow a greater variety of action)."

from "The Friendly Object," by Peter Pragnell (1969, pp. 37-38)

How Much Space Is Enough?

After studying state licensing guidelines and the varied recommendations of other organizations and experts, the Children's Environment Project made the following recommendations as a guideline for adequate space (square feet per child):

	Minimum	Recommended
Child activity space	35 sq. ft.	42
Other support space	25	38
Other facility space (mechanical, corridors)	12	20
TOTAL FACILITY	72	100
Outdoor play area	75	100
Overall site size (parking, drop off area, loading dock, etc.)	190	300

playground. However, vandalism is usually a major concern and the welcome of windows invites problems. Many parents, in this era of fear of random harm, would gladly trade the welcome for the security that sealed boundaries presents. Yet sealed boundaries not only intimidate, they can entrap and hinder quick exit for fire and other disasters. How do you reconcile these factors?

This is a profound issue because in children's first encounters with the world at large they will learn how to perceive and approach the world. Is it inviting, threatening, or a combination of both? If the center is a fortress or haven, disconnected from potentially hostile surroundings or an unprotected setting vulnerable to the world, the child will get the message: "It's all a jungle out there and not for

me." The world of childhood is hidden. For most programs, the goal is an interaction that has a more positive message, perhaps similar to that expressed by a storefront center director:

"Sometimes the children just sit and look at the street. At other times, however, they listen to stories, or talk to their teachers or each other, and the people on the street look in on them and begin to understand what an early education center can do for their children" (Osmon, 1971, p. 22).

There are design compromises that balance openness and protection. Osmon's **Patterns for Designing Children's Centers** (1971) is an excellent resource. Trees and shrubs and ferns can be used to seclude and humanize fencing, windows can be positioned oblique to any

pathways, and places can be structured outside the play area where adults and teenagers can "gather to chat and take in the sun and at the same time casually watch some ongoing activity." Some of the obvious *fortress* protection solutions—high fencing and bars or heavy bars on windows—simply present a challenge and may work less well than design solutions which allow more access and ownership to potential vandals, usually the children of the community. The relationship between program and community has a major impact on the extent of vandalism. It is outsiders—strangers—looking in who wreak havoc, not those who feel they have some connection to the program.*

*Unfortunately, in some places it really is a jungle out there or a refuge for the homeless. There are few, if any, alternatives to sealed featureless settings if the slightest human feature, a shaded bench, attracts society's victims.

A child care director: "Our program lies on the border of a housing project and serves children from the project, as well as many other children up to five years old. The children not enrolled in child care because of funding or because they were too old, many once or future students, were on the outside looking in at a wonderful place filled with toys and food. When they were bored they made our life miserable by trying to sneak in, and by occasionally committing acts of vandalism, minor in cost and major in irritation. We looked for design solutions to keep them out of the building and playground, but they didn't work. It was only when we accepted them as part of the program and worked on how to get them in—involved in the program after hours and on weekends—that our problems diminished."

Protection from the elements is a factor, particularly in wet or wintery climates or in extremely hot areas. Icy or snow-covered sidewalks or long walks with no protection from rain become major irritants in the day-to-day struggle of shepherding children in and out. Building overhangs over key sidewalks are desirable for this purpose. Overhangs also provide protected shaded outdoor play space, rain space and protection from glare, and they help cool the building in hot weather. It is important to pay attention to the precise dimensions of the overhang in the construction process. An architect may not recognize that the difference between a 3 foot and a 6 foot overhang makes a huge difference in the outdoor play potential of the setting.

Keeping the elements out is also important for settings where the floor is prime play space.

Some staging areas on both sides of an entry to and from the outdoors is desirable to shake off the rain or wipe feet; large mats or carpet can be used if nothing else is possible. In wintering climates, foyers may be essential.

The amount of supplies necessary to keep a program going sometimes is underestimated. A medium size child care center may serve 100 children and adults breakfast, lunch, and snacks; this requires a large influx of food and supplies and a large outflow of garbage. The location of delivery entrances and garbage areas will have an effect on everything from back strains to garbage odors.

Mechanical Systems—Plumbing, Ventilation and Heating, Electrical Systems, Security Systems, Fire Protection, Communication Systems

Changing the mechanical systems is usually the most expensive part of renovation because of the amount of licensed skilled labor required. It is important to think through the program needs thoroughly before decisions are made that are expensive to undo. Some considerations:

Plumbing: Underestimating the need for bathrooms or sinks is a serious mistake. The location of the soil stack (the pipe that removes waste from the toilets) is the key element in the design of the plumbing. Adding a bathroom in an area removed from the soil stack may be either impossible or prohibitively expensive. Children will experiment with flushing; multiple clear outs and easy to get at U traps will help to cope with flushed toys and training pants.

Almost every area of a children's center should have access to water for washing hands, for drinking, for activities, for janitors and clean up. Separate shut off valves at each toilet and fixture are useful. The need to restrict the temperature of hot water to 110 degrees is sometimes overlooked. Floor drains in kitchens, laundry areas, and in some bathrooms can be helpful. The role that water plays outdoors (actually and potentially)—drinking, watering, and play—should be considered.

Ventilation and Heating: Effective climate control can make or break a group environment. The position of the thermostat, the location of the heating outlets, and the design of the system should take into account the fact that the most action takes place on or close to the floor. The temperature should be from 68 to 72 degrees a foot off the ground (infants often have fewer clothes on and may require a higher temperature). Radiators and registers need to be able to be covered, thermostats tamper-proof. Children need to be protected from drafts from windows and doors, again at floor level. A warm floor is important, but some programs complain that radiant heating with floor registers is less pleasant than higher wall registers and decent carpet.

Sealed windows deprive children of the feel and smell and sounds of outdoor life and changing seasons; they also make life intolerable during the inevitable air conditioning breakdowns. Fresh air is important for the health of the children in group settings; the ability to air out the room is important. Some heating systems regulate the humidity by reducing fresh air to increase the humidity. Children's programs often need both moist air and fresh air to cope with respiratory illness. A humidity of 50 to 55 percent is desirable. Controlling odors through ventilation is a real concern to anyone who has ever worked in a children's setting. Air conditioning is essential in hot climates; there are already enough stress factors in the setting without undue heat or humidity.

Electrical Systems: To the caregiver who has to make the space work, where the electrical outlets are located and whether the lights are all *banked* or can be controlled more flexibly is no small matter. Outlets must be out of reach of children or safe from tampering and shock proof. An abundant quantity of outlets throughout the space, including central locations through a floor or ceiling grid or power pole, gives teachers much more flexibility. Consider also the cost and convenience of maintenance of lighting. Who is going to get the ladder and change the fluorescent bulb and replace the ballast?

Security Systems: Most communities have a crime prevention bureau to assist in improving building security. Recommendations generally start with dead bolt locks, protective window coverings, key control, outdoor lighting, and alarm systems. Most security measures involve trade-offs. Dead bolt locks may violate fire codes. A reduced number of windows, windows in doors, and security screening can produce a fortress appearance. There is, however, expensive wire mesh screening that looks reasonable. Burglar alarms are effective but they are expensive and subject to human and mechanical error. Outdoor lighting and a good relationship with neighbors are perhaps the most unequivocally positive measures.

Fire Protection: Local building and fire codes determine the need for fire doors, extinguishers, sprinkler systems, and alarms. Consider program factors when planning fire protection. Fire alarm pull boxes are often placed near building entries and exits, 5 feet off the ground. This happens to be a very convenient height for a baby in arms looking for something to do.

Communication Systems: As programs grow in complexity and quality, communication

needs increase. A telephone in the room allows for more communication with parents, particularly important for parents of babies. Allowing parents and children to talk on the phone during the day, during periods of difficult separation, is a nice feature. School-age programs often involve extensive communication with school transportation systems. Some programs use intercoms or two-way radios for communication with groups in distant gymnasiums, art rooms, nap rooms, and on walks (often at the request of security conscious parents and insurance agents). A telephone in the staff or parent lounge, even a pay phone, is a positive feature.

Character

It's hard to define but we know it when we see it. Character can be an attractive construction material like stone or wood, skylights, ornate or novel design features, interesting angles or windows, multi-level flooring, and so forth. The absence of character—Malvina Reynold's "ticky tacky boxes" defines much that is wrong with the modern age—plastic, form-

---

Squares and Angles
by Alfonsina Storni

Houses in a row, houses in a row,
Houses in a row.
Squares, squares, squares.
Houses in a row.
People already have square souls,
Ideas in a row,
And angles on their backs.
I myself shed a tear yesterday
Which was—good heavens—square.

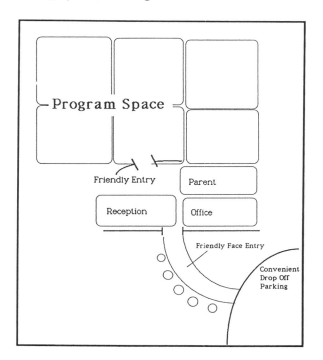

less, artless. But as we seek character in our places of living, we should also make sure we will not come to despise it. *Unforgiving* fixed design features, like skylights that won't darken for naps or movies, quaint spaces that turn into dead space, hallways and stairways, may forever limit possibilities. Screened porches and decks, foyers, and alcoves can provide character with little risk. If there is an unfinished quality that allows the inhabitants to provide the touches that will make the building theirs, that will make it a good place to live, work, and express themselves; the chance of a *soulless* space is reduced. Lofts and creative use of other furnishings can also provide character.

Building Layout

There are essentially three variations in the layout of early childhood programs. They are loosely comparable to homes, traditional self-contained classroom schools, and various open space schools. This is not surprising since three prime sites for programs are homes, schools, and the open plains of church basements.

Homes have a number of small specialized rooms with some common rooms for shared activities; they are designed for small numbers of inhabitants. Many programs in homes flow through the space; some move in groups for definite time periods, some allow individual flow. Programs designed from a traditional school model have classrooms where most everything takes place for a grouping of 10 to 20 children, often including eating and sleeping. Open space models have more dividers and portable walls than fixed walls and usually have shared common areas. Each layout has advantages and disadvantages and can work if the program accommodates rather than fights the layout.

Homes work beautifully until the numbers grow to the point where "she had so many children, she didn't know what to do" (or where they all were). Classrooms have the advantage of providing manageable bounded space. Yet, without places to get out to—common spaces like gyms, art rooms, and the like; outdoors; and field trips—a classroom, however nice, is a rather confining space to spend an early childhood.

Classroom walls that provide boundaries also bind a program to a particular size space and a fixed number of groups. An open shell space provides maximum flexibility and is the lowest cost structure to build. There is the opportunity for multi-use shared space and space adapted to changing conditions. Yet open space is expensive to fill with dividers; the design problem shifts to too little definition of boundaries and too much noise and sensory overload. The more children, the greater the overload.

Open space also requires a staff that has the inclination, skill, and time to plan and coordinate well, as well as expertise in monitoring and evaluating the environment—qualities that high turnover and low salaries work against. Well defined planned space and consistent behavioral expectations replace the walls in providing structure. All children in an open space need a sense of *home base* somewhere within the space, for their own sense of security and to create a sense of group at a more manageable scale. Toddlers also need physical boundaries, real gates that regulate their exploring instincts. Often one finds in open space child care an array of makeshift classrooms.

One does not have to wander too far through the thickets of early childhood programs to encounter teachers in open space settings craving walls and classroom teachers lusting to knock their walls down. Before building, renovating, or moving into a building, it is important to analyze how the particular program and its given philosophy, goals, and staff (or likely staff) will function in the particular space. A relatively *forgiving* classroom-based *modified open space* plan is probably the safest design. A modified open plan "consists of a mixture of several open areas with smaller, enclosed spaces. The open spaces can be subdividable for smaller-group use; the smaller areas can be opened up to each other and to the open spaces to provide a large group area" (Moore et al., 1979, pp. 905-904). One 850 foot classroom may have an accoustical divider allowing division into two classrooms.

The shape of rooms and location of the entries is important. Square rooms are the

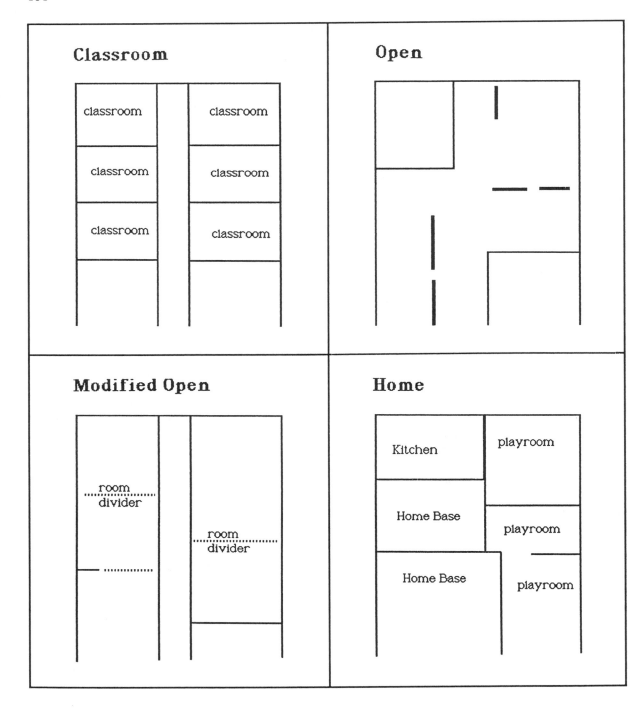

hardest to work with, particularly small square rooms, because it becomes difficult to develop activity areas with reasonable traffic patterns and to achieve any distance between activities. No one ever gets very far from everyone else. Rectangles and L-shaped rooms are easier for teachers to use well. However, if the rooms are too narrow, too much play space is lost to a corridor effect.

Successful adaptations usually stem from a realistic analysis of what the space limitations and strengths really are, what resources are available to change the space or work around the limitations, and what changes in the program will help the space to fit. Both programs and spaces can be shaped to fit. It is when the early childhood professional has a very fixed model of how to run the program (e.g., self-contained classroom groups), or the architects or designers draw from limited experience and impose their vision, that the result is likely to be the same as badly fitting shoes—constant aggravation.

Entries, Exits, Corridors: How adults and children enter and flow through the building will help to determine their identification with the entire program, as opposed to their piece of the program. If a parent and child pass by the office or common space and pass by or through the group they will eventually move to, the sense of program will be stronger and the transitions that much easier. The whole program becomes familiar to parent and child—familiar faces, activities, and space. A daily glimpse into the past—the group they (child **and** parent) grew out of— provides a pleasurable continuity.

Protection versus access is, as mentioned before, a central issue with entries and exits—protection from the outside and protection from the dangers of fire and the like within, access to the outdoors or the common areas, controlled access to the children within. Fire doors that allow quick evacuation for fires also accommodate to the impulsive five year old. Doors that children can use by themselves promote autonomy, but doors that require adult use may protect children from themselves and may draw parents to the door.

Trade-offs have to be made to ensure the most workable solution for a particular setting. A panic bar door to a fenced play yard is very different than the same door to a busy street or alley. Direct access to outdoor play space is a huge positive that will increase the amount of time spent outdoors. It also allows emergency exiting to protected space. A controlled exit that allows teachers to observe as each child is picked up is absolutely essential. A courtyard arrangement that allows children to freely flow in and out without worry is a very desirable feature.

The location of the kitchen, staff room, staff bathrooms, offices, and laundry have their own logic.

Kitchen: The important considerations are the relation to the plumbing and ventilation systems, independent access to delivery and garbage, and clear traffic patterns to and from the area where food is served, free from steps and children. Infant groups have a closer relationship to the kitchen because of the need to individualize feeding and, like the kitchen, have garbage (diapers) that requires frequent removal.

As in many homes, the kitchen often becomes a social room, a second staff room. This could be accommodated by increasing the size of the kitchen or locating the staff room off the kitchen.

Staff Rooms and Staff Bathrooms: These are most convenient if centrally located. If too central, however, the staff room may not serve its function as a place to be away.

Administrative Offices: Generally, it works best to locate them close to the entry, giving parents and visitors ready access. This also helps the administrators in their struggles to collect money and information.

Laundry Area: For prime benefit position it in close proximity to where the most need lies— babies. Laundry chutes are helpful if the wash is done in the basement.

Janitorial Space: If secure from children and designed to make the janitor's job easier, it will result in a cleaner facility and make frequent messy sensory and art play less of a point of tension.

Observation Rooms and Windows: These are useful for all programs for young children, not simply laboratory schools. Observation is essential to learn about children and the workings of setting, both in general and in specific cases. Staff and current and prospective parents can assess the program without changing the dynamics by their presence.

The reflective film often applied to van windows and certain kinds of polished plexiglass for corridor windows are less expensive alternatives to observation booths and two way glass.

Sick Bays or Get Well Rooms: Locate them close to a bathroom and usually to an area independently staffed—a nurse's office or the administrative office.

Corridor Space: New construction often minimizes corridors, but many programs lodged in schools and other buildings have large corridors. Corridor space can be valuable learning space (see Chapter Eleven).

Exercises

1. List **everything** that should happen in and around the building and grounds.

2. Critique a site and building from the standpoint of:

   • a teacher
   • a child
   • a parent
   • a janitor

   Look for built-in positives, dangers, and inevitable irritants.

3. Pick five buildings you are familiar with; evaluate them for *friendliness*.

— Chapter Eight —

Interiors: Walls, Windows, Doors, and Lighting

Walls, ceilings and floors—they shield us, contain us, divide us. Windows and doors are both portals and vistas. Taken together, color scheme, textures and materials, sounds, and light determine the feel of the space—the aesthetic quality of the room. The aesthetic quality needs to be emphasized. If the basic furnishings look good, there is plenty of room for the creative use of *junk* and secondhand materials to develop a high quality learning and caring environment. Amidst tasteful walls and carpets, an eclectic use of donated furniture, cardboard, and various salvage looks creative. The same materials in a drab room with thread-bare carpet and peeling paint looks junky (and parents may evaluate the program accordingly). Money spent *classing up* the basic furnishings is well spent.

Children's programs also need *working* walls and *working* ceilings and floors which can be put to use for communication, storage, display, and activity space. The furnishings work, or don't work, in another sense: together they serve as sight and sound conditioners. When effective, they modulate and direct sensory stimulation in service of program goals.

Ceilings

How high should ceilings be, if we have a choice? Low ceilings would seem to provide for intimacy. However, young children seem to overestimate the size of what they observe, particularly when an object appears large relative to its surroundings. Adults in a place with a low ceiling appear to be even bigger to children (and adult authority already gives them extra size in a child's mind). Osmon (1971, p. 21) concludes that "to minimize the adult presence the ceiling should be at a height where it is not **definitely** perceived by children." He suggests 10 to 11 feet . He goes on to say "whether the ceiling can be too high may not be critical except in terms of economics or acoustics." Because the acoustics and the economics of heating and cooling are often important, ceiling height is usually a trade-off.

Photograph by Jean Wallech

An advantage of high ceilings is that they allow the development of lofts and platforms which increase the amount of usable space. Ceiling height can be varied to provide spatial variety (with less potential for problems than varying floor levels). Parachutes, canopies, and hangings from the ceiling can drop the scale and create intimate spaces. Ceilings that allow the hanging of plants, displays, hammocks, and storage increase the work space of the setting.

Exposing beams, ductwork, and skylights can be very positive; children see how buildings are constructed; natural light reaches the center of the room in interesting patterns. Wallpapering or paneling to a height of 4 to 6 feet from the floor can reduce the cathedral feeling of very high ceilings.

Together, the ceiling and floors need to control noise. An acoustical tile drop ceiling combined with carpeting may make an open space tolerable, but may exert an unnecessary deadening effect in a room where noise is not excessive. To turn a drop ceiling into a working ceiling, a beam can be attached through the ceiling to the beams above.

Flooring

"When you are dealing with a child, keep all your wits about you and sit on the floor."
Austin O'Mally

A balance of carpeted and tiled surfaces is necessary, but what balance? If in doubt, remember, you can always put an area rug over tile but there is no good way to provide temporary tiling. (A plastic tarp attached to a carpeted floor with reinforced plastic duct tape will hold up pretty well until chair legs take their toll.) Varying the floor surface allows better organization of the room. Given sufficient area, going beyond straight line division (this half tile, that half carpet) can be positive.

Wall-to-wall carpeting, fire resistant and washable, is desirable for areas where messy activities are few. The time carpet takes to dry after shampooing is an important consideration because child care programs have almost no *down time*. Carpets differ in their retention of static electricity, which is of more than passing concern to infants and toddlers.

An advantage of area rugs is that they allow for more variety of texture and flexible space use. Avoiding slippery throw rugs on tile and area rugs with *trippable* edges is important.

Tile differs in resiliency and durability, depending on composition and thickness. Vinyl

tile (as opposed to vinyl asbestos tile) is the most expensive surface but the best for both resiliency and durability. Tile also can have texture, an important consideration for wet areas.

Varying the height of the floor is occasionally recommended for the sake of spatial variety, particularly for open settings. This often has disastrous results, however. A two or three tier floor can permanently limit flexibility and create obstacles for wheel chairs, food service carts, and unobservant pedestrians. Portable plywood carpeted platforms on casters are a better alternative.

Photograph by Jean Wallech

Walls

In a high quality program, nearly every inch of wall space has potential use as window space or for display, communication, or activities. Murals and permanent graphics in a classroom are more often than not superfluous, adding unnecessary color and visual clutter, and limiting working wall space. The exception is in very dark, drab spaces.

Color is a useful tool in design, although there is no agreement as to the actual power of the effects of color. Light colors (and mirrors)

Photograph by Jean Wallech

Photograph by Jean Wallech

Photograph by Jean Wallech

do expand the sense of space, and darker colors have the opposite effect. Bright colors or patterns *advance* a wall and thus make it feel closer. Ceilings can be raised or lowered perceptually by using less or more arousing colors and textures. A common decorators' trick is to color opposite walls slightly lighter and darker shades of the same color to make a narrow room appear wider. Beyond the sense of size, warm colors actually stimulate and warm us and cool colors help us to feel cooler and calmer.

Color can be used to dramatize the architecture by directing our attention to beams or to how light enters. Coloring can emphasize or de-emphasize an activity area or art display or signal the active or calm behavior expected. Color also can tie together areas or objects and alter our perceptions of disparities of scale. However, it is precisely the power of color as a tool that has resulted in its regular misuse.

In early childhood settings there is an over-abundance of color. Children's clothes provide color in motion, in addition to the bright colors of toys, artwork, plastic furniture, pillows, and

book covers. Designers, often unable to visualize the setting in action, use too much color and graphics for accent walls. The end result is a kaleidoscopic atmosphere that cheers for a short time and wears on the individual for the other five to seven hours of the day.

In programs limiting children's living to one or two rooms, the use of warm or neutral earth tones on walls and floors, similar to the colors most popular in living rooms, is highly recommended. These colors also show less wear. Color for drama and communication can be added in a less permanent fashion through curtains, displays, and *stain glassing* windows with crepe paper or transparent plastic. Graphics and murals can be used to add character and friendliness to hallways; the building facade; and smaller, special use rooms.

The schools of Reggio Emilia, Italy, mentioned earlier, consider children's programs as art galleries and think through the display of children's materials and other works of art. Corridors, staff and parent rooms, the outside facade, bathrooms—anywhere can be the location for a gallery display. Plexiglass can

be used to protect displays and allow children to touch the materials (through the plexiglass).

For walls to *work*, they have to be made from materials that allow cleaning and the attaching of shelving, cabinets, and displays. There is an endless need/desire to tack or tape materials to the walls. Bulletin boards, map rails, chalk boards, and erasable marker boards will partially satisfy (but probably not quell) a good teacher's primal need to tape or tack. Washable wallpaper is the best surface and the most expensive, followed by a high quality latex paint. Semigloss paint for walls and trim is desirable in high use areas; flats and matte finishes reduce brightness and glare. Combining the use of wallpaper and paint and using paneling in areas subject to hard use (where chairs are stacked or wooden blocks are used, for example) works well.

Remember, for children walls are tactile as well as visual. Textured walls add to the richness and warmth of a setting. In programs where acoustics are difficult, carpeting walls can help.

Photograph by Jean Wallech

Windows

"Penrod was doing something very unusual and rare, something almost never accomplished except by . . . a boy in school on a spring day: he was doing really nothing at all. He was merely in a state of being.

From the street a sound stole in through the open window and abhorring Nature began to fill the vacuum called Penrod Schofield, for the sound was the spring sound of a mouth-organ, coming down the sidewalk. The windows were intentionally above the level of the eyes of the seated pupils; but the picture of the musicians was plain to Penrod, pointed for him by a quality of the calliope, and of cats in anguish: an excruciating sweetness obtained only by the wallowing, walloping . . . palm of a hand. . . . The music came down the street and passed beneath the window, accompanied by the carefree shuffling syncopations on the cement sidewalk. It passed into the distance; became faint and blurred; and was gone. Emotion stirred in Penrod a great and poignant desire. . . ."
Booth Tarkington (1965)

Windows are wonderful as sources of light and openings to the wider world. They give the feeling of more space and of tantalizing adventures just beyond. It is important to remember that windows do have disadvantages—among them lost storage, display, and communication space and, in some climates, loss of heat or cooling.

Nature is never static. Windows allow the drama occurring outdoors to be witnessed and felt. It is a drama that many adults have become quite inured to. The sun streaming through, now blocked by dark clouds bursting with rain that pelts the windows, is exciting. But simply the movement of clouds and trees provides patterns of the quieter drama of light and shade.

Changing days and seasons provide elements of pace to a setting. Street and outdoor scenes—offering a variety of perceptual experiences of sight, sound, and smell—are learning activities and a focus for conversation. But the value of a window depends on its context. An ugly, drab, or distracting view adds nothing.

Photograph by Jean Wallech

Interior windows to hallways and adjoining rooms are useful for observations, daily *welcoming* and facilitating child (and parent) transitions between groups. Daily glimpses of life in other group areas ensures that children move up into familiar spaces.

Windows should be shatter resistant and adequate for the security necessary. Windows that extend 18 to 24 inches off the ground allow for child viewing (and require more cleaning) but are not appropriate in areas where there is a lot of motor activity. Plexiglass panels can be used to protect windows in such areas. High windows can be made accessible through the placement of furniture or platforms.

Protection from heat, thermal glare, and drafts is an important consideration, as is protection from unwanted outdoor noise. The relative desirability of blinds, curtains, and shades depends on the need for durability because of child use and purposes served.

Photograph by Jean Wallech

The Frost Pane
by David McCord

What's the good of breathing
On the window
Pane
In summer?
You can't make a frost
On the window pane
In summer.
You can't write a
Nalphabet,
You can't draw a
Nelephant;
You can't make a smudge
With your nose
In summer.

Lots of good, breathing
On the window
Pane
In winter.
You can make a frost
On the window pane
In winter.
A white frost, a light frost,
A thick frost, a quick frost,
A write-me-out-a-picture-frost
Across the pane
In winter.

Blinds are wonderfully flexible for controlling light but are susceptible to curious hands (as are shades). One program that uses blinds believes the children, most of whom have blinds in their upscale homes, need to learn not to mess with the blinds. One can also buy windows with blinds built into the windows. Curtains tend to be less expensive and more durable, and they can offer some acoustical protection in noisy

areas. Awnings are useful in some situations. Plants located indoors or outdoors can also alter the flow of light.

Windows and window coverings in children's programs receive hard use. One doesn't have to visit many programs to see windows that remain closed or shades or blinds that remain frozen because they are difficult to open, sometimes due to new innovative hardware or simply a need for repair. Window hardware should be selected with an eye toward durability, security, and whether the goal is child proofing or child accessibility.

Lighting

There is a pervasive tendency to overlight all new institutional settings. This may be a reaction both to the old days of dark, drab settings with few windows and other amenities and to the power of the fluorescent light revolution. Banks of diffused fluorescent lighting allow maximum flexibility. At any given spot one can read small print or string beads. But why is this necessary? A mixture of fluorescent light from the ceiling, natural light from windows and skylights, and local area lighting (some on tracks) will allow flexibility that creates "pools of light" (Osmon, 1971, pp. 96-98). Light can also be bounced off a light ceiling. Reducing the dependence on fluorescent lights is also important because there is some evidence that fluorescent lights may have a negative impact on hyperactivity.

Light has the same possibilities as a design tool as color does. Teachers can use light to influence activities and moods; reduced lighting calms, increased lighting can brighten spirits. Lighting at different height levels adds variety. Light dimmers are useful tools, particularly in nap rooms.

Imagine the sense of power and autonomy, as well as the opportunity for creativity, if some of the lighting were designed to allow children to control raising or lowering the light level or to determine the location of the light. Osmon, in his innocence of early childhood ways, offers, as one possible design solution, portable lighting fixtures that a child could carry to different work stations. A crazy idea, perhaps, but think a moment of how a child would react to the idea and what a child might learn in the process.

In planning the lighting, it is important to consider the plan from all angles, literally. Will there be glare in the sight lines of children, including infants staring straight up into the ceiling? Will teachers be able to control the lighting for naps or movies? Can the bulbs be changed easily? (More than one program requires 12 foot ladders or scaffolding to change a bulb.) Warm fluorescent lighting is superior to cool fluorescent bulbs, but more expensive. A design scheme that is based on warm fluorescent lighting may never be realized, as pressure to keep operating costs down takes over.

Furnishings have an impact on the lighting effects. Light wall colors, polished wood or chrome, and mirrors reflect lighting and add to the brightness of the room and, depending on the light source, the glare.

Doors

"What then, I ask, is the greater reality of a door? Well perhaps it is the localized setting for a wonderfully human gesture: conscious entry and departure.

That's what a door is, something that frames your coming and going, for it's a vital experience not only for those who do so, but also for those encountered and left behind. A door is a place made for an act

that is repeated millions of times in a lifetime between the first entry and the last exit. I think that's symbolical. And what is the greater reality of a window? I leave that to you."
Aldo Van Eyke (in Osmon, 1971, p. 30)

It's access versus protection once again. Doors are the subject of fire and safety and health codes which vary in different areas. Whether a room or bathroom entrance requires a full door or allows double dutch doors, an automatic closer, or any particular hardware is often regulated. Ideally, doors serve program goals, allowing the program maximum flexibility—alternately, they can serve as barriers, portals, or windows. A heavy front door that requires adult assistance draws a parent in and at the same time makes it more difficult for would be fugitives to flee.

A program can use hardware that allows child use but also allows adults to restrict access or keep the door open. Simple door stops and hooks can accomplish this. Double doors and screen doors will increase the flexibility by allowing closure with visibility. Using glass or plexiglass panels that extend to 18 inches off the floor for interior doors reduces the number of accidents arising from children being hit by opening doors. Prescott and David (1976, p. 36) point out "that one of the problems with doors from an adult point of view is that children are fascinated with them. They really need to experiment with the concepts of *open* and *closed*, *here* and *gone*, *inside* and *outside*, etc." They note suggestions made by Peller that doors, gates, and pass throughs can be incorporated into play areas indoors and out.

Exercises

1. Take up Van Eyke's challenge: What is the greater reality of a window?

2. Assume you have virtually no money for materials and equipment. All your activities and learning centers have to make do with free and inexpensive materials: water, rocks, computer paper, fabric scraps, string, buttons, materials from garage sales and so on. You do, however, have great funding for renovation and furnishings. Develop ways to really put the walls, floors, and ceilings to work.

3. You have lost your home and have to move into your setting to live for a time. Aside from adding a bed, what changes would make the setting feel livable?

4. Come up with five design ideas that on first glance seem great but over time either teachers or janitors would come to hate.

— Chapter Nine —

Caring

"In an old house in Paris that was covered with vines
Lived twelve little girls in two straight lines.
In two straight lines they broke their bread
And brushed their teeth and went to bed."
by Ludwig Bemelmans (1937)

We all eat, drink, sleep, go to the bathroom, wash, hold and are held (John Wayne aside), love, and do all the other living that accompanies work or play. Some do everything in two straight lines, some sleep in hammocks or on futons instead of beds, some kneel or squat, and some sit in chairs. There are a lot of ways to go about this business of living. In a group setting, the central issue is how to balance the personal and the institutional. When individual personal satisfaction is lined up against efficiency, sanitation and health, economy, and the satisfaction of regulators, insurers, and maintenance staff, it is often no contest. It takes all the creativity and resources that can be mustered to keep care routines from becoming a contest between getting the job done and personal gentle care.

Eating and Drinking

"Man does not live by bread alone. Frequently he needs a beverage."
Woody Allen

In child care programs, it often seems like eating is taking place all the time; in infant programs, this is literally true. Snack, breakfast, lunch, snack, perhaps a late snack for the very late children—a program for 60 children may serve 130 meals and 100 snacks a day. Efficient production and delivery of nutritious meals at set times is essential. For programs serving infants, the need for individualized feeding times and introduction of new foods adds an additional level of complexity.

The Kitchen

More than a clearinghouse for food, the kitchen is often the emotional center to the program.

Programs that prepare lunch for over 50 people greatly benefit from an institutional kitchen—one with a commercial refrigerator, freezer, dishwasher, sinks, and mechanical systems. N.S.F. refrigerators and freezers are often required and necessary because they have a quick recovery time, essential for maintaining the temperature despite the repeated opening and closing that all day program use entails.

A reliable dishwasher that can take the quantity of use and meet health requirements should be coupled with an institutional sink with two or three compartments. Larger programs should have a separate food preparation sink.

The size and layout of the kitchen needs to accommodate what will happen there: the obvious—preparation, cooking, dishwashing, and food storage— and the not so obvious—staff getting medicine, coffee, or taking a break; storage of food carts; storage of bulk food; children observing; and whatever else the program might require. A too small kitchen is a familiar curse. Without ample cupboards, a pantry, and counter space for preparation, appliances, and dirty dishes, the program suffers.

There is never too much storage space. Metal and wire shelving and storage that accommodates plastic containers is effective against insects and rodents. Storage needs to be carefully thought through in terms of access, durability, and security. Cabinets or countertops too high or deep are the bane of many cooks. A step stool is often necessary but in itself increases the risk of accident as something to trip over or fall off.

Sanitation, safety, and concern for a quality workplace for the cook govern kitchen design. Resilient seamless vinyl flooring is easy to keep clean and easier on the feet. Windows and warm fluorescent lighting or indirect lighting that is designed to be flexible and minimize glare (all the shiny surfaces!) and unnecessary brightness provide the best lighting. Heat build up occurs, not just from cooking, but also from the large appliance; and adequate ventilation is critical to remove heat (and odors). Screened windows and doors to the outside do wonders for a kitchen's ambience.

Most regulations do not allow children in the kitchen for safety reasons. As Prescott and David (1976, p. 57) note: "A complete separation of kitchen from the lives of children may be inevitable in centers where food service is done on a large scale. However, some of the nicest moments which we have seen in day care are those where children could perch in safe places and watch, talk with or even help the cook. . . . Food and the people who provide it have special meaning for young children. In family day care, children are not separated from the preparation of food as are children in most center programs. We have been struck by the quality of the conversation which occurs in family day care kitchens." Their insight is an argument for both smaller programs and good design. Pass throughs that allow children to watch and talk, windows that provide visual access, and a preparation area away from the dangerous areas allow children some access.

Photograph by Jean Wallech

Photograph by Jean Wallech

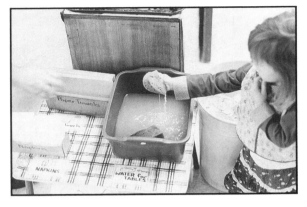

Photograph by Jean Wallech

Programs with infants greatly benefit from having a satellite or countertop kitchen in or off the room: refrigerator, microwave, and food storage. From experience, if the only microwave is in the infant area, general staff use for reheating food and coffee may occur and result in unwanted traffic and a safety hazard, as hot materials are transported.

Bettelheim observed that from the first gulp a baby takes from the mother's breast, eating together is the greatest socialization experience. Mealtimes are potentially positive group experiences—social, convivial times to touch bases and recount experiences. They may also be harried, hectic occasions with tired, hungry children and adults fluttering around like mother robins trying to satisfy incessant needs. Or mealtime may be a stern, no-nonsense *let's get the job done we have a schedule to keep* operation. The goal for most programs is a relaxed social occasion that balances children's development of self-help skills with limited time for eating and cleanup. Location and layout of the eating area and choice of furniture and utensils are important.

Separate eating areas have their advantages, most notabably in more contained and less

hurried clean up, proximity to the kitchen, ease of serving, and freeing the classroom from the need for tables. For groups largely confined to a classroom, the daily trips to the cafeteria can provide a welcome break. But the disadvantages usually outweigh the advantages. Most programs do not have the space to set aside for limited use; a separate dining area usually results in more transitions and a more regimented mealtime in a larger group. Eating in the room requires adequate tile space, suitable tables and chairs, and the clean up of materials and equipment. When a program has a choice, experimenting with both alternatives and analyzing the trade-offs is useful.

Encouraging self-help is possible with the right utensils—small *freezette* pitchers, bowls and glasses with wide bottoms for more stability, and room enough between children to allow for body language. A dishpan with water and sponge, paper towels, and a mop *right there* make clean up easier.

Tables and Chairs and Other Places to Sit

In most early childhood programs, mealtime is the only time there is a real reason to have

of very limited value. Yet, at mealtimes, proper tables and chairs are very important if a child is going to be granted some degree of independence in serving and if adults are to feel comfortable about the whole thing.

The solution is to select or adapt tables for maximum flexibility. Flexibility, ease of cleaning, and the ability to adjust to the right scale so that the child can sit at the right height relative to the table (with feet on the floor) are the important criteria. Small half-round tables, rectangle, and trapezoidal tables can be combined to form larger units and can be flipped

Photographs by Jean Wallech

every child seated at a table at the same time. At those times, it makes sense to have tables where five to ten children can be seated with an adult. At other times, large tables waste space because the floor, cubes, and smaller tables are more suitable. With a table 10 to 18 inches off the ground, a child can kneel or stand and, Anita Olds points out, use the full leverage of his entire body to act on the materials.

A variety of tables is useful. Large tables work better for projects or where supervision is necessary. Small tables allow one to four children to attend to a task with less interference. Too many tables and chairs is a major problem for programs with tight space, especially in toddler programs where large tables are

Photograph by Jean Wallech

Photograph by Jean Wallech

upside down on top of each other if necessary. Most useful, a texture table can be used as an eating table by making a 3/5 inch plywood top (three coats of polyurethane) that extends 6 inches beyond each edge for legs to fit under.

There are now many chairs to choose from. Some are easy to clean, some stack better than others, and some (like Educubes) are wonderfully flexible and useful as tables, stools, and building pieces. For young toddler bodies, Community Playthings' wooden chair is far superior for providing support. It is also a pain to clean. Educubes work reasonably well with toddlers and preschoolers, offering flexibility in height and use; but they are big and blocky and do not stack. (They do fit under a table preschool height.) If teachers do not recognize their value as tables, push toys and props in dramatic play and building, they take up usable space.

There is no law that classrooms have to have all the same kind of chairs. Stools, cubes, armchairs, rocking chairs, and chairs of different heights are valuable to a child learning to come to terms with a differentiated world. The complicated negotiations over who sits where and on what, and coping with disappointment, is what social learning is about. Chairs that a child can move around allow a child a sense of control. It also helps to consider Peller's observation: "Only in our Western culture have we given up squatting or kneeling positions which bring us nearer to the floor than the average

chair. Children like to sit tailor fashion on the floor, or to kneel on a flat cushion, sitting on their heels as the Chinese do. Both positions are healthful for the child" (Prescott and David, 1976, p. 39).

Infant Feeding

In some infant programs, the idea of a high chair is an anathema which forces a child into an unnatural and unnecessary position. In programs where infants are being fed from bottle or breast, there is an obvious need for comfortable adult furniture in pleasant surroundings.

Most other programs have never seriously considered any alternatives to the high chair. For infants ready for finger feeding and spoon feeding, high chairs are most frequently used; but they take up space when not in use (which is much of the time). Inexpensive high chairs rarely last.

If space is limited, using a car seat with an attachable tray is an alternative which allows flexibility. The seat can be used as a car seat and

Photograph by Jean Wallech

for individual play; it can also be moved around easily. It can be used on the floor or secured to a cabinet top. The Community Playthings chairs mentioned earlier have trays and work well with older infants. The portable seats that attach over the table top work successfully for some programs. An *eating corral* reduces the spread of mealtime disorder.

Drinking

Access to water is important. Drinking fountains with simple hardware or floor mechanisms, adapted with steps for child height both in the room and on the playground, are not a luxury. A paper cup dispenser is a more

expensive alternative, but it is more appropriate for toddlers unless the fountain has controls a toddler can coordinate.

Aside from the autonomy issue, it is valuable to teach children that water, as opposed to other beverages, is a wonderful drink when they are thirsty.

Bathrooms and Diaper Areas

"The old Lanham Act Centers in California had large bathrooms with windows and often long benches for sitting. We were struck with the relaxed tempo which this light, roomy area seemed to promote. The teacher often sat down, relaxed, and gave children help and individual attention. The children enjoyed a bit of water play and the pleasure of some time with pants off."
Prescott and David (1976, pp. 52-53)

Rarely do we think of bathrooms in terms of pleasure and social interaction, unlike the Japanese who give much thought to the color and feel of the tile and stone, the shape of the bath, and the view from a window (often to the garden). Prescott and David pointed out that economy of construction often dictates a central location for bathrooms; a typical bathroom is designed to be small and efficient to make more room for play space. "As a result, much of the teacher's energy will be directed to keeping *the show on the road* and snuffing out any illicit water play or questions about anatomical differences" (p. 52). Toddler bathrooms, where adults are needed to help with clothes and provide moral support, are often a tight squeeze. Because of the frequency of slippery floors, bathrooms (even with floor drains) can be dangerous places under crowded conditions. The preschool bathroom should be large enough to comfortably allow an adult to help a child change messy clothes amidst other children using the facility.

Immediate access when the child needs it is very important. Programs where indoor and outdoor access is difficult tend to be forced into an unpleasant degree of regimentation. Access means door hardware that allows the child to enter and exit and a sufficient number of stools. In one program, because a health inspector required self-closing bathroom doors and did not allow a window that would open for acoustical access, two year olds were continually being trapped in the bathroom. Ultimately, the door had to be propped open, defeating the health inspector's purpose. This was a less satisfactory solution than the lighter doors with

plexiglass windows which the program originally sought.

Unfortunately, for the logistics of group living, waiting for a toilet is not something very young children do well. Wet pants and unauthorized water play to pass the time are the inevitable result. A bathroom attached to each group area is desirable.

For children under five, segregation by sex is generally considered unnecessary, but it does vary by community. One mass bathroom for 30 or 40 children is much less desirable than two smaller bathrooms, even if they are side by side. Two entrances improve the traffic pattern and reduce the crowding, making a significant difference. A toddler bathroom that serves more than 15 children will make life hard on the staff. If possible, one stool per ten preschoolers is preferable, and, to avoid the use of potty chairs, one per five or six toddlers.

There is no consensus on the need for child size stools, particularly in small programs. They are expensive and adult toilets can be adapted. However, child size toilets tend to result in more autonomy and more sanitary bathrooms, particularly for children under three. Toddler size toilets remove much of the fear of falling (an extra load to an already loaded issue). Urinals can be useful for preschool and older.

Maintenance is a critical concern in bathrooms. Nothing turns parents and staff off more than smelly, dirty, wet bathrooms. It is a given that little boys will have problems with accuracy, unintentional and otherwise. Seamless flooring, easily cleanable walls, and a tight seal between wall and floor are important for sanitation. A wet mop in the bathroom and a fixture off the sink that adults can operate for filling buckets (and water tables) aid spot cleaning.

Bradley sinks are wonderful only if expense, both in purchasing and maintenance, is of little concern. Because this is rarely the case, purchasing two or three individual sinks with simple hardware and an aerated reduced flow is often wiser. Hot water is not necessary.

A drinking fountain outside the bathroom, preferably in the classroom, reduces congestion. In a child care center, a bathtub or child shower area with a flexible hose is of real value, for instances of diarrhea or other dramatic messes.

Hand dryers are useful for wet hair but do not replace paper towels because most children (and many adults) will not wait to dry their hands. There is no *right* dispenser for towels. Children should have access to the dispenser and be able to get one towel and not a handful. Personal wash cloths work for some programs but need space to hang on a line or hooks.

Toothbrushing is one of those socialization experiences that child care programs should aspire to but are only possible when staffing and space are accommodating. A roomy bathroom with multiple sinks can help make it possible. It is even easier if sinks are available outside the bathroom.

Ventilation, acoustics, and aesthetics are key ingredients in bathroom ambience. An exhaust fan directing air, moisture, and odors out of the building will also provide white noise to cushion the acoustical hardness and the noise of flushing toilets, which can be a major classroom distraction.

Bathrooms are often overlit rooms with considerable brightness and glare emanating from the tile and glossy paint. This can produce a harsh rather than cheery setting to learn bodily control. Softer overhead lighting with focused lighting on mirrors (child height), windows, plants, and a calming color scheme—blues or greens—will help to produce a relaxed atmosphere.

Bathrooms are often storage centers for wet clothes, cleaning supplies, and assorted materials relating to art or messy play. Cabinets or shelving and an area for drying clothes are important.

Bathrooms are expensive additions; many programs adapt to circumstances. One program uses a chemical toilet for its basement gym/ sleeping area. While not an ideal situation, the alternative was sending children on a solo 50 yard journey up a flight and a half of stairs, unsanitary accidents occurring along the way.

Diapering

Diapering a child should be an unhurried, one-to-one interaction between baby and adult, rich with language, eye contact, and adult responsiveness. Staffing, group diapering logistics, and layout all too often result in a rushed, impersonal experience. A diapering area in or adjacent to the play area, enabling the caregiver to remain in sight and hearing range, decreases the need to hurry.

If this is not possible, a play area in the bathroom (a holding area) that allows one or two babies to occupy their time while another child is being diapered might help matters. A diaper table in a crib room makes good sense as children are typically diapered before and after naps.

One diapering table for six to eight children is reasonable. For programs serving children under 16 months, a toilet should not be necessary (although required in some locations). Some programs use a flush sink unit built into a countertop (designed for hospitals). A sink or other source of water for handwashing is essential. If nothing else is available, a keg or coffee urn with a tap will provide running water for handwashing, a better alternative than relying on wet wipes.

Health and safety considerations and the need for diapering to be a positive experience for both adult and child guide the design of a diaper area. Ideally, the area is laid out so everything is right there—diapers, plastic bags, sink, soap, medication, disinfectant, and covered garbage container. It is when the adult has to reach or interrupt the diapering to retrieve something that the danger of falling occurs. Given the frequency of diapering in an average program (12 children x 4 times a day x 250 days = 12,000 diapering incidents), the risk of a serious accident from a 3 foot fall is high. Diaper tables with 3 inch rims may reduce the risk of accidents, but I suspect they also engen-

der a false sense of security. Use of a strap to secure a wiggly baby makes diapering an unpleasant experience. The solution is making it a cardinal rule for staff to always have one hand on a child, posting reminders of the procedure, designing the area thoughtfully, and installing resilient flooring just in case a child does fall. Diapering on the floor in a group setting almost always results in very poor sanitation.

Layout is the key to sanitary procedures, and sanitary diapering is the key to a healthy infant area. It is no small achievement to undress a child, change a diaper, reclothe the

Photograph by Jean Wallech

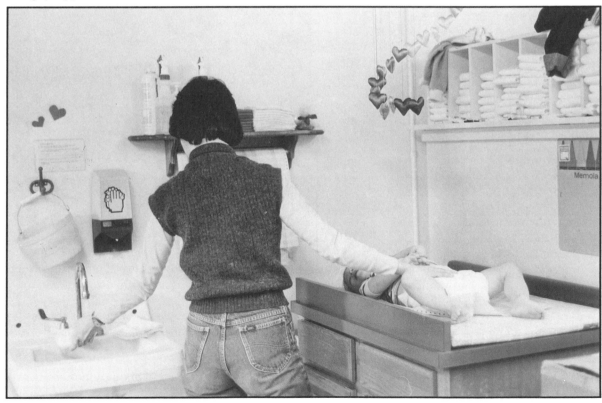

child, wash your hands and the child's hands, and return the child to the floor without contaminating any surfaces. Monitoring and analyzing the procedure and tinkering with the layout of equipment and paraphernalia is necessary.

Toddler diapering should occur in a bathroom. A ramp or stairway up to the diaper table will over time greatly reduce the amount of lifting, but it may be tricky in terms of the space available and the child's safety climbing onto the changing table.

Janitor's Sinks and Art Sinks or Where is the Fish Tank Cleaned?

Ideally, there are sinks in addition to bathroom sinks. There should be a sink in the group area for art and messy play and for hand-

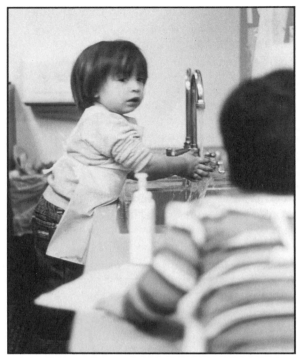

Photograph by Jean Wallech

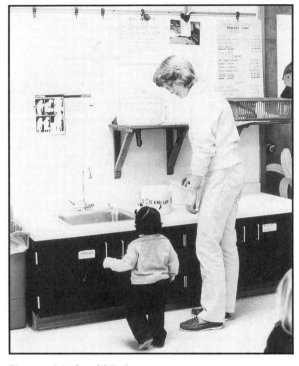

Photograph by Jean Wallech

From Experience—Diaper Table

• Plastic bags and bag holders (like those found in supermarket produce departments) can be mounted on the wall for a great addition to diaper areas and bathrooms.

• Computer paper works fine as a changing pad's disposable cover.

• Good quality paper towels (medium weight, c-fold) soaked in water work fine as wet wipes. (Cleaning requires soap.)

• The most useful sinks are either the Lady Vanity by Kohler with a sloping bottom or a stainless steel institutional kitchen sink which is deep enough for bathing a baby—both with spray attachments.

• Sink hardware that allows elbow control of the faucets is useful.

washing. This sink should be child accessible and deep enough to prevent splashing. It should have a high curved spout and be large enough to allow buckets, fish tanks and other oversized equipment to be cleaned. A flexible hose attachment for filling tanks and water tables makes life easier. Janitors sinks may serve the same purpose but usually are not child accessible.

Sleeping

"Sleep is the gift of many spiders
The webs tie down the sleepers easy."
Carl Sandburg in "Drowsy"

A child care setting needs an area where each child has the opportunity to sleep free from interruption for some portion of the day. Infants and some toddlers need to be able to nap in the morning in a quiet space, separated from active children and adults. The acoustics need to ensure muting of the cacophony of snores and hacking coughs, loud cries, whispers, and so on. A darkened room allows fewer distractions. Supplied with adequate air flow and free from drafts, the space should be large enough to allow 2 to 3 feet between each sleeping child. Also needed are places where a child can crash for a time without leaving the room.

The setting helps to determine whether the periods of easing into and out of sleep are gentle times. Falling asleep at one's own pace with one's own quirky actions and rituals, to soft music and a back rub, soothes a restless or exhausted spirit. Warm sunlight, breezes, and some music are natural arousers and provide a pleasant transition to wakefulness.

How important are separate crib rooms and nap rooms? Programs that have them are convinced they are a must, those that don't often see them as desirable but nonessential. For preschoolers, having a separate sleep area in a gym or multipurpose room allows teachers a chance to restore the order and set up for the afternoon. It also results in a space in the classroom for children who do not sleep. The lack of a non-sleepers' space often justifies forcing children to stay quiet on a cot for an

---

from **Sleep and Poetry**
by John Keats

"What is more gentle than a wind in
summer?
What is more soothing than the pretty
hummer
That stays one moment in an open
flower,
And buzzes cheerfully from bower to
bower?
What is more tranquil than a musk-rose
blowing
In a green island, far from all men's
knowing?...

What, but thee, Sleep? Soft closer of our
eyes!
Low murmurer of tender lullabies!
Light hoverer around our happy
pillows!
Wreather of poppy buds, and weeping
willows!
Silent entangler of a beauty's tresses!
Most happy listener! when the morning
blesses
Thee for enlivening all the cheerful eyes
That glance so brightly at the new
sun-rise."

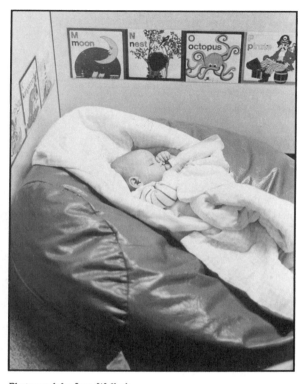

Photograph by Jean Wallech

oppressively long time (probably anything over 45 minutes). Avoiding regimentation and an institutional, military-like atmosphere should be a goal, eliminating the drill sergeant and forced uniformity if not the barracks.

Toddlers benefit from the security of sleeping in a smaller, more familiar space than a large multipurpose space. Infants, however, are more adept at tuning out external stimuli, and many programs get by without crib rooms. This is harder on the staff, who are usually struggling with far less than optimal conditions on all fronts. With more than six infants, an acoustically separate crib room is a large plus. This does not rule out simultaneous use of the room for quiet nurturing, staff planning, and other

Photograph by Jean Wallech

generally prefer them. Portacribs work well; non-institutional quality will last for a reasonable length of time, if cribs are not used as play space and if children are taken out as soon as they desire it. If children spend more time in their cribs, a standard size, heavier duty crib is necessary. There are now cribs available with plexiglass sides, cribs that rock, hospital cribs built to last for decades, and waterbed cribs. None of these are essential.

Children attending on the same day should never share a crib (or cot or mat). If part time children share, each child should have her own bedding; and the crib should be disinfected after each use.

The space under cribs can be used for storage. Bags for personal items can be attached to each crib. Charts above each crib detailing the child's sleep habits should **never** be tacked.

Whatever older children sleep on will have to be washable and stored. Children seem to sleep perfectly well on mats, molded plastic cots, sheets on soft carpeting, or blankets on grass. As adults we make judgments about what is comfortable and may prefer one or another surface for our children, but children seem to get used to anything. Mats and plastic cots require less storage space and are lighter. There are toddler size cots available for use with children under two. Storage of blankets should be considered; children often bring standard size blankets and quilts from home.

Sick Children

All programs care for sick children. The issue is whether moderately ill children are taken care of for the shortest possible time (until picked up by parents) or for longer periods in sick bays or get well rooms. Minimally, a quiet,

quiet activities. A window to the playroom or an intercom can maintain contact, because few programs can afford to continuously staff a crib room. (Some states do require it and programs should comply.)

In good weather the capacity to sleep outdoors on a porch, shady deck, or shady grass is a wonderful asset. In Europe, sleeping outdoors is common.

It is a given that children have to sleep. What they sleep on is not a given and depends on regulations, parent and staff preferences (children's preferences more rarely), cost, and storage.

Cribs, portacribs, playpens, cradles, crib mattresses, and floor mattresses are all used in various combinations in different programs. Cradles attached to the wall stretches crib room space and does not result in the kennel-like appearance of cribs attached to the walls. Cradles only work, however, with infants unable to pull themselves up, generally under four months old. Some programs use bean bag chairs for young infants. Infants making the transition to a toddler group can sleep on toddler size cots.

Most programs rely on cribs for babies as the perceived safest alternative, and because cribs are what children use at home and parents

Sizes of Furnishings

Floor Space

Standard crib	30" x 54"
Porta crib	24"-27" x 42"
Changing table	18"-24" x 34"-40"
Toddler cots	24" x 42"
Preschool cots	24" x 52"
Rest mats	20"-24" x 38"-48"
Rocking chair or armchair	24"-30"
Couch	30"-40" x 60"-84"
Storage units	11-1/2" or 15" x 24"-28" x 24"-48"

Heights of Furnishings

Child size chairs (seat heights)	8" to 13"
2 year olds	8"
3 year olds	10"
4-5 year olds	12"
Child size toilets	
Toddler/preschool	11"
Kindergarten	13"
Table heights	
1-3 year olds	Adjustable 16"-18"
3-5 year olds	Adjustable 16"-20"
4-5 year old	Adjustable 21"-30"

semi-secluded space away from the action is necessary for children who become ill. Often a corner of the office or a quiet nook in the play area performs this function.

In an ideal world all programs would have a separate, staffed sick bay with the capacity to serve up to 10 percent of the children—complete with sink, separate toilet, separate entrance for children with chicken pox, room for cots and cribs, and a quiet play area. Another alternative to a sick bay is a satellite *sick home* or *center* that the children become familiar enough with so that they perceive it as part of the center.

Without some way to serve moderately ill children, even in spaces less than ideal (no separate toilet in the sick bay, for example), the end result is more moderately ill children in the general program population, to say nothing of parent and staff stress. Because of the hesitancy by regulators and health professionals to approve of sick child arrangements admittedly less than ideal (but more affordable), sick child programs are few. For any change, standards for sick bays need to take the real world trade-offs of limited resources into account.

Living, Loving, and Being

What makes an institution a good place to care for others? It's the same furnishings that one finds in homes to accomplish the tasks, only now selected with an eye toward the rigors of group living and for flexibility. Homes have **10 to 20 times** the amount of square feet per occupant, and home furnishings receive much less wear. Caring for children means **many** soft places to hold and snuggle—couches and chairs, preferably covered with washable throws. Flip chairs with heavy duty fabric and futons make marvelously flexible places to nurture, almost as flexible as a soft floor and pillows. Bed pillows with pillow cases and throw pillows are washable and can be combined with blankets, small rugs, and other fabric pieces to allow children to create spaces. Caring requires rocking chairs, swings and hammocks, and out of the way

padded places to help children through moments of lost control, humiliation, and inconsolable loss.

Exercises

1. Analyze your own feelings about eating, going to the bathroom, and sleeping. What aspects of the environmental context do you find help make the circumstances pleasant or unpleasant?

2. List as many different possible sleeping surfaces as you can (cot, barn loft, etc.) and the advantages and disadvantages of each in terms of comfort, flexibility, safety, economy, and so on. Be as creative as humanity has in its history.

3. Close your eyes. What do you remember about settings where you were cared for as a child?

4. Take a child along and together critique a setting.

— Chapter Ten —

Storage

"The doorknob was dusty and the door creaked as it slowly opened. I quickly stepped back, recoiling from the fetid air, and narrowly avoided being crushed by the large box hurtling down towards me. I took it all in at a glance: the violent disorder, the rubble, the sad soft creatures with missing limbs, the half-empty crates, and, here and there through the chaos, glimpses of once strong airplanes and garages and other remnants of the Fisher-Price civilization. I now understood the knowing looks and cruel laughter of my new colleagues when, in my innocence, I volunteered to organize the storage room."

There are probably few programs with adequate storage. Even in new buildings designed for child care, the sheer quantity of *stuff* required for quality early childhood programs is underestimated. In 1976, Prescott and David commented that storage has not been given enough attention as a key factor in providing good child care. Little has changed. Prescott's finding that better and more conveniently located storage was often the first step to program improvement is an insight quickly affirmed by nearly all who are working to improve programs.

Good storage allows a program to:

• Maximize the use of its resources. If you can't find it or unsort it, you can't use it. If it's hard to get or far away, you won't use it very often.

• Accumulate resources. If you can't store it, you can't keep it.*

• Teach children about relations between things. If you can't organize things in a way that children understand, you can't expect children to maintain an order.

• Extend and elaborate children's play. Prescott and her colleagues found that organized storage led to more complex and longer lasting play. Apparently, open storage enabled children to visualize relations and plan future actions (Prescott, 1984, p. 48).

• Teach children to take responsibility for things. A well organized book display connotes far more respect for books than a pile of books on a shelf.

• Maintain harmony among people. If adults and children are not allowed personal storage,

*While too much storage is impossible, ample storage does allow programs to keep junk that may never be used and distracts from useful junk. If it hasn't been used in a year or two, it probably never will be used.

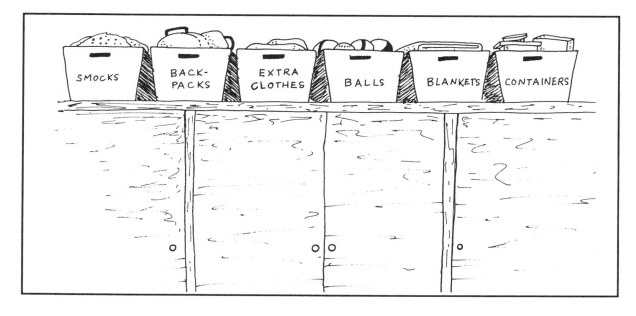

whether the teacher's scissors or the child's mittens, conflict will inevitably ensue. A new director traced a long standing cold war between two teachers to an allegedly *stolen* stapler.

It is helpful to categorize storage along three dimensions:

Open or Closed: Open storage is visible and accessible to potential users. Closed storage is usually out of sight or reach of unauthorized users, but may be closed through symbolic signals like a stop sign or "hands off" label. Problems occur when storage is, in fact, observedly open, yet considered closed ("No using the block area now, Johnny").

Fixed or Movable: Storage that takes tools or additional strong bodies to move is for all practical purposes fixed (and stable). Small units or units on casters allow flexibility.

Multi-Use or Specialized: Some storage is designed specifically for storing certain objects or materials: cots, large blocks, books, etc.

Photograph by Jean Wallech

Other types of storage have standard compartments and a range of uses.

Every program requires a balance of storage in all three dimensions. Closed storage is of obvious use for food, janitorial supplies, personal possessions, valuable materials, and materials harmful to children. Open storage is necessary in any program encouraging responsibility or autonomy in children or shared use among staff. Too much fixed storage limits the program's ability to adapt the environment. Movable storage is necessarily limited in size. Specialized storage can be helpful in fitting specific spaces or solving problems (such as

The storage unit pictured below transformed a center's use of a texture table. Storing rolled oats, cedar chips, sand, and other materials within a few feet of the point of use increased the amount and variety of experiences dramatically.

Photograph by Jean Wallech

storing cots under a platform or using a cabinet as a divider which enables two groups access to specific equipment).

Good storage is sufficient to organize and store whatever resources the program might be able to obtain to improve the program. Good storage is:

• Located close to the point of use. This is the cardinal rule. When things are nearby, people make more use of them.

• Able to comfortably hold and distinctively display the contents when open. If it is too deep, materials are hard to remove; if not deep enough, objects protrude; if too long, clutter is inevitable as more is placed on each shelf. Distinctive display advertises the potential of the materials.

• The right size and shape for the space. Floor units that are too high block necessary sight lines. Units that don't fit a space may leave protruding corners or irritating gaps that collect dust and worse.

• Aesthetically pleasing. A too odd assortment of storage units can be a jarring, disjointed landscape, even when units are connected through color.

• Clear and understandable to its user, whether 20 months or 20 years old.

• Safe. This last criteria deserves special mention. Almost every program has at least one harrowing tale of a cabinet or shelf collapsing or pulling out of a wall, or a floor unit tipping over and narrowly missing a child. Children **have** been killed and seriously wounded by falling storage units and by heavy materials falling from storage units. Also of concern as a hazard

Photograph by Jean Wallech

is tripping over the *feet* extending from the bottom of storage units to stabilize them. Serious injuries are possible due to sharp corners on units at a child's eye level.

Closed Storage

This section could have also been titled *adult* storage, because young children are rarely allowed to control storage of any kind, even of their own possessions. Closed storage is necessary for materials dangerous for children and materials likely to be misused or disappear. It is needed to allow for rotation of materials and for personal possessions. Teachers and parents need places to safely stow their coats and

purses, which are often loaded with lethal materials like keys, medicine, pins, and so forth. Teachers need a secure place to accumulate the tools of their trade: scissors, tape, markers, staplers, and the *stuff* they deem essential. Poor storage that allows open *borrowing* inevitably results in needless irritation and conflict.

Wall Cabinets, Shelving, and Hooks

Wall cabinets are useful because they allow the space underneath to be used for storage or play. It is absolutely essential that they be attached securely to the studs in the wall or the cinder block. The longer the cabinet or shelf, the more support necessary. Don't assume the volunteer putting them up for you, or whoever put them up for the last occupant, knew what he was doing. From experience, well made kitchen cabinets with good hinges from a home improvement store are adequate.

Shelving is cheaper and provides more flexibility than cabinets, and the height restricts child access. The primary disadvantage of shelving, visual clutter, can be reduced by using storage boxes or fabric covers. Some shelving systems hold more weight than others, and staff vary in their sensitivity to issues of structural

Photograph by Jean Wallech

integrity. Flexible shelving using tracks and metal brackets is not designed for heavy loads. It is always dangerous to store heavy materials up high—record players, boxes of computer paper, paint cans.

Open spaces on shelves and counters is necessary to prevent cubby tops, diaper tables, and table tops from being used as inappropriate resting places for wayward bottles, unidentified objects, and temporary storage.

Walls are wonderful places to store things, provided the right storage hardware is used.

Photograph by Jean Wallech

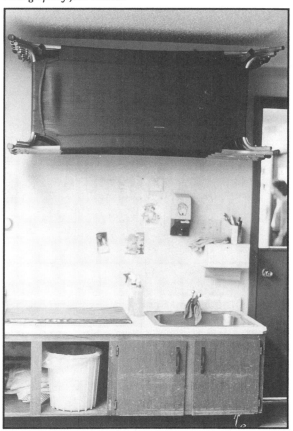

Wheel toys, trikes, and wagons can be hung on hooks or pegs, as can jumpers, wading pools, ladders, and all sorts of indoor and outdoor maintenance equipment. Pegboard systems for smaller tools are useful; flexible metal track systems are available for larger items. Devoting an entire wall to storage covered with sliding doors or curtains has proven successful.

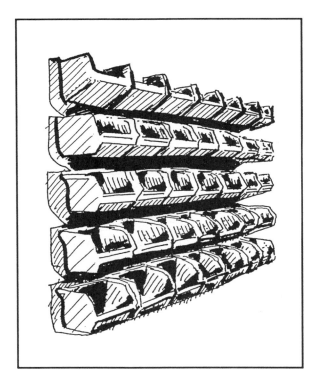

Storage Rooms and Sheds

Storage rooms are the stuff of center legends and rarely as useful as imagined on paper. They do, however, have their place—close to the point of use of the materials. Centrally located supply storage rooms and outdoor sheds can be effective if superbly organized and maintained. Taking advantage of the burgeoning science of

storage evident in home magazines, storage rooms need flexible shelving, compartments, hooks, and whatever else will organize the contents. Because the room has multiple users who change over time, the method of organization should be visible and proclaimed with labels, pictures, and outlines.

Floor Units

Particularly in large rooms, closed floor units are often necessary in order to provide more convenient access to a central location. Open storage can be made closed and flexible by combining two units with a hinge and closing them off, or by using inexpensive fabric curtains to shield the contents from view.

Creative Closed Storage

It is the programs with the fewest resources or the most restrictive conditions that have the greatest need for storage. There are alternatives to costly cabinets. Pillows can be used to store extra dress up clothes and fabric. Fabric sacks can be hung from the wall or ceiling in an artful, charming fashion. The space under cribs can be

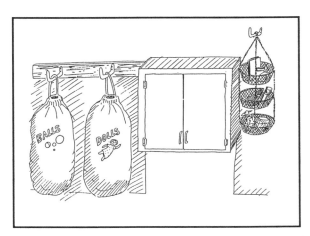

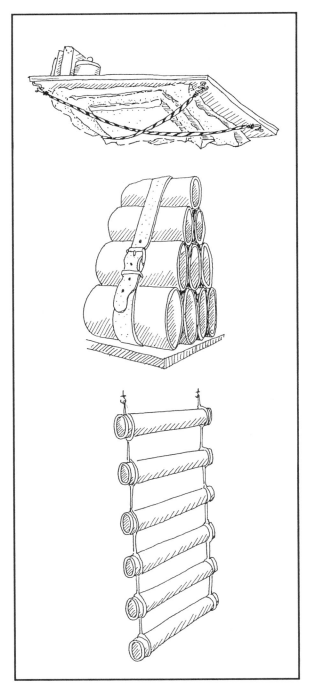

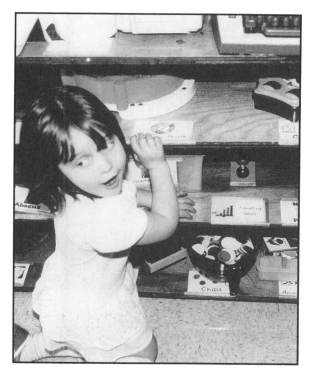

Photograph by Jean Wallech

used and hidden by fabric panels. Storage boxes can become tables, the space under platforms can be designed for cot storage, the ceiling can be used to store projects and works in progress.

Open Storage

Good open storage allows children to be independent and responsible. It is necessary because, as Peller points out, "a young child's intentions or plans are not well defined or fully conscious. He cannot put them into words with ease or precision. The layout of the nursery school enables him to translate into action impulses which are vague and fleeting. This too is part of the *self-expression* offered in nursery school" (Peller, 1972). Loughlin and Suina (1982, p. 6) add, "Since displaying materials

---

> ## "Write what you want but we live in the real world," my Grandfather said to me
>
> It is easy to write about the power and utility of organized storage, the wonderful potential for storage to teach. It is also true that organization can oppress and restrict. There is a place for toy boxes and casual storage where speed and convenience take precedence over teaching concepts. The materials, staff-child ratios, and time schedules may dictate when and where toy boxes are appropriate.
>
> It is also important to recognize that organization takes an incredible amount of time to establish and maintain, easier for programs with *down time* or lots of volunteers or student teachers than for understaffed child care programs always awash with children. Lab schools and parent coops are often models of organization, not only because they have to be able to work with an ever-changing staff, but also because they have the time, the people, and the energy to organize.

side by side strongly suggests connections between them and the possibility of combining them in some way, combinations of materials can suggest activities."

The point has already been made that the layout of materials can teach. Materials can be organized around a property: color, shape, size, transparency, etc.; a function: communication, pull toys, tools, building; a relationship: pencil and paper, dolls and clothes, *my* work, cultural materials; an action or effect: sound making, dissolving; or other concepts. Layout of materials can teach left-to-right sequencing, perceptual discrimination, or a sequence of motor skills.

The organizational scheme, both the conceptual scheme and the distinctiveness of the display, has to be appropriate for the developmental level of the user. Distinctiveness can be achieved by limiting the number of items on a shelf, by defining compartments or clear boundaries with tape or color, or by juxtaposing

contrasting items. The younger the child, the simpler the concept and the more distinctiveness necessary in display (e.g., for infants, the concept of *sameness* and one item per compartment).

Photograph by Jean Wallech

Personal Storage

All children need a place of their own to store their considerable assortments of personal possessions—multiple sets of clothes, diapers, boots, blanket, artwork, and personal treasures. Older children need space for works in progress. Programs use lockers, cubbies, storage tubs, hooks, pockets, and various combinations of all of these. Some of the issues to consider include:

Protection: How are a child's clothes and possessions kept intact and safe from curious cohorts and the child's own actions? Preschool and older children should have at least one relatively protected space, at least the top of a cubby; but a separate tub, shoe box, or folder is more desirable. Labeling with a name and a picture make this space their space. Storage for oversized art work (computer paper and larger) shows children that their art really is valued. Infant/toddler diaper bags often contain pins,

Photograph by Jean Wallech

medicine, and other unsafe materials, so the bag needs to be stored safely or the offending items must be removed.

Ventilation: This is an important factor for wet or soiled clothes. Pegboard backs improve cubby ventilation; but, ideally, an open place to hang wet clothes or set out wet boots makes sense in areas where snow and rain are major factors.

Aesthetics: Nothing adds more to visual clutter than loaded open cubbies. Hinged doors are desirable but require more space in front, are fun to bang, and limit the inside space. Fabric curtains that children can pull aside are simple and inexpensive.

Activity: Cubbies or lockers are at times centers of activity—the sites of dressing and undressing, sulking, lounging, rummaging. In an all day setting, the personal space is not simply a functional space, it is an emotional space, generally the only *my* place in the setting. Having a *my own* place is important in an institutional setting lodged within a culture that from birth invests enormous importance in personal property.

The more personal storage is confined to one all purpose location, the more activity will take place there. Is a cubby a place for a child to sit and be alone, or a place to put on a boot, or a social place to show off personal treasures and exchange tokens of affection? If not, where are those places? The cubby design should take into account all the activity that will take place there.

Location: Where storage is located has a bearing on all other factors. Often cubbies and other personal spaces are either in high traffic areas like busy corridors or in isolated areas like hallways and foyers. In either case open storage

Photographs by Jean Wallech

Photograph by Jean Wallech

Out of necessity, early childhood programs have been resourceful in creating low cost efficient storage. Cinder blocks, milk crates, barrels, and other supports combined with planks can make effective shelving units. Salvaged office cabinets, bowling ball lockers, department store units, and literally *whatever* have been put to use.

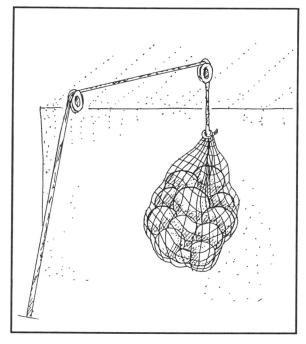

may result in lost or pilfered items. Hallway storage restricts use.

Activity Storage

Flexible storage is a key to a successful learning environment. Too much fixed storage or uniform storage limits a program. Built in storage often becomes sacred ground; covering or blocking part of it with a couch or display becomes unthinkable. Storage that is too specialized, with some exceptions noted below, has the same effect.

Some uniformity in height is aesthetically positive; but the ability to vary shelf size and length, compartmentalize, and have or not have a back that allows two sided access increases the

utility of the shelf storage. Shelves are only one way to store materials. Hooks, bags, barrels all have their place.

Portable Storage

Storage that is easily portable allows a program to continually expand and contract spaces as the need occurs. Small shelf units and units on castors provide that capability. The disadvantages of the latter on hard floors can be overcome by using rubber stops or carpet underneath. Plastic milk crate storage can be relocated and recombined easily.

Portable in another sense is storage that can be raised or lowered from the ceiling. Using pulleys and table tops or nets, a program can develop space to store projects and bulky equipment. Hanging baskets and shelf units may work for particular kinds of storage.

Add on storage may be useful like under-shelf racks and cabinet hooks attached to shelf units.

Transportable Storage

For multi-purpose space and hallways, transportable storage is useful. This may be a trolley, a wagon, a suitcase, or a duffel bag within which is an activity and/or the makings of a space—a reading or writing suitcase, a block cart, a make believe prop bag (picnic with dolls at the beach with dolls, towels), a science kit. The storage could contain a rug, or sheet, or rope for defining the boundary of the activity.

Adapted Storage

If all the powers of the environment that might work for the program are to be utilized, the staff should view nearly all furnishings and equipment as adaptable. Remove the back of a shelving unit that serves to divide two groups to create a shared zoo with fish tanks, gerbils, and birds. Cubbies laid on their side may make

acceptable shelf units, enabling a program to design or purchase more workable cubbies. Some items like cages and tanks benefit from rims along the edge of a shelf to keep them from being pulled out too far. **Note:** It is important to check to make sure that adapted units are stable and otherwise safe.

Walls and Backs

It is important to consider the backs of storage units as potential display or storage space. Pegboard backing allows the most flexibility. Other options include easel space, mirrors, book display.

Storage Containers

The kind of container used to store materials can work for or against the program's goals and objectives. Some considerations:

Visibility: Does a child have to take the container off the shelf to see the contents? Younger

children will invariably dump it out and then decide whether to use it. Inexpensive, clear plastic shoe boxes will crack and break; it is better to spend more and purchase clear soft plastic. The shape, color, or texture of the container can highlight the materials displayed.

Motor Skills Required: Does a child have the motor skills to safely remove and transport the container to where it will be used? Does the container require the child to use different motor skills? The act of transporting buckets with handles, dishtubs, single handle bowls, baskets, trays and different size

Photograph by Nancy P. Alexander

containers are all different activities in themselves.

Social Skills Required: Storing materials in a container that requires two or more children for transport stimulates cooperative activity.

Classification: Defining the nature of the activity and/or the location of the activity by the color, shape, material (wood, metal, etc.) or kind of container (basket, tub, box, etc.) can build in classification and develop an order that younger children can understand and help to restore.

Aesthetics: Do containers help to set off the materials in an attractive manner? Do the containers contribute to excessive visual clutter?

Room to Learn (1974) by Joan Dean and **School Zone** (1975) by Anne Taylor and George Vlastos are particularly valuable resources for ideas on how to adapt space and storage to help programs allow children more experiences, develop greater independence, and make teachers' lives easier. Both books have many illustrations of creative use of found materials and made materials to better use walls, floors, and corridors.

*Illustration adapted from **Room to Learn** (p. 36).*

Exercises

1. Think of as many ways as possible to store things without using shelves.

Visual Access to Materials

One of the most thoughtful and complete works for preschool and elementary school teachers on putting together classroom environments that work is **The Learning Environment: An Instructional Strategy,** by Catherine Loughlin and Joseph Suina (1982). In great detail they discuss the teacher's major tasks in arranging the basic structure of the learning environment: spatial organization, provisioning for learning, materials arrangement, and organizing for special purposes. The chapter on arrangement and display alone is worth the price of the book.

Following are some of their points on visual access to materials (pp. 125 -148):

• Stacking hides materials.

• When items are spread across a shelf, specific items don't show clearly.

• Empty spaces, contrasting color, or framing around materials focuses attention.

• Sets in commercial boxes look alike when left in the box.

• It's easier to remember where materials belong when they don't look alike.

---

2. Design a useful piece of equipment that also serves as cot storage.

3. Design an outdoor piece of play equipment that incorporates storage.

4. Design a *space in a box* and a *space in a sack.*

5. Design an orderly storage system that uses an organizing attribute other than color.

— Chapter Eleven —

Room Arrangement

Molly stretched out to build the roadway and glanced over at Jamal's tower. She thought, "It's awful close to my toes. It's a good thing that I'm not any longer or don't stretch and OOPS."

"I'm telling! You knocked down my tower!"

"It's not my fault. It hit my feet."

The room arrangement grows out of the fixed space, inhabitants, program goals and philosophy, and resources. In this chapter the predominant focus is on room arrangement for all day settings, in which the goal is an open program structure where teachers have the opportunity to **be with** children in a relaxed and enjoyable fashion—to have conversations, to nurture, to guide, to spark learning, and to teach. It is also a space where parents are welcome when they have the time. Children spend much of their time choosing and moving freely and competently in an environment designed for caring and learning—choosing activities, being alone or in a group, being quiet or active.

The *look* of this kind of space is a far cry from a traditional classroom with the teacher's desk facing a row of smaller desks. The logic of such an arrangement is clear: all attention is focused towards the teacher, traffic patterns lead to and from the teacher or out of the room, materials are stored around the perimeter, out of

the reach of students. Traditional classrooms emphasize teacher instruction and solitary study; the business of living takes place outside the walls. Programs organized for active, individualized learning, autonomy, and social interchange have much more to think about. If these programs are environments for living in six to ten hours a day, and all the dimensions discussed earlier have to be taken into account because the day-to-day quality of life is important—eating, sleeping, privacy, softness, adult

Photograph by Nancy P. Alexander

ease and comfort—staff have a job worthy of city planners or architects.

Unlike city planners and architects, programs don't have to live forever with their latest thinking. The pathways and intersections, activity areas and rest stops, can be reworked as children and adults learn and develop. When children grow autonomous and the expectations of behavior are more clearly understood and ingrained in teachers and children, and when

Photograph by Jean Wallech

interests change and skills develop, or when everyone just needs a change, the arrangement can change. The less set in concrete any environmental system of space or time or roles is, the more the environment can be shaped to serve program goals.

Children and adults tell us how the room *should be* by their behavior. People seek the right fit for themselves in space. In open spaces, we seek whatever enclosure we can find and create our own landmarks. In closed spaces, we

periodically seek to break out. If we watch closely the struggle to use a space and to adapt it to human needs, we can design better spaces. One simple test is *how many places are there to be?* Just one large place? Or enough places for individuals and groups to find their place?

In **With Man in Mind** (1970), architect Constance Perin discusses how important it is, although often neglected, that places are designed so that people can carry out their everyday lives with a sense of competence. Assessing a children's setting from the standpoint of the child's sense of competence in his or her everyday life is a simple but powerful idea. Child care settings are where the child first experiences a public self; the importance of feeling competent in public will have a great bearing on self-esteem. Anita Olds points out some guidelines: "Ultimately the ability of children to work

competently and productively is affected by (1) the number and variety of things there are to do, (2) the number and variety of places there are in which to do them, and (3) the organization and accessibility of those things and places within the classroom space" (Olds, 1982, p. 18).

As Francis Wardle asserts, there may be a conflict between a child's sense of competence and the teacher's idea of what should be a child's competence. Ability to wait, maintain order, behave, or share are areas in which staff may expect too much of children (or sometimes too little), as they mold children to their image of them.

One can easily apply the *competence test* to the staff's sense of competence as workers within the space or to how competent the

---

Whose Space Is This Anyway?

"I just can't afford a sprinkler system. What good is it anyway? I can see the point of another exit; that will save lives. But the sprinkler system won't do anything," insisted the child care director.

"Sprinkler systems save my firefighters' lives and other people's houses. That damn well counts, too," replied the fire marshall.

It is easy to forget that spaces serve and are serviced by more people than the caregiving staff and children, people with legitimate claim to consideration of their needs. "Every time I come in on Monday after the janitors have been here, the space is different," laments a teacher with a wonderfully elaborate and precisely arranged room. Room arrangements need to accommodate everyone with a function in the space; and this often includes maintenance people, evening or weekend groups, other program groups at the beginning or end of the day. It is human, but not particularly useful, to insist on total accommodation to *our* space, particularly if the result is Monday morning resentment. Planning the arrangement with an eye to all the parties involved may save aspirin. This may involve posted floor plans, some built-in flexibility, or necessarily simplified arrangements.

parents feel in their *work* of leaving and picking up their children, well aware of the eyes of caregiving staff.

Activity Settings

All space has pathways and activity settings. *"Activity setting* describes the place and any objects in the place that must be there in order for the activity to occur. These space-time-units provide the life of the program" (Prescott, 1984, p. 50). Examples include a diaper area, art area, teacher corner, reaching area for young babies, table toy area. A home base, or classroom itself, can be considered an activity setting further broken down into activity settings.

Activity settings are places, with **boundaries** and **entries**, which may or may not be clear. The clarity of the boundary to children and adults is a crucial attribute in determining a setting's use, both in terms of amount of use and the kind of use it sustains. A "boundary can be as solid as four walls, as fluid as taped lines on the floors, or somewhere in between. Regardless of its permanence or fluidity, however, each area must have a definite boundary that signals where the area begins and ends" (Olds, 1982, p. 20).

Activity settings exist in **time** which may or may not be structured. Some are experienced in defined time segments (e.g., 30 minutes in the gym, no more because there is another group waiting—no matter what wonderful experiences are taking place).

Activity settings exist to accomplish **tasks**. Prescott categorizes settings as **essential**—areas for caring and areas for play. All aspects of the setting should work toward accomplishing the tasks in line with program goals and philosophy.

Activity settings have **size** and **shape** and **height**. The size should be tailored to the number and size of the users and the activities planned. If it is too big, the area may result in a larger group than desirable. If too small, the area may simply not work.

Areas may be as small as a window or a rug. When it comes to shape, adults typically square off corners. However, round and oddly angled areas are appealing to children. Areas with varying heights through the use of canopies, platforms, overhangs, or raising or lowering the floor height add character and charm and clear definition.

Activity settings have **surfaces** for work or play: floor space, table or counter tops, walls or dividers for mounting materials or for use as easels.

Activity settings have **personality**, an ambience or mood produced by the combined effects of all the elements: business-like, cozy, chaotic, cheery, noisy, bland, serene, perhaps melancholy (a womblike place where we can go and feel sad). The mood is created by the activities, sounds, and smells; by the aesthetics of the colors and textures; by the feel of the place. Artwork, certain furnishings, ritual behaviors—all the things that create an ambience in our personal spaces—can be used to create an ambience in a child care setting.

Activity areas usually have **signals** (open/closed signaled by a gate, a sign, a sound, or a light). There are other signals like a new picture or object that catches a child's eye and gives the message *check me out* or a smell that sets off a stampede to the eating area.

Activity areas can have understood **rules**, expectations of behavior: How shall the tasks get done? How must the inhabitants interact? The more these expectations are built into the space through arrangements of furnishings and

Photograph by Jean Wallech

Photograph by Jean Wallech

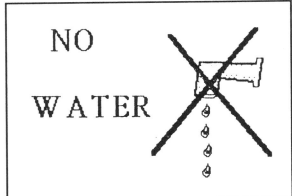

materials and written or symbolic instructions in the area, the less need for indoctrination and supervision. We all, but children especially, pay more attention to what actually happens than what is supposed to happen. If the rule is *no running up the slide*, but it is only enforced intermittently, children understand that it is not really a rule.

Interest Areas and Learning Centers

Typically, classrooms which are more open are organized into interest areas often called **learning centers**—curriculum defined activity areas where materials are stored and used: art area, table toys or manipulatives, block area, and so on. What areas to have depends on goals, space, and staff. In limited space, a *wet* or *messy* area encompasses art, sensory play, and projects. Quiet areas become multi-purpose sites for quiet activities. A table area becomes the site for table toys and projects. When more space is available, areas can develop a more specialized function. What is fundamental to the learning or interest center idea is that the space is planned and that children can function in the area relatively autonomously. In a learning center based program, interest areas are the basic units of planning. It is an efficient structure to ensure a daily balance of experiences and to allow for child choices.

One drawback to interest areas is that, when defining an area by content, art, or science, for instance, it is easy to lose sight of the reality that the content exists everywhere in many activities. Instead of a grand conception of art as both an approach to the world and a manifestation of life's grandeur, art becomes a narrowly defined set of activities in a set location. Science is viewed not as a process of investigation that occurs whenever a child investigates the properties of objects or the forces that underlie existence, but as a selection of materials and experiments.

A similar drawback is a tendency to become inflexible about boundaries and where activities may take place: "Reading belongs in the reading area and block building in the block area." But because of restricted space, the areas rarely are able to contain the potential range of experiences. In the case of reading, few reading corners can accommodate both solitary reading and the giggly social sharing of books, and listening with headsets. In most block areas, there is not room for long chains of *falling soldiers* or elaborate forts and roadways.

The tendency to compartmentalize is overcome by an articulated program philosophy and curriculum that clearly expresses the place of art, science, language, music, and so on in daily life. When teachers understand that "Art is science in the flesh," as Jean Cocteau expressed it, the art corner becomes a convenient place for *some* art experiences, and it is recognized that the activities involved in the area involve scientific and motor learning. Training staff and visibly expressing the philosophy using wall posters and signs will break down the limitations.

An understanding that the physical boundaries are flexible resolves the other limitation. Books can be read in other quiet spaces, including the outdoors. Some block building requires double the normal space and necessitates moving boundaries.

Recognizing that a learning center doesn't have to be big or permanent removes another drawback: limited experiences. A **learning station**, a one person learning center, could be a wall easel, a writing desk, a mirror, a cushion. Again, what is important is that it be a defined space, organized for children to learn autonomously.

Developing a Layout

It helps to begin at the beginning, to set aside preconceptions and knowledge of the present room use and empty "the room psychologically, if not physically, of all movable objects" (Olds, 1982, p. 20).

• Begin with the fixed space—doors, windows, dows, bathrooms, sinks—and get a picture of the primary flows—people traffic, things like food and supplies (and ensuing noise, dirt, etc.), light, and cool and warm air.

• What's going to take place in the room? List absolutely everything, including items like dressing for winter, outdoor play, parent sign-in and parent-staff evening chats. At this point it

Photograph by Shawn Connell

Photograph by Jean Wallech

also helps to ask: What other possible spaces are available: closets, hallways, outdoors? What are the essential activity settings? What are the activity areas we need? Which areas will be multi-purpose (eating, table toys, messy play) and which are generally permanent (dramatic play, book corner)?

• Given all of the above, what flow of communication and materials is necessary?

• What transformations are necessary (to a nap room, a large muscle area, or back to a church meeting room)?

• What features exist in the setting that lend themselves to locating one activity in a particular area (windows, sinks, electrical outlets, heat)? Olds suggests thinking of **neighborhoods** (a warmer concept than zones) "defined both by the fixtures they require and by their personalities. All the areas which need water

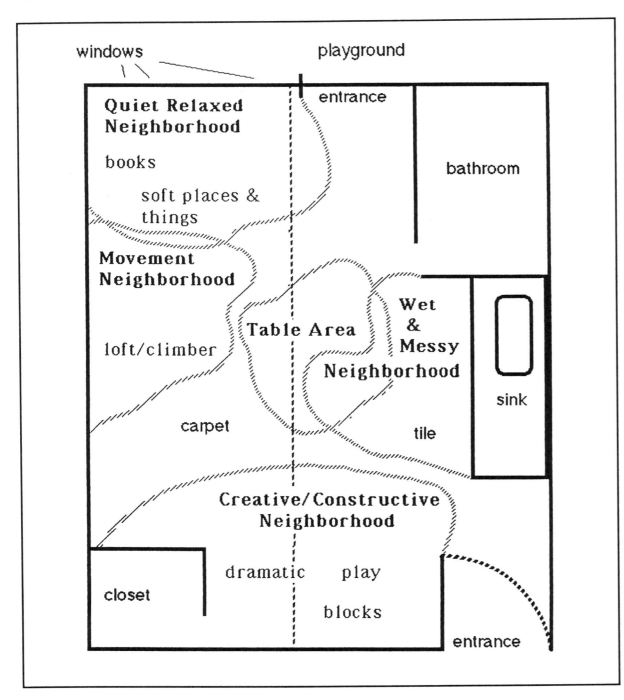

should be grouped near the sink. But it is probably better to put painting, rather than water play, close to the reading corner. The movement and talk that occurs around a water table is distracting. In creating areas, think about separating messy and neat, quiet and noisy, expansive and contained activities" (Olds, 1984, p. 14).

• Are there any minor physical alterations that would greatly enhance the space (more outlets, wall storage or display, counters)?

It helps to keep in mind the following:

• Children (and most adults), like bag ladies, take seriously the maxim: *materials placed close together will be used together.*

Thus, if construction projects can be painted, adjoin the construction area and the art area. Unless the guinea pig can swim, keep animals away from the water play area.

• Children, like bats, integrate noise and movement to maneuver.

Children punctuate with noise. Some activities lend themselves to noise: steady chatter, explosive noise, outbursts of song, or Gregorian chanting. Others need silence or whispers. Protecting the opportunity for silence and the variety of vocal accompaniment is important.

• Children, like bowlers, often need their whole bodies to perform a task.

Children need room. It is sad that most programs for young children are struggling with minimal space. A child needs room; he or she is always getting used to a rapidly changing body that doesn't seem to respond quite as competently as he or she imagined it would.

A child not only needs the freedom to move around in the space, but to use his or her whole body when engaging in an activity, whether painting, building a tower, or grasping a toy. When allocating space to an activity area, we need to consider this, to visualize the child stretched out with paintbrush in hand, or lying extended while focusing on a toy. Conflicts, accidents, and messes follow cramped space.

There is a psychological dimension as well. Henry David Thoreau at Walden Pond lamented: "I sometimes experienced in so small a house, the difficulty of getting to a sufficient distance from my guest when we began to utter the big thoughts in big words. You want room for your thoughts to get into sailing trim and run a course or two before they make their port" (Thoreau, 1960, p. 98). The big thoughts of children need room as well.

An area being too large may cause difficulty, if the space is intended to be a quiet cozy spot or a place to concentrate and the size results in more children than necessary.

Some Strategies for Layout

The Maze

"We have provided open space although we are operating in a series of small rooms. It's like the difference between the football field and the maze strategy. In the football field, you provide a huge open space for children to roam around in. In the maze strategy, the open space is broken down and specific opportunities are offered in specific places. Children can see and move into other areas, but they are always within an enclosed space."
Rambusch (in Osmon, 1971, p. 39)

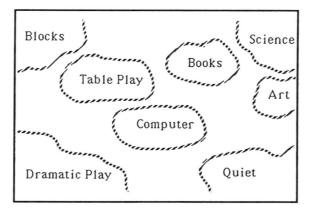

A Perimeter Strategy

"Whenever possible, work areas should be located around the perimeter of the room, with a central space left for moving from one area to another and for group meetings and action games. In classrooms that can't have a central area, one of the work areas should be big enough for group meetings."
Hohmann et al. (1979, p. 36)

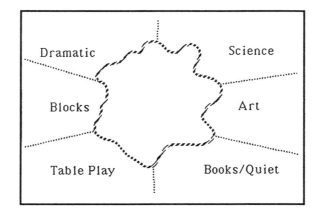

A Central Activity Area Strategy

*"The **central room arrangement plan** is a system I've devised to arrange the primary play—learning—study areas in the center of the room, with the open*

areas on the periphery. The purpose of centralizing the individual activity centers is so that whenever children look up, they see and are near other persons instead of walls. This results in more natural conversation, more interaction between children of varied temperaments and interests, and a more relaxed and casual atmosphere. . . In the central room arrangement plan, the proximity of various types of centers encourages the fullest exploration of all the activities available. . . ."
Cherry (1981, p. 39)

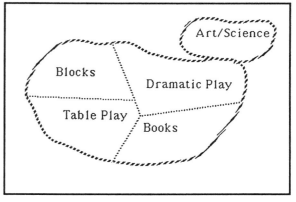

Whether any of these strategies works depends on the size and quality of the space—windows, entrances, sinks; the staff; the age of the children; and the program goals. A maze can become just that, a space that confuses children and staff. The potential drawback in a periphery strategy is that the open area in the center can become, for much of the time, a dead space and the site for wrestling and the like. The perimeter of the central activity can become a race track. Variations of each strategy can work or not work depending on the circumstances. A child care setting may have to consider how the arrangement works for nap and lunch and for times when understaffing occurs.

No matter what the strategy, clear pathways are essential. As discussed earlier, pathways encourage different kinds of behavior. A meandering pathway with forks and T's encourages *shopping* for an appropriate activity and perhaps observing the activities of others. A straight pathway with one beginning and one ending emphasizes reaching the destination. Unbroken paths encourage, perhaps even insist upon, running.

Pathways can encourage different motor experiences. The pathway can involve motor experiences by using tunnels, balance beams or planks on a rug, outlined footsteps, rough or smooth surfaces, or surfaces with give like foam.

Dividers

Dividers are an essential aspect of a good room arrangement. Anything can serve as a room divider as long as it is safe. In many programs **everything does**—all kinds of furniture, storage units, cribs and stacks of cots, easels, blankets, and so on. Child care programs, like shanty towns are skilled at adaptation. Dividers can be as solid as concrete and as symbolic as the edge of a carpet. What makes a good divider depends on what you want to do with it. It may be furniture or storage. What we use as dividers often involves a trade-off of form, function, and cost.

Permeability: What is it that needs to be blocked—a child's vision, aimless wandering in and out, light, or unwanted sound (the most difficult and costly element to block)? An 18 inch bolster provides a mini-wall to enclose a space for a baby; an opaque curtain can seclude. Neither will block sound. Using carpeting, cork, or tile, or padding a divider can create some sound conditioning.

Photograph by Jean Wallech

Size: Small dividers, 40 inches or less, restrict children's visual access yet allow adults to see the whole field of action. Since the floor is a natural place for children to be, some dividers within a group only have to be 30 inches or less to provide partial seclusion.

In open programs where classroom groups share space, an open visual field can be hard on adults, and so can the noise. The classic divider, a wall, either floor to ceiling or partially to the ceiling, is usually the first option. But if only visual access is the problem, fabric panels suspended from the ceiling may be preferable. Solid dividers affect the distribution of light, breezes, and heating/cooling.

Photographs by Jean Wallech

Stability: Falling dividers have caused serious accidents. The stability of free standing dividers—cubbies, storage units, commercial office dividers—depends on their design and dimensions. Stability comes from the ratio of height and width, from the mass, and from the width at the base, either *feet* or supports of some sort. A storage unit that is 16 or more inches deep and under 5 feet high will not topple; a cubby only 12 inches deep needs feet to be stable. To test for stability, try to tip the divider over from the child's vantage point of 2 to 3 feet from the base. Attaching feet at the bottom can increase stability but may provide another thing to trip on if corridor space is narrow. Added width increases stability but results in less floor space and a bulkier unit. Heavy items should be stored at the bottom.

Dividers can be hinged together into L shapes or bolted into T formations. They can also be bolted to floors and walls for more fixed arrangements.

Portability: The more dividers can be re-arranged easily by adults, the better, as long as they remain stationary for children. The only drawback is that portability may mean sacrificing some other qualities: aesthetics, acoustical separation, perhaps stability. Walls do have their place.

Multi-purpose: Most programs struggle with minimum floor space. Using essential furnishings like couches and storage units to divide space kills two birds with one stone. The potential drawback, if it is a large space with lots of different dividers, is a lack of visual harmony that disturbs some adults. However, if the basic furnishings and other elements are aesthetically pleasing and well coordinated, most adults will accept the trade-off, and the children will thrive on the variety.

Dividers are potential units for display. Making them out of pegboard or flannel board, building in busy boxes, attaching telephones, providing holes to peak and poke through, or adding mirrors makes a divider an activity setting in itself.

Kinds of Dividers

Walls as Dividers: Programs lodged in basements, ex-supermarkets, and warehouses, and buildings designed with the assumption that 100 children and 20 adults in an open setting is desirable, all crave walls. Programs with a lot of small rooms periodically lust for sledgehammers.

There is a range of commercial acoustic portable walls, freestanding and on tracks, to choose from, all relatively expensive (although often available from resale companies). Demountable walls provide flexibility, but only in terms of 4 foot adjustments when most often the need to tinker with the space is only a foot or two. Portable partitions that serve as walls have to be designed to be stable, not always an easy thing to do. Dividers with slotted bases are stable and work beautifully in interior spaces because the base creates small spaces. But the base will also protrude if one side is needed to define a corridor. Bench dividers are designed to solve that problem. Floor to ceiling beams, 3 to 5 feet apart, allow the creation of portable walls of fabric, but of course the beams limit flexibility.

Curtains or Panels: Our society thinks in terms of solid walls. But lattice work, fabric, blinds,

The Window
by Walter de la Mere

Behind the blind
I sit and watch
The people passing by,
Passing by.
And not a single one can see
My tiny watching eye.

They cannot see my little room
All yellow with the shaded sun
or even know that I am here
nor guess when I am gone.

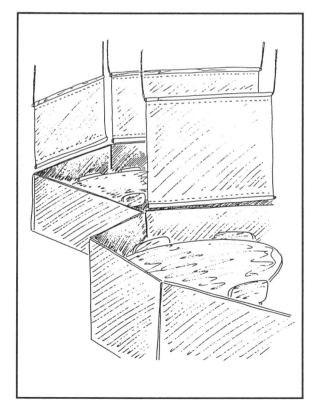

Photograph by Jean Wallech

Photographs by Jean Wallech

wicker, or bamboo curtains all divide space. Provided a program is able to establish clear expectations about children's behavior (don't bend the blinds or eat the wicker), curtains and blinds are a good way to adapt some spaces. Fabric panels hung from a ceiling give relief from unlimited adult visual scope and provide interesting visual experiences with light if different fabrics are used. Canopies can bring a space down to scale and create cozy private spots.

Mini-dividers: Dividers 3 feet high or less are invaluable for creating small spaces. Five inexpensive and functional designs are:

• Slotted bases with plywood, tri-wall, cardboard, or plexiglass;

• Toy chest or benches with extended backs;

• Pegboards with feet;

Photograph by Jean Wallech

• Foam or carpeted risers; and

• Cinder block shelving.

Symbolic Dividers and Boundaries: One program stained glass windows with tissue paper to match the green and the orange carpets. When the afternoon sun flowed through the windows, the effect was identical to the Emerald City in the land of OZ. The space was clearly defined by color. Another program established a curtain of standing and hanging plants. The area was defined by the sight and smell of plants. An *usher's rope*, a taped line on the floor, or a change of flooring are divisions that children respect, if we adults respect them.

Lofts and Platforms

Lofts and platforms have tremendous potential to enhance space, particularly since most centers and homes struggle with minimum space. A loft can increase the quantity of usable space, providing both over and under space, and the quality of the space, by creating alcoves and building in motor and social learning space. Two story space increases the spatial variety and charm of a setting and may allow children access to a heretofore unreachable window. A platform or loft can provide clearly defined space bounded by railings, an overhang, or support beams that corral materials. And, of course, lofts or platforms are fun: children literally get high. They survey the world from a different vantage point, one that may allow them to look adults in the eye.

Unfortunately, unless well designed (which is no mean feat), a loft or platform can become a bulky white elephant that **reduces** the quantity and quality of space and is a constant headache to staff. Even a well designed loft can become a negative unless adults and children know how

Photograph by Jean Wallech

to use it. Programs should be very cautious before constructing loft spaces.

Designing Lofts and Platforms

What is the purpose? Do you want to add to your space with a multi-purpose site for activities, including small groups; a motor center ; a dramatic play area; built in storage space underneath; or small hide-aways?

What is the rest of your space like? Is a platform going to overwhelm the rest of the room?

Who is going to use it, or not be allowed to use it? Are teachers going to need to be on the upper level or underneath it? Will they need to be able to reach into the farthest nook which may harbor a little fugitive? Can teachers see the children at all times?

How do the important adults, staff, and parents, feel about children being up high or being able to squirrel themselves away, or climbing up and down in a group center?

Loft or Platform: A platform 4 to 12 inches off the floor provides defined elevated space and maybe some under storage. Railings are not necessary if the children are preschool or older. A loft 3 feet or more off the ground creates additional under space for storage or play. Platforms are far simpler to create, and there are fewer possibilities of design mistakes. Lofts have far greater risks but higher potential payoffs.

Size: Bigger is not necessarily better, and it is a lot more difficult to do a big loft well. Large lofts (50 square feet and up) may allow you to have small groups up or down and increase your usable space. However, unless the loft is 5 feet or more off the ground to give sufficient clearance underneath, the under space may become dead space. Lighting underneath is a critical factor, particularly with younger chil-

Photograph by Jean Wallech

dren. Deep dark under space will usually not be used much for play. The relationship of the under space to windows and to electricity is important, although spot and trac lighting can correct some unforeseen problems.

Shape: The shape and layout of a platform or loft will also determine its use. Two entries on opposite sides can create a corridor effect which might be useful if the main purpose of the structure is motor and if getting up and down is the activity. But it is negative if the goal is less movement. Only one entryway creates dead end space for play; alcoves or using an L-shape

Photograph by Jean Wallech

achieve the same thing. One entry can create congestion depending on the use patterns.

Safety: Most children over a year old are concerned with their own safety and are learning to deal with or avoid the threats that they recognize. Unfortunately, they are also driven to try and do everything, and there are a lot of dangers they do not recognize. Further, children under three tend to be oblivious to the safety of others. Thus, the design needs to minimize the chance of crowding and traffic jams.

It is bad form for children to fall off the tops of lofts or platforms. Preventing it is not quite as simple as it seems. Obviously, the two key design factors are the railings and the entry and exit ways. Railing height varies depending on the age of the children and the use of the loft. If there is anything on the loft that children can stand on, they will; and the railing height must take that into account. If the railing is not solid or slatted vertically, children will climb on it.

So what's the problem? We'll just make the railing bigger. Okay, but now the problem is more limited visual access, both for caregivers and children, and perhaps an adult needs to be able to reach over the railing. Some solutions to the visibility issue are using plexiglass or a railing that incorporates mesh.

The thorniest problem is the entrance at the top. There has to be a space large enough for child and, at times, adult entry. Thus, it becomes an opening more than sufficient for a child to accidentally tumble through. A gate may present an answer but create two new problems—traffic jams at the entrance and on the stairway and gate banging. Curving or L-ing or staging the stairs may provide a solution, but may in some spaces have side effects that will need to be dealt with. A ramp solves the

problem but requires a lot of space. A padded landing surface helps. Hand holds at the top are an important safety aid.

Another safety issue derives from a child's delight in testing gravity on all the little Isaac Newtons down below. Allowing the dropping of soft things into a bucket or making it a cardinal sin to drop things over the railing alleviates the issue at least for children over two years old, but it is another issue to think about before jumping into two level spaces.

This discussion is short on answers because the best solutions all depend on the context. Gates work and don't work depending on the age, the means of entry, and the program climate.

Entryways: How do adults and children get up and down? The choice of various ladders, ramps, and stairways depends on the children's skills, adult sensibilities, and how much space is available. Trade-offs in a nutshell: ladders take up the least space, offer motor challenges, and are probably the safest means of getting up because children have to concentrate. But adults aren't wild about climbing them, and children

Photograph by Francis Wardle

may have trouble climbing down. Carpeted ramps or slides can offer easy entry or exit for adults and children but have the potential to become runways and, like stairs, require quite a bit of space.

Stairs are the most expensive to build, require railings, and have probably the greatest potential for accidents. However, stairs work for both adults and children and stair climbing is a valuable and necessary experience in itself. Steep stairs or stair-like ladders set at an angle are less safe than ladders because children usually come down face forward and jump the last steps. Combinations of ramps and stairs can solve some problems of tight space.

When designing an entry, there needs to be a staging space to get on and off or accidents will result. There should be sufficient space around a platform so that if children do fall, they will not hit furniture or playing children. Calculating play space gained needs to take into account the space lost to the staging areas. Multiple means of entry are positive because

Photograph by Jean Wallech

be? What stress does the loft have to withstand and where? Who is going to maintain it and periodically inspect for wear and tear? How is it to be cleaned? A consideration I gained from experience: Will the structure need to fit through a doorway?

Using Lofts: How the adults behave will determine loft use, particularly with infants and toddlers. With babies, planning attractive activities for the loft space and encouraging babies to use the space is not enough; adults have to themselves be up or under the loft or the space

Photograph by Jean Wallech

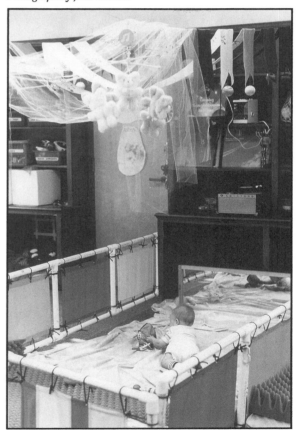

they reduce crowding and confrontations similar to Robin Hood and Little John on the narrow bridge, but again take up more space. When an entrance requires concentration and skill, like the dinosaur spine ladder or the eiger board, a separate exit reduces the confrontations that occur when two climbers meet at midpoint. Two methods of going up also afford different motor challenges.

Play and Storage Spaces: The lower depths have great potential as either play or storage space, provided the lighting issue is resolved. As an area for dramatic play, or as a pit or corral for activities with a lot of parts (e.g., poker chips, Legos), or as a quiet area, the space can be quite

valuable (if it is cleanable). Or, if storage is a pressing concern, storage of cots or large equipment can quite easily be built into a loft design.

Building Lofts or Platforms: Successful loft building is the result of combining a child care and early education expertise; a sense of goals and purposes for the structure; and a knowledge of sound design, construction, and safety. Without these, lofts more often than not tend to be structures that are unsafe, unusable, or both. There are no perfect designs that work everywhere, only designs that best fit the space and circumstances. Some considerations for building include: How portable does the loft need to

Photographs by Jean Wallech

will be underused. The appearance of safety is often as important as the reality of safety. It goes without saying that if staff or parents have safety concerns or feel the loft is not worth the effort, it will not help the environment.

Pits and Corrals

The bane of a caregiver's existence, particularly one caring for children under three, is how to provide a wealth of materials to be sorted, arranged, counted, and connected without seeing them scatter—Fisher-Price people and pieces, poker chips, Legos, blocks. Loose parts can be contained in a pit or corral that physically encloses the floor on three or four sides, even if the border is only a 4 by 4. Borders can be beams, carpeted plywood, covered foam risers, or a sunken floor (which of course you have to live with forever). A plastic wading pool is a useful corral. The walls of a block corral can be the planks that enhance block play.

Nooks, Crannies, and Hallway Learning

In crowded homes, dormitories, and office complexes, people seek out places for privacy and small group interaction. A hallway becomes a conversation place, an empty room a private space. The bathroom, laundry, or garage may be our only place. Or perhaps we have to go outside, under or up a tree. One way or another, we usually find a place.

The same needs exist in children's settings; and we are faced, or stuck, with the same possibilities for spaces. Staff rooms and offices are empty at times, corridors not always used, crib rooms and classrooms sometimes vacant; even bathrooms can serve the purpose.

Photograph by Jean Wallech

Mindsets

A friend visiting a farmer was astonished to find the farmer out back in the apple orchard holding a pig up to the tree. "Have you lost your wits, Vern?" the friend called out. "What are you doing?"

"Feeding the pig," Vern replied.

"That's the silliest thing I've seen. That's a big pig. Do you know how much time that's going to take?" the man asked.

"What's time to a pig?" Vern replied and went back to feeding the pig.

What's time to a child? Teachers often have difficulty with temporary spaces that may last only five to ten minutes before collapsing. The adult sense of time works against them. Taping a blanket to a wall (but not a painted wall) is a good illustration. The first time the blanket is taped to the wall and draped over a chair to create a tent (a three minute teacher effort), it may only last two to five minutes with a group of two or three year olds. But pulling it down is more fulfilling, and just as educational, as using it as a hideaway. The second, third, or fourth time, the children begin to use it as a tent.

The mindset that sees taping and retaping as a waste of time for small returns often coexists with a mindset that views the effort we make to produce an activity with a product as worthy. Consider the time spent in preparation and clean up for an activity where the primary event is attaching a cotton puff to a cut out bunny's behind, provided the child hasn't eaten the paste. For the farmer above and everyone else, it sometimes helps to step back and consider our mindsets.

Nooks and crannies and their makeshift equivalents are not frills, but psychological necessities. They are places for us to rest and recharge our batteries with the energy we need to adapt to group living. If privacy and intimacy are considered a right and if the same inventiveness and tenacity we use in our homes is allowed in centers, then these areas can be found or created. The very best spaces are those we find or create ourselves. Some ideas:

• Attach eye screws to walls in corners to allow snap on curtains. Use map rails or velcro strips to create temporary wall coverings that define small spaces. Children can adapt these spaces themselves.

• Attach a hammock to two walls.

• Create packaged porta-spaces in boxes, bags, or carts that transform a space into an activity setting: pillows, carpet squares, rope or snake pillow boundaries, slotted tri-wall barriers, materials, and so on. Porta-playpens can work well as planned protected space, not as cages. Mini-tents, or cone-like structures that suspend from the ceiling when not in use, are possible. Children appreciate having blankets available to create their own spaces.

• Crates, refrigerator boxes, fiberboard barrels, spaces underneath tables, kneeholes in desks, spaces underneath stairs are all places that children will use if we let them. Overturned tables provide four-postered bounded spaces, complete with rims to contain loose parts.

• A blanket or fabric attached to the wall and draped over something or attached to the floor creates sheltered tent-like space.

• Inflatable domes are essentially big baggies held up by air pressure which is maintained by a fan. They serve as portable mini-rooms, ideal for church basements.

• A roomy bathroom may be a good place for a water play area (separated from the toilets) or a rocking boat. This could allow a leisurely diapering of a toddler while the caregiver supervises two to three other children at the same time.

• A corner of an office can be the site of a listening station with headphones.

• A play spot may be next to the washer and dryer.

• An area for explosive noise—when a scream is absolutely required—may be made possible by padding an open stairwell, using a closet, or defining an outdoor space right by the door.

• A space with music and headphones becomes a quiet place.

Serving Children with Special Needs

Serving children with special needs—perceptual or learning disabilities, emotional problems, retardation, or physical handicaps—requires an environment that provides them with the cues to perceive and understand how the setting works: physical spaces, time, materials, and relationships.

Mario walks along the path to the books, his stocking feet feeling the smooth tape on the carpet. In other places he's guided by a texture strip or the sounds and smells coming from an area. After his first few tumbles, the children and staff have taken care to keep pathways clear. Labels made out of textured fabric and paper allow Mario to find and return things. Most important, things have their place; changes are minimized and introduced to Mario as they occur. Visually impaired children can use their other senses to function with other children. Activities that involve touching, hearing, and smell assume a special importance. Having a safe, secure space to run, climb, and slide is achieved by regulating the number of children involved and carefully monitoring the space.

Kelly's learning disability is not as obvious as Mario's. She has trouble organizing sequences of time and space in her head and often seems lost or wandering. Confronted with too much perceptual stimulation, complexity, ambiguity, or change, Kelly becomes hyperactive, even panicky or desperate. Kelly requires a familiar space, organized as a coherent whole, that allows her to see her choices. Time is predictable, and transitions are telegraphed to avoid surprise or time pressure. The same sensory cues that guided Mario are useful for

Kelly. Visual coding by color, shape, and size may help her. Children like Kelly often need multiple and repeated cues to function effectively. Marked pathways and boundaries, signaled choices, and simplicity are important for children with perceptual problems. A profusion of colors, images, shapes, and sizes, that might be charming for other children, will throw them off.

For Leland, whose hearing is very limited, the classroom acoustics have been designed so that much of the extraneous classroom sound is absorbed and he can clearly distinguish speech. Leland's classroom's floors and some walls and dividers are carpeted, ceiling fans provide some white noise, acoustical ceiling tile keeps the noise from bouncing, and draperies are occasionally pulled to keep out street sounds.

Many, if not most, settings for young children can be adapted for children with disabilities. Children with physical disabilities may need wider corridors, more room, and flooring which is neither slippery nor shaggy to accommodate crutches, walkers, or wheelchairs. Higher or lower work surfaces and special chairs may be necessary. Most important is attending to what the children can do and building from there.

Ideally, a setting recognizes all special needs and special strengths. The child who lives with several siblings in a tiny high rise apartment with no playground has a special need for space to move and to be alone. A child gifted in art, sports, language, or mathematical reasoning has a special need to fulfill that part of herself—as does the withdrawn child who needs time and certain situations in order to engage other children. Most of the adaptations of space for special needs children serve to make the environment a better place for all children: more

room, greater clarity, and plenty of options for use.

Children aren't the only ones who need space adapted to help them perform competently. Older workers and adults with disabilities often require the same kind of sensitivity and recognition of limitations of motor or perceptual skills, or strength, or stamina.

Exercises

1. It is often hard for adults to think of pathways in an ordinary sized classroom. Diagram some actual classroom traffic flows and characterize the pathways. Look for forks and T's.

2. Think about what inspires delight, wonder, and affection in spaces that you frequent. Then list ways you might inject personality into activity settings that would inspire the same feelings in children.

3. View a room from a child's eye level. Isolate and map the following attributes: shape, size, color, and mass of the objects. If the objects were all buildings, what would the skyline be like? What does it feel like to walk among them?

4. Think of five activity settings in a suitcase, each including the materials that would transform a hallway, table, or other defined space into a bounded setting with an activity and a personality.

5. Design a classroom layout to accomplish a specific set of program goals (e.g., autonomy, security, increased language usage, development of more peer assistance).

— Chapter Twelve —

Indoor Learning Environments

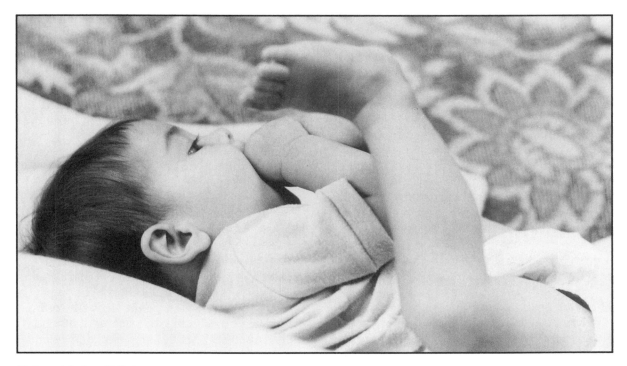

Photograph by Jean Wallech

"If you want to do something good for a child . . . give him an environment where he can touch things as much as he wants."
Buckminister Fuller in **Letter to Children of Earth**

"Richness of experience, not tidy perfection, is the point of the whole thing."
Katherine Whitehorn

What is to be learned? Everything!

An infant emerges from the body of another into William James' world of blooming, buzzing confusion. Oblivious to the complex differentiation of people and things we take for granted, babies have a lot of learning before them to become the wise and worldly readers of this volume. Armed with already sophisticated

motor and perceptual equipment and an innate drive to explore and construct meaning out of experience, all infants at birth immediately begin to **make** sense of the world.

The world that began with two categories—things I can suck and things I can't—becomes a world of distinguishable sights and sounds, people and things. A largely all or nothing reflexive motor response becomes a consciously controlled interrelated perceptual-motor instrument of great power.

"Who am I?" "What can I do?" "What can I be?"

The newborn has to learn where she stops and the world begins; the toddler learns that he is an independent force. The four year old learns the powers of his increasingly capable body and imagination, and six and seven year olds begin to assume the tasks and responsibilities of the cultured.

From the infant discovering his hand with unbridled fascination, to the four year old writing his name, to the surgeon learning a new technique, the questions of *Who am I?* and *What can I do?* continue. Hopefully, most of us learn that we are somebodies—strong, capable, resourceful problem-solvers with marvelous physical equipment that enables us to live in this world.

"Who are you?" "What are you to me?"

The process of defining oneself in relation to others and understanding others never ends. "Who are these people I live with?" "What does it mean to be a son, a mother, a sister, a friend?" As children grow they experience both fleeting and lasting relationships with other children and adults, and find themselves having to negotiate increasingly numerous and complex social interactions. They learn the social structure and skills to maneuver within these interactions.

Photograph by Nancy P. Alexander

"What is all this?" "What is it made out of?" "What can it do?" "How does it work?"

By age six that world of suckables and non-suckables is now composed of things with both perceptual properties —color, shape, weight, mass—and conceptual attributes—function, ownership, beauty, worth. By age 15, that world can be ordered and reordered, imagined and reworked in the head of a child daydreaming far from the concrete objects of his dreams. The unseen forces of gravity, electromagnetism, love, and the complicated relationships that hold physical and abstract systems together are, if not understood, beginning to be acknowledged.

Beyond any doubt, active experience in the physical and social world is necessary for the child to develop. At the core of Piaget is the understanding that to know an object or understand a relationship is not to look at it or hear it but to act on it. The assumption inherent in this discussion is that children construct physical and social reality out of their experience.

Learning in Early Childhood Centers

There is a general, time tested consensus about the kinds of experiences that young children need to thrive: sensory, motor, language, perceptual-motor, and so on. There is general agreement that children learn through both play and teaching, that both active experience and instruction are important. Early childhood programs have long recognized the critical role of hands-on concrete experience in development. There is less agreement, when time and space are limited, on the relative value of different kinds of experiences.

The age-old issues as to the relative value of play and instruction, structured play and free play, and the issues of what experience to prioritize (both intrinsically for all children and for particular categories of children) have continued. The concern for giving disadvantaged children a head start on school, and the belief that any child's development could be maximized by intervention or enrichment in the years before school, fueled the interest in structured curriculums and concentrated teaching.

Equally important, the growth of day care and Head Start brought a huge increase in both teachers and parents whose common reference point was not nursery schools, where play held a large role, but schools, where teaching dominated. The assumption that early childhood education was *schooling* conducted in much the same way was often taken for granted. What exactly play is and the relative importance of play and teaching in early childhood settings often result in spirited discussion.

For the most part, this chapter sidesteps those issues and leaves them to the works on development and curriculum. In all day settings, the whole range of experiences that children require need to be present in child care; and, if play is a critical aspect of childhood, it needs to occupy a prominent role in the setting. The relative importance of teaching skills and information will depend on parent desires and program goals.

Certain assumptions seem important to note before wading into the nuts and bolts of learning environments:

The entire setting is a learning environment.

The environmental dimensions, the structure of time and space, the behavior of adults and other children, and the nature of the routines teach children.

All experience is not equal.

While many believe that children select the experiences they developmentally need, children can only select from what is present. Entertaining children is not the same as educating them, a point made earlier. Johnny and Mary may be be kept active and happy all day with Fisher-Price toys, play dough, big wheels for Johnny, housekeeping for Mary, and a dash or heap of television. But this is not developmental education (or combatting sex-role stereotyping). It should be pointed out, however, that simply entertaining children without harsh coercion or periods of boredom is often an achievement in all day programs with minimum resources.

Information does not equal experience.

"Everybody gets so much information all day long that they lose their common sense," said Gertrude Stein. Information that leads a child to active inner or external experience may be reduced by information overload. More (displays, activities, enrichment) is not necessarily better.

Teaching and learning are not the same.

Teaching is something one does. Whether learning results from teaching is something else again. Good settings are always learning-based; they recognize that the learning, not the teaching, is the end and measure of success.

Play is child's work, *but* . . .

Montessori may have been the first to proclaim that "play is child's work." In the sense that play is the major vehicle for discovery and understanding, for testing and integrating ideas, and for developing mental and physical

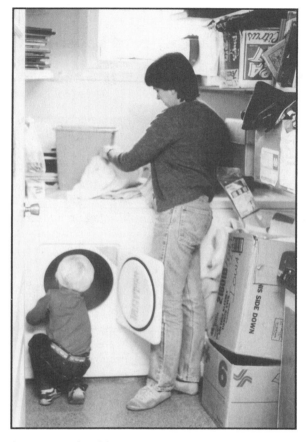

Photograph by Jean Wallech

skills, play is the child's major occupation. Montessori's statement also denotes the seriousness of play. It is not simply for pleasure or recreation in the adult sense, or mere surplus energy:

"The playing adult steps sideward into another reality; the playing child advances forward to new stages of mastery. . . . The child's play is the infantile form of the human ability to deal with experience by creating model situations and to master reality by experiment and planning" (Erik Erickson).

But, in a point made earlier, play is not work—that is, play is voluntary, spontaneous, and undertaken without instrumental purpose. What appears to be play becomes work when it is compelled or bound to exterior goals or restrictions. Many programs, including many Montessori programs, allow far less actual play than may be immediately obvious.

Play is essential, but so is work. The playful element in mastery is what makes life worth living. Work is essential because children need to enter the fabric of society in a responsible way and be taken seriously by having real tasks to perform, both as members of the family or the program society and as small citizens learning the skills necessary to succeed in school and society.

Characteristics of Good Learning Environments

• Experiences are developmentally appropriate for all children. The experiences need to encompass both the developmental levels of the children and cover all aspects of development. The difficulty with teacher-directed formats is the near impossibility of allowing for all the developmental levels, learning styles, and interests of the children. However, learning environments can be designed to be rich with experience; and materials can be developed that allow different levels of use and learning styles, without depending on the teacher's pinpoint knowledge and accuracy.

• The experiences are balanced. All play media lends itself to different uses on a number of dimensions. A good learning environment is characterized not only by a rich assortment of materials and activities, but also by an allowance for these to take on different forms:

Nicholson's Theory of Loose Parts

Simon Nicholson's (1971) theory of *loose parts* is powerful in its simplicity: "In any environment, both the degree of inventiveness and creativity, and the possibility of discovery, are directly proportional to the number and kinds of variables in it.

Creativity is for the gifted few; the rest of us are compelled to live in environments constructed by the gifted few, listen to the gifted few's music, use the gifted few's inventions and art, and read the poems, fantasies, and plays by the gifted few.

This is what our education and culture conditions us to believe, and this is a culturally induced and perpetuated lie. . . .

The result is that the vast majority of people are not allowed (and worse—feel that they are incompetent) to experiment with the components of building and construction, whether in environmental studies, the abstract arts, literature, or science: the creativity—the playing around with the components and variables of the world in order to make experiments and discover new things and form new concepts—has been explicitly stated as the domain of the creative few. . . . This is particularly true of young children, who find the world where they cannot play with building and making things, or play with fluid, water, fire, or living objects, and all the things that give us the pleasure that results from discovery and invention. . . . The simple facts are these:

1. There is no evidence, except in some special cases of mental disability, that some young babies are born creative and inventive and others are not.

2. There is evidence that all children love to interact with variables, such as materials and shapes; smells and other physical phenomena, such as electricity, magnetism, and gravity; media such as gases and fluids; sounds, music, motion; chemical interactions, cooking, and fire; and other humans, and animals, plants, words, concepts, and ideas. With all these things children love to play, experiment, discover, and invent, and have fun.

All these things have one thing in common, which is variables or *loose parts*. . . .

It does not require much imagination to realize that most environments that do not work (i.e, do not work in terms of human interaction and involvement in the sense described), such as schools, playgrounds, hospitals, day care centers, international airports, art galleries, and museums, do not do so because they do not meet the *loose parts* requirement; instead they are clean, static, and impossible to play with. What has happened is that adults—in the form of professional artists, architects, landscape architects, and planners—have all had fun playing with their own materials, concepts, and planning alternatives, and then builders have had all the fun building the environment out of real materials; and thus has all the fun and creativity been stolen: children and adults and the community have been grossly cheated. . . ."

One can quickly assess the creative potential of a setting for adults or children by looking for loose parts and materials like water or sand that transform themselves. A television has none. A field or vacant lot has thousands. As Robin Moore (in Coates, 1974) points out in support of Nicholson (speaking specifically about outdoor settings): "Kids really get to know the environment if they can dig it, beat it, swat it, lift it, push it, join it, combine different things with it. This is what adults call *creative activity*, it is what artists do . . . a process of imagination and environment working together."

Teachers also need loose parts and autonomy to turn their creativity loose and create wonderful learning experiences. Teacher-proofing with prescribed curricula and materials leaves their jobs mindless and them as poor role models. Teachers need to avoid being the last in a line of playing adults robbing children of experience and inventiveness by constricting the loose parts in the child's environment.

Active—Quiet: Reading, building, painting, or pretending can be exuberant or boisterous; or the same activities can be quiet, contemplative, or intense.

Social—Solitary: Even for babies, the experience is different if it occurs in association with others.

Novelty and Challenge—Familiarity and Practice: Children require variation that adds challenge (sometimes called mastery play) and the opportunity to repeat the same activity or use materials the same way (practice play).

Open—Closed: A dimension discussed by Prescott (1984, p. 51), open materials or "activities have no *correct* outcome and do not have an arbitrary stopping point. . . . Closed activities involve a right answer or a clear ending." Blocks, painting, and play dough are open; puzzles, Montessori materials, and worksheets are closed.

Simple—Complex: Also discussed by Prescott, "The simple unit has one obvious use and does not have subparts or a juxtaposition of materials that enable a child to manipulate or improvise. Examples include playing on a swing, jungle gym, rocking horse, or tricycle.

The complex unit has subparts or a juxtaposition of two essentially different play materials that enable children to manipulate or improvise. Examples include a sand pile with digging equipment, a doll bed with dolls, and single play materials and objects that encourage substantial improvisation or have a considerable element of unpredictability, such as play dough or paints, a table with books to look at, or an area with animals such as guinea pigs or rabbits" (1984, p. 51). Simple materials challenge children to supply the complexity in their use of the material.

Realistic—Non-realistic: Children need a balance of realistic materials and activities

Photograph by Jean Wallech

(Tonka trucks, making cookies) and materials that allow fantasy and imagination (boxes and cartons, clay, wood, and fabric pieces).

3. Time and space are appropriate. Whether organized into a structure of interest areas and

Photograph by Shawn Connell

Building-In Constructive Play

Some of the most imaginative ideas on building learning into the environment and equipment are contained in **Constructive Play: Applying Piaget in the Preschool** (Menlo Park, CA: Addison-Wesley, 1984), by George Forman and Fleet Hill.

The authors illustrate how using pulleys and pendulums, inverted furniture, crazy brushes, and other original ideas provide children with the learning encounters critical for maximizing development.

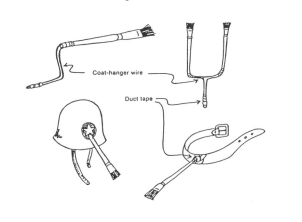

Toys

"A good toy leaves room for free exercise of a child's imagination. It can be used in different ways. It is handsome in shape and color and is good to touch, beautiful in line, and interesting in texture. It is sturdy and will take heavy use."
Caplan and Caplan (1973, p. 43)

The toy market has exploded in the last decade. Amidst the here today, broken or forgotten tomorrow junk is a wealth of good toys. Toys for children in groups need to be exceptionally well made to stand up to the heavy use. For many toys such as dolls, furniture, puzzles, and wheel toys, it is usually wise to pay the higher price for equipment found in catalogues by companies like Community Playthings than to look for discount bargains. On the other hand, many items like Fisher-Price sets, Legos, small blocks, and the like can be found new at discount stores and used at flea markets and garage sales.

Before purchasing a toy, ask yourself:

• What experiences will children really have with this toy?

• Is this something that could easily be made out of junk or could the same experience be provided with found materials?

• Will I actually take the time to find or make the alternative?

• Will it be used appropriately or remain intact in my setting?

• Will it wear gracefully and safely or become unsafe or useless once damaged?

• Is it something that children will all have at home anyway?

Photograph by Francis Wardle

own excitement, often through aggression or other non-sanctioned activities. Too many choices may paralyze children or lead to flitting from choice to choice.

Trying to put scarce dollars to work in the service of varied experiences often creates a problem because duplicate materials are essential for toddlers and wise for other age groups.

• Adults are able to prepare, monitor, and change the environment. They are able to plan the arrangement and the type and quantity of materials, observe, define problems, and generate solutions.

• Adults are able to **be with** children. This is essentially an outcome of the first six characteristics. The adults are more than planners, instructors, and tenders. They are mentors and facilitators, which means they are able to listen and observe, ask the right question, provide the correct tool, empathize with the frustration, share the joy. They are aware of when to redirect, reinforce, intervene, and (not lastly) teach and set clear expectations.

learning centers or not, the space and time have to fit the experiences. Too little room or time or lack of definition will make everyone's life difficult.

• Learning is built into the environment wherever possible. The less set-up and clean-up, the more learning goals are incorporated into routines and the space, the easier it is for teachers to facilitate learning. Built-in learning does

not mean garish rugs or wall displays with shapes or letters in primary colors. It means easels attached to walls rather than hauled out of a closet, storage containers that require the cooperative effort of two children to carry, or pulleys that raise and lower a storage bag.

• The experiences and materials are measured. Too few choices results in boredom and repetition and challenge the children to create their

Sample Daily Environmental Planning Sheet—Toddlers

Monday	Early AM	Late AM	Early PM	Late PM
Messy area water table	Pipe pieces	Bubbles water	Water	Large pegs
Couch area	Books	Climbing with pillows and planks	Lullabyes	Bears
Small motor action area	Lock boards	Lock boards	Fasteners	Fasteners
Vehicles		Wagons, wheel barrows with stuffed animals		Riding toys
Table area	Smearing	Smelling with teacher		
Playhouse	Dolls	Dolls	Dolls	Pots and pans
Pit area	Beach balls	Juice cans and poker chips	Soft	Soft
Large motor	Slide	Slide	Slide	Planks
Hallway			Blocks	
Outside		Walk with teacher	Hill—roll and slide	

In young children, motor experiences are essential to all aspects of development. Climbing, as Clare Cherry points out (1976), not only strengthens muscles, develops postural control, and builds self-esteem, but also orients children to varying views of the world. Swinging and rocking force children to orient their in-motion perceptions to a constant world. Jumping causes the child to learn that a constant—the ground—feels very different relative to the height of his fall. Motor activities constantly challenge children to "integrate body, mind, and space" (Cherry, p. 55). Children are scientists with their whole bodies.

Large motor play has other values, particularly in a setting where one is very small, faces long days, and must fit into the schedules of adults and other children. It is in climbing, swinging, sliding, and so on that experiences of ecstasy, unbridled joy or power, concentrated tension, and wild physical abandon are most likely to occur. On the grayest of days, motor play affords children the opportunity for power and pleasure and emotional release.

Similarly, children can *lose themselves* on a swing, a rebounder, or a rocker. For a short time

Photograph by Jean Wallech

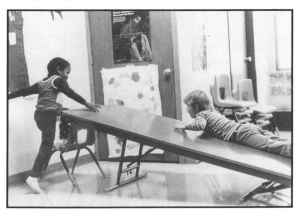

Motor Play

Relative to schools, most early childhood and school-age child care programs recognize the value in large motor experience. Yet it is rarely a strong area in most programs, both because of space and because many adults are unable to really **feel** its importance. Large muscle experiences are more than emotional outlets and exercise (each critical in all day programs), more even than body *building* and basic skill development and practice.

Photograph by Jim Greenman

they are alone, focused on the motions and sensations. Children can release physical tension and recharge emotional batteries.

Making use of the outdoors as the primary arena for large muscle play is sensible, but not if it is the only arena, particularly in climates where weather limits availability or in programs where space is limited. Maximizing the use of multi-purpose space or rooms and hallways tends to be essential in all day child care to provide at least for the non-explosive motor experiences. This often depends on creative selection, storage, and use of equipment, and, perhaps most important in many programs,

coordinating between groups and handling the internal politics of sharing space.

Sharing common space is never as easy as it appears to be. In those centers where meeting time and time away from children are limited and staff communication thus becomes more difficult, the result frequently is that staff become more room bound and less flexible. Large motor play often suffers the most.

In the classroom, platforms and lofts can provide climbing equipment, slides, a porch swing, even a fireman pole. Portable climbers can do the same thing. A jumping pit may be pillows stuffed in a large refrigerator box with the sides cut away. Small rebounders and trampolines are fairly inexpensive, as are rocker or swivel boards. A slide can be a plank, or a table with legs folded down, leaning on a couch. Planks on the floor and large wooden blocks, or even tape on the floor, can form challenging walkways from point to point; easy to make stilts can also build in challenge. Sweeping, mopping, dusting, and carrying larger equipment like planks and large pillows provide large motor experiences. Transporting equipment (or pals, real and stuffed) in wheelbarrows, trikes, wagons, *two-man* containers, and push carts do the same.

In multi-purpose rooms and corridors, planks, milk crates, triangles, chairs, and nearly anything a child can climb or balance on, go over or under, or jump off of or onto can become part of an obstacle course. Bean bags and foam balls allow throwing and catching; punching bags are used for punching, kicking, pushing, spirited hugging, and swinging. Hula hoops and streamers, scarves and parachutes facilitate rhythmical movement experiences. Roller skates, scooter boards, and skate boards challenge school-age children.

Balls—from small golf ball size to huge earth balls—belong in early childhood programs. For holding, dropping, rolling, kicking, catching, sitting or rolling on, balls allow children to practice nearly every motor and perceptual skill they possess. As they use balls they have to attend to the size, the roundness, the *give* that makes the ball hard or soft. Consider what is involved in just blowing up a beach ball, rolling it back and forth, and bouncing it up and down. Air pressure; depth perception; perceptions of space, gravity, visual-motor acuity, perceptions of color as the ball rotates and colors appear to blend; and all sorts of muscular coordination skills come into play.

Photograph by Jean Wallech

Photograph by Jean Wallech

development of topological (spatial) concepts of near, far, in, out, and so on; counting; and symbolization as the child uses abstract forms to represent cars, things and people.

As architect and builder a child employs all of his knowledge about how the physical and social world works. Building roadways, schools or cities, children must hold the structure or layout in their minds and apply their understanding of form in the re-creation. They run smack up against the laws of nature as towers collapse, hard materials refuse to bend to the child's will, round blocks prove different from square ones, and limited materials necessitate structural change. The ability to gauge distances and precise muscular control determine the size of the tower or length of the chain of dominoes. Cause and effect is often simple and dramatic: crash and ruin.

In building children also need to contend with the reality of a crowded planet. Without cooperation or at least a live and let live stance, child-made earthquakes, territorial seizures, and misappropriation of limited resources ruin the experience. Carting a 36 inch board or wheelbarrowing a load of blocks through a building area without committing mayhem taxes a child's

Older children derive challenge from all sorts of ball games like basketball and croquet-like games.

Construction and/or Building

"I wanted to see them build a world; I wanted to see them re-create on their own level the life about them, in which they were too little to be participants, in which they were always spectators."

"A simple geometrical shape could become any number of things to a child. It could be a truck or a boat or the car of a train. He could build buildings with it from barns to skyscrapers. I could see the children of my as yet unborn school constructing a

complete community with blocks."
Caroline Pratt (in Provenzo and Brett, 1983, p. 29)

To create a world, piece by piece, and for a short time hold dominion is a powerful and important experience for children, particularly those who spend much of their time in a group setting. That alone makes building an invaluable activity. But building with blocks and other construction materials offers much more and is perhaps the most complete activity a program can offer. As she plays with blocks and other building materials, most of the child's cognitive, perceptual, and motor abilities come into play: classification by form, function, and size;

Accidently
by Ishikawa Takuboku
(translated by Carl Sesar)

accidently
broke a teacup—
reminds me
how good it feels
to break things

powers of concentration, muscular control, and social conscience.

There is more to building than unit blocks and Legos, versatile as they are. A variety of building materials multiplies the learning experiences. The weight, shape, size, and substance of the material change the activity in terms of motor behavior, risk (of getting bopped), sense of power, sound, and construction possibilities. Large construction (or demolition) with heavy hollow wooden blocks and identically sized cardboard, plastic, or foam blocks creates different experiences. Having hundreds of domino size blocks opens up the possibility of table top worlds. Materials that adhere—bristle blocks, snap blocks, slotted panels, foam blocks with velcro, tinker toys, and other interlocking building systems are valuable, as is supplying tape or twine for props in construction play. Using temporary materials—cardboard boxes, plastic sheeting—not only enhances construction, but teaches children (and adults) about recycling and resourcefulness. Programs need to apply the same resourcefulness that humanity has shown in construction materials for building shelters—shanties, igloos, lean-tos, domes, caves, bridges, and other structures of brick, glass, paper, and so on.

Construction play lends itself to props that add complexity to the experience of building and props that encourage dramatic play in building. The use of wheelbarrows, wagons, pulleys, and lifts does more than add drama—it allows the child to begin to experiment with mechanics, physics, and cause and effect.

Maximizing construction play requires organization and plenty of room and materials. There are few things more frustrating for children than trying to build in constricted space or time or without the materials to finish a

Community Playthings

The equipment made by Community Playthings is an artisan's delight. No other manufacturer shows the consistent care and quality in design and construction. Their wooden materials set the standard for the industry: furniture, building and riding toys, toddler carts, wooden trucks and trains, platforms and easels.

Community Playthings is the business name of the Hutterian Brethren, a Christian fellowship of families and singles seeking to live as the early Christians lived through 200 A.D. The love and care for the community's children is evident in the craftsmanship of the materials. Under the name Rifton, the Brethen produce an equally high quality line of equipment for children with disabilities.

For catalogues write:
Community Playthings
Route 213
Rifton, New York 12471

vision. A teacher's tolerance for construction play is directly related to the amount of conflict engendered and the ease of clean-up. Boundaries and efficient storage are important. Block areas that are expandable as the need arises or the use of a gym, multi-purpose room, corridor, or the outdoors are usually necessary given space limitations. Mobile carts that turn empty corridor space or multi-purpose space into building areas are valuable to have.

Block storage that requires classification is usually a positive, but sometimes ends up reducing use of the area, if clean up is either too time consuming or expectations of children are not established. A block bin that facilitates easy use is better than restricted building play .

Allowing children to create personal boundaries is valuable in a group setting (think of our own needs for boundaries). Giving them string or tape to carve out space on a table or floor can ease social tension.

The older the child, the more important the element of time becomes. Four year olds and older are capable of complex visions constrained by short time blocks. School-age children particularly need some experiences that carry over from one day to the next.

Surfaces: Level tile floor, low pile carpet for sound absorption, table tops, sheets of cardboard. (This format is adapted from **Young Children in Action**, Hohmann et al., 1979.)

Equipment: Blocks of any sort, boards, boxes, crates, couch pillows, styrofoam pieces, plastic milk crates, sheets and blankets, plastic sheeting, cardboard tubes, plexiglass, pvc pipe.

Props: Connectives (tape, rope, twine, etc.); dolls and animal figures; cars, trucks, and trains;

Photograph by Nancy P. Alexander

construction machines—levers, pulleys, cranes, conveyers; wheelbarrows and wagons; rocks and sticks; diagrams and photographs.

Keep in Mind

There are now a huge number of commercial construction materials available: blocks of all sizes and shapes and materials; log, pipe, and tinker toy systems; large and small Lego-like materials; and panel systems. Each type of equipment seems to have its fans and its detractors. When purchasing keep in mind:

• Variety is a positive, but should not be at the expense of a sufficient quantity of any one set. There should be enough large blocks, unit blocks, table blocks, and parquet building

systems (two dimensional tile systems) for the number of children envisioned building at one time. New materials should be added with the same principle in mind: two or three sets of one material often are better than three different materials.

• Programs differ in their *hard use* of materials (because of staff-child ratios, philosophy, training, etc.). Cardboard blocks may stand up well in one school-age program, but have a short life in another program where they are more likely to be smashed. Some large plastic blocks (Superblocks) have quite sharp corners.

• Some building systems that allow you to build climbers and vehicles—Quadro, for instance—require time and school-age skills to assemble. Once something is constructed, it will likely stay up for a while.

Artistic and Creative Experiences

"Art permits them to share with others what all consider something higher—something that lifts them out of the experience of everyday experience to a vision greater than themselves . . . art's unique role—that of guiding the individual to a personal vision of the world, and of his place in it."
Bruno Bettelheim (1979, p. 417)

Art is universally appealing to children. Smearing, scribbling, painting, sticking together, shaping into forms, experimenting with color, and all the other possible means of self-expression begin in infancy. Art is a way children create beauty, powerfully impose their order and will on objects, explore color and substance, and create offerings to proudly share with and bestow on others.

A good art area is characterized by easy cleaning—flooring, walls, clothing—access to a sink and **plenty**—plenty of room to maneuver, plenty of surfaces, plenty of media, of tools, of cleanup materials, and of storage. A smaller, flexible area that allows a variety of experiences over time will do.

Looking at the huge wall or floor size canvases of Jackson Pollock in a museum, one can visualize the sweeping action and energy of the strokes and the room necessary for him to move. In the sculpture of Rodin, one can almost feel the pounding and chiselling that went into the piece. In another museum room, the precise, intense lines of Japanese miniaturists or the exquisite detail of a fine carving bespeak of silent concentration. A site for art needs to encompass bold, energetic expression and studied time-consuming precision, solitary work and social kibitzing.

Art is a process that may or may not include a product. Children as individuals and at different ages differ in their interest in the product. Many are content to explore the media and their skills. For all children there should be a recognition that the greater the range of media, the more opportunity for learning and expression. Painting with tempera or water colors and

Photograph by Shawn Connell

> *"It's a journey—when you start, you don't know where it will take you, how it will all come out. . . . Sometimes I just start by throwing the brush at the blank surface. Then I try to respond to that mark. I enter into a dialogue with the surface. Then I try to deal with the surface tension. With enough tension, the piece comes alive, it begins to breathe, it swells, there's a fullness. I try to puncture the surface, to go deep inside, to build up the layers. I love to listen to music as I work . . . painting becomes sort of a visual music. It's abstract, but there's a sense of the world in it. I love to take walks in the park, see the way the branches intersect and sway, the swooping of the birds. I love looking down on the city from the rooftops—the clean verticals and horizontals, the movement of traffic. All that gets filtered in. But above all, it's feeling—feeling that is then carefully composed and constructed and integrated. Feeling that breaks apart and then comes together again."*
> Harold Shapinsky (Wechsler, 1985, p. 84)

drawing with markers are quite different experiences.

A successful art area is organized to allow children to use it with a minimum of adult assistance. There is a logical order implicit in the space which is easily understood by the children because of the visual clarity of the layout of smocks, paper, tools, and drying area. Put on a smock, select the materials, use the materials, store the artwork for drying, clean up, and put the smock away.

Surfaces: Floors, table tops, counter tops, floor easels, wall easels, chalk boards, linoleum tacked to walls, high chair trays for babies, bodies. For drying: racks, clothesline, walls.

Media: Tempera paint, liquid starch, finger paint, soap flakes, water colors, food coloring, markers, crayons, chalk, pencils, ink pads and stamps, moist clay, modeling clay, play dough, sawdust, wood scraps.

Paper: All kinds of paper of different sizes, colors, textures, shapes—including computer paper, tissue, newspaper, foil, paper plates and towels, cardboard, cards.

Tools: Brushes of all shapes and sizes, plastic squeeze bottles, sponges, screening, rolling pins, molds, muffin tins, containers, scissors.

Collage Material: Literally anything—rocks, leaves, sand, twigs, feathers, pasta, cardboard, ribbons, cotton, buttons, styrofoam, fabric.

Connecting Media: Glue, paste, stapler, rubber cement, tapes, paper clips, pipe cleaners, rubber bands, thread, string, wire, yarn, ribbon.

Clean Up: Smocks, sponges, paper towels, rags, mop, floor drain.

Keep in Mind

With children under three, the logical canvases are their bodies and their clothes. Their natural inclination is also to use their whole body as a brush. Tasting the media is the first order of business. Body art, using high chairs and car seat trays as easels for babies, and careful use of smocks and washable paints for older toddlers, reduce the mess.

With a single back-to-back easel, social interchange between the painters is difficult and will probably lead to spills. Two side-by-side easels allow for more conversation. A designated easel with an extended time limit for turns promotes extended painting.

Older children enjoy art that requires time to paint or construct. Joint projects appeal to school-age children.

Photograph by Nancy P. Alexander

Photograph by Jean Wallech

Water and Other Sensory Play

Probably nothing is as appealing or as valuable as water play and play with other sensory materials. Water soothes and calms. It is mysterious, compelling, capable at once of surprise and reassurance. Water forever is connected to sensual memories of bathing and being bathed and perhaps atavistic memories of the womb.

Water lends itself to action. Containable but always illusive, dripping and slipping between fingers, evaporating, receding, water is alive to children (of all ages). Its pleasures are visual and auditory as it drips, splats, pours, foams, gushes, ripples, and foams. Sometimes clear and transparent, sometimes opaque or reflective, an unbroken surface now, a mosaic of millions of bubbles seconds later—water can be broadly obvious and exquisitely subtle.

Water play encompasses the entire range of valuable learning experiences. It is something to measure and experiment with as it reacts to action, other substances, and temperature. Water provides an avenue for make believe with dolls, and boats, and kitchen supplies. Equally important, water play can be real work, real cleaning of toys and tables and floors and bodies.

Water play works both as social and solitary play, as a time for language and a time for contemplation. Perhaps most valuable of all, water play requires no expensive or elaborate equipment, props, or sophisticated staff training— simply a recognition of its value and common sense.

Sand and Other Good Things

Sand is nearly as versatile as water. It moves and reacts and lends itself to action, experiment, drama, and sensual reassurance. Children can pour, sift, bury, pattern, fill, dump, ad infinitum. All sand is not equal. Fine sand allows building and shaping, coarser sands do not.

Water tables and tubs become texture tables if, instead of water, sand or other substances are used: snow, grass clippings, leaves, grains, styrofoam pellets, coffee grounds, flour, mud, and so on. The potential mess or damage to floor or carpet can be controlled by using washable rugs or plastic sheeting under the table or tub, depending on the nature of the substance. Individual tubs for each child generally result in much less spillage. A mop or portable vacuum nearby reduces aggravation. Shelving near water play needs to be impervious; non-slip flooring or non-skid bath rugs reduce the safety risks.

Equipment: Water tables, sinks, baby baths, garden tubs, dishpans, wading pools, mops, towels, sponges, smocks.

Props: Kitchen utensils, plates, pipes, funnels, dolls, boats or pretend boats, corks, straws, containers, brushes—literally anything that sinks, floats, absorbs, contains, or sieves water or sand.

Keep in Mind

The process of preparing a baby for a bath, bathing the baby, and dressing the baby is an absolutely wonderful activity that at once calms and cleans a child and, at the same time, creates the closest possible relationship between the child and the adult. It provides the context

Photograph by Michael Whelin

for real language exchanges and other learning.

Using individual tubs in a water table, setting them into a table, or separating them reduces the spread of germs.

Often some of the mess of sensory play comes from its popularity and subsequent crowding. Increasing the number of tubs or reducing the number of children will help.

Language

"Books must be read as deliberately and reservedly as written."
Henry David Thoreau (1960)

Just as a home does not require a study or a den, a program does not have to have a reading or language area. And certainly it is a mistake to confine *language* to one location. It is important for children to have opportunities to explore books, alone and together; to have opportunities with spoken language that convey the power and pleasures of the spoken word; and to have the chance to solve the problems and practice the skills that understanding and using language presents.

Language should be built into the entire environment through organization of space, time, and materials, and expectations of adults and children as to verbal and written communication. Written labels, notes, and conversations are evident in language rich settings.

Books and magazines should be clearly displayed so that children can browse and select for themselves. Books that children enjoy looking at or reading by themselves should be on display. The number of books displayed

---

Little Girl, Be Careful What You Say
by Carl Sandburg

Little girl, be careful what you say
when you make talk with words, words—
for words are made of syllables
and syllables, child, are made of air—
and air is so thin—air is the breath of God—
air is finer than fire or mist,
finer than water or moonlight,
finer than spider-webs in the moon,
finer than water-flowers in the morning:
and words are strong, too,
stronger than rocks or steel
stronger than potatoes, corn, fish, cattle,
and soft, too, soft as little pigeon-eggs,
soft as the music of hummingbird wings.
So, little girl, when you speak greetings,
when you tell jokes, make wishes or prayers,
be careful, be careless, be careful,
be what you wish to be.

---

depends on the ages of the children. Nooks, corners, carrels, and quiet out-of-the-way spots that hold one or two children are important, as are areas for social reading and giggling. Local lighting enhances the space.

A listening center with a phonograph and/or tape recorder and headsets provides opportunities to attend to the sounds of language. Children can be lulled to sleep with poetry recordings—lulled to sleep by the rich voices of people like Julie Harris and Cyril Richard. Filmstrip projectors allow children another enjoyable experience.

A communication center for children may involve bulletin or marker boards, magnetic letters, tape recorders, and a self-service writing

Photograph by Shawn Connell

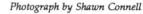
Photograph by Shawn Connell

Photograph by Nancy P. Alexander

Keep in Mind

If books are going to be treated with respect, then bookcase displays should not allow books to tumble out or be stacked in a pile, and an optimum number of books should be on display.

Books can be made using cardboard, contact paper, and magazine pictures or photographs.

Writing can be incorporated into nearly any activity by including paper or notebooks and pencils.

Music

Language and music areas are often combined or adjacent because of the joint need for a record player and tape recorder. Yet a music area requires the opportunity to make noise and move freely:

"There seems to be more lack of spontaneity in the music program of most preschool centers than any other activity.... Due perhaps to the

station. Typewriters and computers encourage children to write.

Furnishings: Book and magazine display racks, bulletin boards, cabinets for not-in-use materials, pillows, couch, easy chairs, table, lamps.

Equipment: Record player, tape recorder, head sets, filmstrip projector, typewriters.

Materials: Picture books, read aloud books, newspapers, magazines, photographs, mail, catalogues, writing notebooks, filmstrips, records, tapes, rubber stamps, wooden, plastic and magnetic letters, writing materials.

"There's nothing like dancing—creative, expressive, physical movement—to open up all we've got. Dancing picks up the impulses and inspirations from the spirit itself which sweeps through the mind and out through the body, picking up all we've got, mopping up anything lying about: spare feelings, desires and desperations. Dancing to music knows how to identify and release man's capacity for exuberance and exhilaration, even to ecstasy, which purify and unshackle happiness. Body and spirit marry each other, and their offspring is joy. Dancing is a language, a composite language of spirit, senses and body. It can be a language of fine joy or fine despair, telling what we cannot otherwise tell. Dancing communicates all."
Sylvia Ashton-Warner (1972, p. 161)

tradition of music and dance no real middle ground is recognized between passive listening and skillful performance. The folk attitude which accepts music as a form of expression for all people is completely forgotten in most schools" (Hartly, in Osmon, 1971, p. 82).

At home and on the street, many children turn life into an ongoing operetta. But at the center, the group setting and space available inhibit this. Skillful acoustical design and maximizing the use of space may allow the creation, if only for a time, of music **and movement** areas.

For music children need access to instruments, records, and tapes. Tapes are easier for children to use, and it is inexpensive to make multiple copies of library albums. Battery-powered cassette recorders with an a.c. cord are inexpensive and can power a listening station for headsets. Children can be taught how to use phonographs and recorders with the aid of pictorial labels. Using pictorial matched labels for cassettes and their containers and for albums and their jackets, and storage that allows children to browse and select records or cassettes without rummaging is useful.

A piano, autoharp, or electronic keyboard are nice to have, as is a set of children's instruments. Instruments made from containers and *junk* save money and also reinforce the notion that music can be everywhere. Dividers on casters that allow expansion of the area for movement are useful. A mirror, scarves, and streamers will encourage movement.

Furnishings: Low pile carpets, mirrors, ballet rail, platform.

Equipment: Record player, tape recorder, headsets, instruments, piano, auto-

harp, keyboard, microphones (or look-alikes).

Materials: Records, tapes, photographs, paintings, scarves, streamers, dancing clothes and shoes.

Dramatic Play

Through dramatic play, children come to terms with the world. They *absorb* their experience. In their imitations, replay of events, role playing, and scene setting, they work to understand **what is** against a back drop of **what might be**, who **they are** in light of who they might be or who they will become. What exactly are mommies or police officers, mice or dogs? Why do children live the lives they do, the maddening blend of dependency and unwanted responsibility, the complex social order that rules their lives? What are older brothers good for? What am I good for?

Photograph by Jean Wallech

Young Children in Action

Young Children in Action by Hohmann, Banet, and Weikart (1979) describes the *cognitive curriculum* developed by the High Scope Foundation. This work is supported by other books, pamphlets, films, and numerous training opportunities provided by High Scope, but in itself is a valuable resource on establishing a learning based environmental curriculum. Clearly written, thorough, and well illustrated, the book belongs in every program library. Some of the prop boxes listed in their section on dramatic play (pp. 40-42) include:

grocery store box:
  outside—pictures or photos of a check-out clerk, packer, meat cutter, customers
  inside—toy cash register, empty food containers, play money, paper bags

carpenter's box:
  outside—pictures or photos of carpenters at work and their tools and equipment
  inside—carpenter's apron and hat, ruler, some tools, empty paint cans and brushes, sandpaper

plumber's box:
  outside—pictures or photos of plumber at work and his tools
  inside—coveralls, wrench, faucets, plastic and metal pipes and pipe fittings

post office box:
  outside—pictures or photos of mail carriers driving trucks, emptying mailboxes, delivering mail from house to house; people inside a post office
  inside—old shoulderstrap purses or paper bags with shoulder straps stapled on, canceled stamps or seals, envelopes, paper, postage scale, rubber stamp and ink pad

doctor's office box:
  outside—pictures or photos of doctors and nurses
  inside—white shirts for uniforms, nurses' caps (can be made out of paper), bandaids, gauze, tape, tongue depressors, pill bottles, small suitcase or purse for doctor's bag, stethoscope, plastic syringes with needles removed

farm box:
  outside—pictures or photos or animals, barns, farmers, farm machinery
  inside—overalls, rubber boots, hat (whatever kind local farmers wear), pail, straw, calf feeding bottle and nipple, oat bag, bridle, saddle

gas station box:
  outside—pictures or photos of gas stations, gas station personnel, gas pumps, cars being filled, washed, and repaired
  inside—workclothes, hats, empty oil can, hose or tubing (for gas pump), paper towels, plastic spray bottles, car jack and lug wrench

fire station box:
  outside—pictures or photos of a fire station, fire trucks, firemen in the station, on the trucks and fighting fires
  inside—firemen's hats, a child's rubber raincoat, a pair of boots, rubber hosing

hamburger shop box:
  outside—pictures or photos of hamburger places, people working in them, customers, hamburgers, French fries, soft drinks
  inside—chef's hat, apron, cups, napkins, straws, plastic ketchup and mustard containers, French fries (cut from foam rubber or styrofoam), hamburgers (cardboard or clay), cash register, play money

shoe store box:
  outside—pictures or photos of shoes (child, adult, male and female shoes), people having their feet measured, people trying on shoes
  inside—a variety of shoes, ruler (or something to measure feet with), shoe boxes, shoe horns

---

Mirror! Mirror!
Deborah Ensign (age 7)

As I look into the mirror I see my face.
Then I talk to myself.
Then I play like I am in jail.
I pretend that I am bad.
I pretend sometimes that I am on a stage.
I sing to myself. I introduce people.

In dramatic play, children can always have impact that often escapes them in the real world. The child can order events and stack the deck, turn the tables and be the dominant power—the rule setter, the bread winner, the dispenser of rewards. Or the child can return to babyhood, become the family pet, the magical fairy. Machines and people will bend to their will. Dolls or Fisher-Price people can experience the pain the child imagines inflicting.

Dramatic play is more than imitation and pretending; it often encompasses complex problem-solving; science; and a range of motor, cognitive and sensory experiences. The world of housekeeping involves water, ordering and classifying utensils and clothes, challenging fine motor experiences with hangers, egg beaters and other utensils. The garage involves tools and uniforms; the beauty shop, water, styling accessories, and a wealth of *cosmetics* to classify and order. Storage and display of dramatic play props are made to order opportunities for classification and seriation.

In many programs, dramatic play areas become exclusively housekeeping and dress-up areas. These are always appealing to children, reflecting the world they know the best. But many children's active experience in the world outside the home is narrowing. Child care needs to widen the child's world by extending children's experience through walks and field trips and books, subsequently offering dramatic play opportunities to allow children to absorb the experience.

Housekeeping

Furnishing: Child sized stove, refrigerator, sink, shelves, desk, ironing board, tables and chairs, steps, easy chair, child bed, lamps, blankets, sheets, pillows, mirrors, plants, etc.

Equipment: Literally anything, not dangerous, found in a kitchen—adult sized silverware, utensils, pots and pans, coffee and tea pots, table settings, colanders, molds, crock pot, can openers, mixing bowls, rolling pins, paper towels, napkins, sponges, scrubbers, child size (cut down) brooms and mops. Also items from around the house—clocks, telephones, television and radio, ad infinitum.

Props: Empty food containers, plastic food, bottle caps, poker chips, styrofoam pieces, paper, seeds, grains, nuts, containers, bags, tablecloths, towels, dress-up clothes, suitcases, baskets, purses, dolls, stuffed animals, doll furniture, doll clothes, photographs.

Fantasy/Storybook Area

Furnishings: Over-under space, fabric, cardboard boxes, lamps, tables, planks.

Equipment and Props: Materials from a story like **The Wind in the Willows** (motorcars, boats, small animal figures, materials to make caves and river banks) or for space adventures (helmets, metallic items, boots).

Keep in Mind

Furniture can be made or adapted using tri-wall cardboard or packing crates. For example, a stove surface can become a doll examining table by altering the surface with contac paper.

Photograph by Nancy P. Alexander

Workshop Area

Furnishings: Tables, work lights

Equipment and Props: Aprons, caps, tool belts, machines and appliances to take apart, tools, containers, wood pieces, tree stump, nails, screws, glue, pencils.

Manipulatives

If anything is clear about the learning environment, it is that children need *stuff,* loose parts to manipulate, things to take apart and put together. Manipulatives encompass small or fine motor, perceptual motor, cognitives, dramatic play, science, and math. Whether open materials—blocks, clay, poker chips, pebbles— or closed materials—puzzles, beads, Montessori materials—children will manipulate them and test their physical powers of motor and perception, their cognitive understandings, and their imaginations. The items will be arranged, classified, counted, put together and taken apart, stacked, moved, and explored with the senses. They will be used to represent other things such as people, animals, weapons, vehicles, and money (a list that perhaps sums up civilization).

Literally anything can become valuable stuff; *unstructured* materials that the child structures—lids, bottle caps, pen tops, key chains, stones, poker chips, pieces of wood or pipe.

Manipulative areas need room to store and clearly display the myriad stuff available at the moment, boundaries to contain all the loose parts, and defined spaces that allow individual territory and one-child, two-, or three-child size spaces. This may be accomplished with small tables or cubes, trays, carpet squares, or rugs.

Nearly anything that is safe can be used in a manipulative area. Containers that vary in size, shape, handles, and so forth and require different motor and perceptual skills add to the experience.

Areas can be ordered by color, containers, or location.

Photograph by Shawn Connell

Furnishings: Small tables and chairs, rugs, carpet squares.

Materials to sort and build with: Beads and strings, cubes, parquetry blocks, small blocks of different sorts, bottles and jars, sensory (smell, sound, texture, visual attribute) bottles, buttons, rocks, shells, washers, marbles, and anything else that can be sorted.

Materials to order and build with: Nesting and stacking materials—jars, cans, rings etc.; cuisinaire rods and similar materials; pipe fittings, boxes.

Materials to fit together and take apart: Different size pegboards and pegs, tinker toys, Legos, puzzles, nuts and bolts and screws, gears, clocks, small machines or appliances, magnets, string, straws, popsicle sticks, and tape.

Materials for representation and perception: Fisher-Price plastic people, animals, dinosaurs and other figures, puppets, photographs, wood, rocks, and scraps of cloth.

Keep in Mind

Small pieces will travel within the center, and as *pieces of the center,* they will be sneaked into pockets and taken home. Some materials— teddy bear counters and small cars—seem designed for that purpose.

Authorizing certain pieces to travel back and forth—such as buttons, prized cars, or icons made from junk—will help make strip searches and airport-like metal detectors unnecessary.

Games and Projects

School-age children need a game area where they can play two to four person games ranging from checkers or card games to monopoly. The crucial ingredients are space off the beaten path and time.

Project space is important for older pre-schoolers and school-age children—space to create, store, and display the crafted works. At a minimum, they need an area that is protected over a sufficient time period to complete an elaborate block project or a jigsaw puzzle.

Optimally, a program would enable the children to construct and store in process elaborate projects out of cloth, papier-mache, cardboard and landscapes, or reliefs such as dinosaur habitats out of natural materials.

Photograph by Jean Wallech

Equipment: Creative storage, large surfaces.

Materials: Games, decks of cards, models, project materials.

Electronics

From Speak 'n Spells to computers, early childhood settings have entered the electronic age. If it is clear that electronic toys, games, and computers are not substitutes for hands-on experience with *stuff* and are extras to be considered when budgets are relaxed, this equipment can have real value, particularly as software grows more sophisticated and the child's interaction with the hardware becomes more active and varied. Electronic classifying games, drill, and *jack in the boxes* have the same virtues and drawbacks as their non-electronic brethren or teacher directed call and response activities. The virtue of electronic drill is that it can be a quiet solitary activity and fun.

As software allows young school-age children to move beyond drill and to program using languages like logo, and as more staff are trained to understand and appreciate computers, the computer will have a more legitimate role in the classroom. Computers can be a *loose parts box* for mental *messing about*, a tool for testing possibilities and designs, as well as a medium for reading and writing. But as an expensive electronic Etch A Sketch or flash card drill, it is hard to justify a computer educationally. And they are actually harmful when used as a marketing gimmick or when they reduce time spent in more valuable play activities.

Science

Science is a process of knowing about the world. It is observing, making inferences,

Photograph by Jean Wallech

testing hypotheses, classifying, and integrating and communicating insight. All too often, science in the early childhood program becomes merely a category of facts and tasks, often a nature center to learn facts about nature, perhaps taking care of animals and plants. But science is more than that. Science is the passage of time, the distance between objects, the change of days and seasons and bodies, the light and shadows and whispers in the room. Classifying experience and puzzling out cause and effect through observation and trial and error is science. Care needs to be exercised that the science area does not become *the place where science happens*.

A creative science area is more laboratory than museum. It is also a sort of take out area: a place where the materials exist to conduct experiments in chemistry, plant and animal sciences, physics, mechanics, and perception; to carefully observe animal and plant life/death; to develop the tools and report the results of experiments occurring throughout the particular setting and other settings the child occupies.

A science area demands a tolerance for interaction, yet many of the materials and live creatures are fragile. While no substitute for teaching children care and gentleness, the design and layout of a science area is important. Cages and aquariums that allow all-around viewing and discourage poking or shaking (Osmon, 1971, p. 83), ample counter and table space for projects, a convenient sink, hardy plants in sturdy containers, carefully laid out accessible storage of tools and props, and secluded places for contemplation and individual experimentation are important.

Animals offer children important experiences when they are more than caged specimens. Children over two years old can learn to coexist respectfully with cats, dogs, guinea pigs, and rabbits. Gerbils, mice, rats, frogs, toads, salamanders, and the like can spend time in more open enclosures. Birds add an element of life and charm to a classroom. Fish fascinate children and provide interesting soothing aesthetics.

The literal ins and outs of life are all present in the life cycle and food cycle. Feeding pets, cleaning cages, growing plants or earthworms or

Photograph by Shawn Connell

meal worms for food, collecting bugs to feed the toad, watching animals being born and die provide the stuff of mystery and wonder.

Science and math are often understandably lumped together as one area in early childhood settings or math may end up in *manipulatives*. What is important is that children have the opportunity for concrete experiences with numbers: counting, matching, measuring, dividing, and so on. For that they need all the *stuff* mentioned in manipulatives and all the measuring devices of a good science area.

Furnishings: Large table or counter, small tables or individual work spaces, sink, window, storage and display adapted for intended use, blackboards, varied lighting.

Equipment: Tubs, tanks, aquariums, cages, containers of all kinds, pails, watering cans, microscopes, magnifying glasses, fans, wind chimes and streamers, pinwheels, watches, timers, pulleys, levers, kaleidoscopes, scales, hot

plates, thermometers, gauges, tape measures, rulers, turntables, notebooks.

Materials: Earth, sand, gravel, rocks, driftwood, shells, bones, all different sorts of plastic pieces, fabric, metal, paper, all sorts of liquids and malleable materials.

Plants, Animals, and Health

There seems to be no consensus as to the legitimate restrictions to make for health reasons on the tending of plants and animals in group settings. It is one of those issues that depends on where one draws the line in comparing programs to homes or institutions like hospitals. Some municipalities (or individual regulators) ban all flora and fauna. Generally, though, plants are okay unless found to have toxic elements. All plants should be cleared by the local poison control. Most areas restrict turtles under four inches in diameter and allow fish, gerbils, and hamsters. In some areas cats, dogs, birds, rabbits or guinea pigs are restricted. No one seems to pay much attention to snakes or lizards. Restrictions are usually based on the concern that animals will transmit disease or cause problems with children's allergies. This is another issue that would benefit from the recognition that childhood, like Marianne Moore's description of poetry, is "a garden with real toads."

Plants: Easy to grow plants like ivy, coleus, geraniums, succulents; plants children can tend like avocados, beans, sweet potatoes, grasses, bean sprouts. (Check poison control if in doubt about toxicity.)

Animals and pets: To be handled—domesticated animals like rabbits, guinea pigs; to mostly observe—reptiles, birds, rodents, larger turtles, fish, amphibians, caterpillars, worms, ants.

Beyond Preschool

Infants and Toddlers

Many of the issues that distinguish infant and toddler care and learning were addressed in Chapter Three. But it is important to dwell on

Photograph by Jean Wallech

Photograph by Jean Wallech

some of the differences. Babies are not just shorter and less capable, they are smaller; the scale needs to take that into account. Their mobility is different and motor experience is central. Their capabilities and interests are different; and they lack social graces and work alone, even when together.

Built-in learning is critical to allow caregivers to concentrate on one-to-one nurturing and learning interactions. The learning environment needs to stem from what they do, not the tried and true categories for older children like art, music, and science. A small 6 square foot area might form a reaching area or a texture spot with a mirror. The space between a couch and a wall could be a discovery corner or a sounds area. Under a table or a counter is space for sorting, or building, or a texture cave. Busy boxes, telephones, pictures, or fill-up containers can be attached to the back of any shelf. Dividers can become peek-a-boo or poke-through boards. High chairs are art spaces.

For older toddlers, pick up and collection points for hauling and dumping, a throwing or dropping corner, telephone booths, sorting spaces, and other small activity areas work well.

School-Age Children

At the other end of the spectrum, it is not uncommon to see five to ten year olds in before and after school settings that are primarily preschool settings. They sometimes suffer because no one pays enough attention to the developmental differences between school-age children and preschoolers. There are also school-age programs that don't seem to acknowledge the context of the child's life. School-age or latch key care wraps around three to six hours a day of a child's institutional life. In both cases the children's experience tends to be narrowed rather than broadened.

The learning environment for school-age children should acknowledge their capabilities, their greater size, and their developing interests in playing a role in the real world. They need bodily challenge that requires concentration and discipline like using larger wheelbarrows, building cardboard castles, or using tools; intellectual challenge that adds the complexity of many parts like jigsaw puzzles, trial and error problem-solving and discovery, carrying ideas and activities over time and space. The world of machines fascinates them—uncovering how things work, how things are put together. The world of commerce—producing, buying, and selling—and communications—corresponding, producing newsletters, plays, and shows— provide rich school-age material.

By age seven, play is distinct from reality for school age children and rules and roles become important elements. Games, plays, and clubs reflect the child's increasing interest in the social fabric of life. School-age children reflect much more than younger children; they reflect on their own reality, on the reality of others, and on what might be. The scope of the setting's experiences should match the growing boundaries of their

Photograph by Shawn Connell

minds. Their visions can become real, given the tools and materials. They can take an active stance in planning and evaluating experiences and activities.

In past societies, and some present ones, elementary age children are accorded nearly the same responsibilities as adults. Children thrive on being given responsibilities they can handle, being involved in the work of the program, assisting the staff and each other. Involving children in planning activities, routines, and

space and in doing chores necessary for the program to function is important. But the *work* should be considered in the context that they *work* at school and also need time to be free from adult compulsion. Being trusted with responsibility and chores can be fun in reasonable doses.

Special Needs Children

All children benefit from individualized settings. Children with special needs—learning,

emotional, or physical difficulties—**need** settings geared to their strengths, as discussed earlier. Successful experiences are particularly important to children with disabilities. Organization must be clear with appropriate spatial, sensory, and language cues. The setting may need simplification for some children. It is possible to have a rich learning environment that is simplified through rotation of experiences and limitation of choices at any one time.

Exercises

1. Imagine that you have no playground or multi-purpose space. How could you build motor experiences into the setting?

2. For a five minute time period, observe all the experiences available in a child's setting that could be considered science related (e.g., the death throes of a cockroach). Do the same thing for art, music, and math.

3. List activities that would work using the space under a table for the activity setting.

4. Assess a children's setting for loose parts.

5. How could you double the number of loose parts with free materials?

6. Imagine that all the children in your program were extremely well behaved and your staff/child ratios were suddenly doubled. What changes in the learning environment would you make?

— Chapter Thirteen —

Outdoor Learning

In Minneapolis there is a skyway system that connects the second floors of buildings throughout the downtown area—offices, hotels, stores, and residential developments. There is also a domed stadium and there are domed tennis courts, skating rinks, swimming pools, and indoor fountains. In Minneapolis and many other places, one can seriously ask: Why go outside to the world of snow and ice, heat and mosquitoes, auto exhaust, and rain?

Happiness
by A. A. Milne

John had
Great Big
Waterproof
Boots on;
John had a
Great Big
Waterproof
Hat;
John had a
Great Big
Waterproof
Mackintosh—
And that
(Said John)
Is
That.

Photograph by Nanette Seeler

The outdoors has weather and life, the vastness of the sky, the universe in the petals of a flower. But many programs, following the model of schools, have seen the very qualities that make the outdoors different as obstacles or annoying side effects. The openness is tightly constricted; weather provides a reason to stay in, and landscape and life are things to be eliminated. A playground, considered the primary, if not the only outdoor setting, performs the same function as a squirrel cage or a prison exercise yard—it is a place for emotional and physical release and a bit of free social interchange.

Playground Types

Traditional playgrounds in schools, centers, or parks are open areas dotted with various pieces of unrelated commercial, usually metal, large muscle equipment such as slides, swings, climbing domes or bars, spring animals, see-saws, and so on. Children play on one piece of equipment until bored and then move on to the next. Play tends to be disjointed. These playgrounds encourage large motor play and little else. Children have no way to change the setting. Creative and social play tends to be limited to adding an element of risk in using the equipment, such as swinging together or jumping off slides. The amount of motion and varying heights, and an often inadequately impact-cushioning surface, result in safety problems. Children *least prefer* traditional play areas when given a choice (Noren-Bjorn, 1982).

Developed as an alternative to traditional playgrounds, **creative playgrounds** are coordinated and designed or adapted for a site. These include both modular coordinated play installations (e.g., Big Toys) and *one-off* architectural designs which have a sculptural or natural quality in the forms and materials. Often the landscape is used to create berms for slides and tunnels. There usually are multiple levels of platforms, steps, and slides for climbing, chasing, and hiding. At first largely static except for occasional cargo nets and wobbly bridges (a reaction to the dangers of traditional playgrounds), today there are installations that include varieties of swings, moving parts, and cable slides. Creative playgrounds can support a variety of motor and social play in a compact area, if they include moving parts. They are usually attractive to both adults and children. They rarely, however, have any provisions for loose parts.

Typical nursery and child care play areas lean toward a blend of traditional and creative, with perhaps a playhouse and sandbox thrown in, and a trike path if size permits.

There are alternatives common in other countries but relatively rare in the United States. **Adventure playgrounds**, found in Europe, literally grew out of the rubble of World War II.

Photograph by Nancy P. Alexander

The Door
by Miroslav Golub
translated from Czechoslovakian by Ian Milner

Go and open the door.
Maybe outside there's
a tree, or a wood,
a garden,
or a magic city.

Go and open the door.
Maybe a dog's rummaging.
Maybe you'll see a face,
or the picture
of a picture.

Go and open the door.
If there's a fog
it will clear.

Go and open the door.
Even if there's only
the darkness ticking,
even if there's only
the hollow wind,
even if
nothing
is there,
go and open the door.

At least
there'll be
a draught.

Sometimes called workyards, adventure playgrounds are the ultimate expression of the power of loose parts. The idea, expressed originally in the 1930's by Danish architect C. Th. Sorenson, was "sort of a *junk* playground in which children could create and shape, dream and imagine, and make dreams and imagination a reality." Virtually nothing is static (or expensive). They are filled with junk—wood, rope, canvas, tires, wire, bricks, pipes, rocks, nets, logs, balls, abandoned furniture, wheels, vehicle and unimaginable assorted artifacts.

Adventure playgrounds have play leaders who help children to build, demolish, repair, incinerate, dig, flood, and play safely. Tools are provided and their use supervised; fire and water are considered important elements of the playground. Children are allowed to create complex structures, both physical and social ("Girls keep out on Tuesday"). There is a wide variety of cognitive, social, and motor play. As a play leader expressed, "The secret of a successful adventure playground is in its continual development, it is never complete, never developed. It is sort of a *terrain vague* that can be many things to children."

Adventure playgrounds are most often designed for school-aged children. Supervised adventure playgrounds have an excellent safety record and have proven to be highly popular with children. Despite this, they are rare in the United States and likely to remain so. The extreme caution due to the insurance crisis, the likelihood that adults would have trouble accepting the unsightly "junkiness" of the play area (Spivak, 1974), and just the lack of tradition of such playgrounds makes the spread unlikely in the near future.

However, a variation of adventure playgrounds, also called Creative Playgrounds, originating in Sweden, incorporates loose parts to allow children to construct their own environments. Instead of junk and tools, modular building pieces and panels are available for construction. This form of adventure play as

Photograph by Nancy P. Alexander

part of a child care program or school is eminently feasible as demonstrated by Play Mountain Place in Los Angeles (Ellison, 1974).

Environmental play yards, which encourage an active interaction with plants and animals, water and dirt, weather, and the life cycle, offer children education at its most compelling. The Environmental Yard at Washington School in Berkeley, California, offers the most fully realized expression of the idea. A one and a half acre asphalt traditional playground has been transformed to incorporate miniature ecosystems—*the meadow, willow island*—ponds, pathways, gardens, and animals.

Here and there throughout the country are child care programs in semi-rural areas that are able to incorporate many of the same experiences. For urban programs a garden, shrubs, a birdbath, and trees are a start.

The Outdoors in Children's Lives

Richard Dattner (1969, p. 44) gives testimony to a vision of a playground very different from the exercise yard, one reflecting Buckminister Fuller's view that playgrounds should be renamed "research environments":

"A playground should be like a small-scale replica of the world, with as many as possible of the sensory experiences to be found in the world included in it. Experiences for every sense are needed, for instance: rough and smooth objects to look at and feel; light and heavy things to pick up; water and wet materials as well as dry things; cool materials and materials warmed by

---

April Rain Song
by Langston Hughes

Let the rain kiss you.
Let the rain beat upon your head with silver liquid drops.
Let the rain sing you a lullaby.

The rain makes still pools on the sidewalk.
The rain makes running pools in the gutter.
The rain plays a little sleep-song on our roof at night—

And I love the rain.

Photograph by Jean Wallech

the sun; soft and hard surfaces; things that make sounds (running water) or that can be struck, plucked, plinked, etc.; smells of all varieties (flowers, bark, mud); shiny, bright objects and dull, dark ones; things both huge and tiny; high and low places to look at and from; materials of every type, natural, synthetic, thin, thick, and so on. The list is inexhaustible, and the larger the number of items that are included, the richer and more varied the environment for the child."

Most programs do not have the outdoor playground space to create miniature worlds. But a program playground exists in a larger outdoor context. If the playground is planned as part of that whole, the child's outdoor experience may reach Dattner's ideal. The context includes:

• all the accessible outdoor space—the sidewalks, the city parks, the stream nearby.

• all the time the children have access to the outdoors—daily, weekly, seasonally.

• the outdoor experiences that children have outside the program—in the yard, on the street, in the park.

Glendale Child Development Center Playground

Many of the photographs in this section were taken at the Glendale Child Development Center in Minneapolis. In 1983, the center began developing a playground for children from infancy through early school age using inner-city high school students, volunteers, and trained supervisors—and whatever advice or expertise they could get free. Located in a housing project on the edge of a traditional city park, they set out to design a playground open to the public that used landscape, water, pathways, loose parts, and skeletal structures that children could add planks, ladders, fabric, or rope to (ladder, hurdle, or bench-like made structures, dead trees) that would be the sort of place a child in urban child care would be able to experience a full, rich outdoor childhood. The playground continues to grow as new ideas develop and old ideas prove flawed.

Photograph by Shawn Connell

Photograph by Francis Wardle

WHOOSH—moving through a big space with each swing. They can be short—a fast-moving, back-and-forth, round-and-round kind of ride" (Moore, R. in Coates, 1974, p. 233). Add the short circular motion of tire swings, the back and forth of porch swings and hammocks, the experience of standing or lying on the swing, swinging together or in tandem and the variety of learning experiences are evident. Three-chain tire swings are very versatile and safe; they work well with very young children and with children with disabilities.

Places for Sliding and Rolling: High, low, wide, narrow curvy, straight, fast, slow. Slides offer wild release, experiments with friction, social experiences, and all sorts of physical challenge. Set in a hill, slides can be safe for the youngest children and for children with disabilities. Wide slides offer more possibilities for experimentation with the body and for social sliding.

Photograph by Jean Wallech

In urban areas and areas with harsher climates, the outdoors is a precious resource to be carefully maximized when it is available. In some fortunate areas with year round gentle climates and open spaces, the outdoors is a way to extend classroom boundaries to the horizon daily.

Outdoor Places

What outdoor places benefit children?

Places for Active Motor Play

Children need physical challenge from a playground: the opportunity to literally *reach new heights* and *run wild*. They need the stimulus of risk; they need choices in climbing, sliding, swinging, and so on so that they can determine the excitement and challenge they are ready for. Playgrounds are where reputations are made—whether 4 or 14 years old—and structures are necessary that allow derring-do with which to build self esteem. Equally important are *break away points* for those who change their minds or need time to act (much like adults on a ski slope)—alternate routes up and down, graduated challenge, and a range of accomplishment opportunities that allow all children to build self-esteem without pressure.

Places for Swinging: Swings with seats, tire swings, rope swings, porch swings, hammocks. Different swings provide different experiences with time, motion, and body control. "Swing ropes for example can be long, suspended far above the ground, giving a long incredible

Photograph by Jean Wallech

Places for Climbing: Trees, live or dead; platform climbers; ropes; ladders; sculptures; tire trees; pole mountains. **Anything that can be climbed will be climbed.** The exhilaration and the challenge of climbing depends not just on the height but on the size and spacing of footholds and handholds, whether the climbing structure moves like ropes or branches, whether the surface is wood or metal, whether it is open underneath, and so on. Large metal frames and jungle gyms often take up a lot of space and get relatively little use, unless loose parts are available for adding on. Climbing structures need multiple levels of difficulty and stopping points. Creative play installations with platforms, timbers, tires, and nets fill this need.

Places for Jumping: Platforms, poles set in the ground, climbers, anything that allows a secure launching point and a safe, absorbent landing area away from the traffic flow. Plato saw the model of true playfulness in the need of young

Children love to roll themselves and objects down slopes. Walking, pulling, or hauling up a slope provide challenge. Summer's rolling hill becomes a water slide with a plastic tarp or winter's sliding spot. Tires, balls, and teachers all roll nicely. Railings can become courses for rolling objects by adding pipe or tubes.

Photograph by Francis Wardle

Photograph by Francis Wardle

"Once, on a summer day, I was busy in the shop, and Mequsaq and Pipaluk were playing outside with their little friends. Their game was to crawl up on a big slanting rock and slide down its smooth side. Up and down they went in one wild tumble. Then I heard their grandmother, Kasalum, come out and shout to them: 'Oh no, dear children, don't do that! Think of your poor father who has to drive long stretches in the cold and dark to get skins for your pants. Now you are wearing off the fur. It is unreasonable, you must not do it!'

Then she went back inside, and the children resumed their sliding down the rock, a wonderful game in any latitude!"

from **The Book of Eskimos,** by Peter Feuchern (1963, p. 83)

Of Boys and Men

"Dr. Fritz Zwicky last week tried to hurl some metal slugs out into space, free of the earth's gravitational pull. Dr. Zwicky stood in New Mexico and tossed from there. He was well equipped: he had a rocket that took the slugs for the first forty-mile leg of the journey and then discharged them at high velocity to continue on their own. The desire to toss something in a new way, or to toss it a greater distance, is fairly steady in men and boys. Boys stand on high bridges, chucking chips down wind, or they stand on the shore of a pond, tossing rocks endlessly at a floating bottle, or at a dead cat, observing closely every detail of their experiment, trying to make every stone sail free of the pull of past experience. Then the boys grow older, stand in the desert, still chucking, observing, wondering. They have almost exhausted the earth's possibilities and are going on into the empyrean to throw at the stars, leaving the earth's people frightened and joyless, and leaving some fellow scientists switching over from science to politics and hoping they have made the switch in time."
E. B. White (Elledge, 1984, p. 268)

children, animal and human, to leap. Leaping expresses faith in yourself and your environment. The opportunity to jump from different heights and land safely is incomparable, a test of self and gravity.

Places for Running: Open space, pathways, or tracks which allow all kinds of running. Children run this way, thatta way, back and forth, round and around. Toddlers and other unsteady walkers need smooth, flat surfaces.

Places for Throwing and Kicking: Walls and nets, hoops, barrels, trees, as targets; balls, bean bags, frisbees, and (when appropriate) rocks and sticks as missiles. Throwing, heaving, hurling something to someone, at something, into something belongs on a playground.

Humankind probably began kicking during the first boring walk—kicking rocks and sticks and small animals. Children love to propel things and feet do the job with dispatch.

Photograph by Jean Wallech

Places for Bouncing and Balancing: Beams of different sizes, widths, and heights; logs, poles, boulders; wobbly balancing surfaces, movable balance beams and planks. Children will balance on everything from a crack in the sidewalk to railings on a deck. They love to balance on their feet, stomaches, heads, and hands.

Bouncing requires knees; variations come from different surfaces—planks with give, spring platforms or spring animals, trampolines or rebounders.

The best spring equipment is produced by Kompan. Because spring animals only hold the interest of children under four, they are of limited value and are too often purchased in greater quantity than necessary.

Places for Traveling, Riding, and Transporting: Children love pathways and sidewalks that provide a here and there and routes in between: to journey, to race, to haul, to ferry, to caravan. Institutional wheel toys are far superior to home-use models. Vehicles that encourage hauling or two child use have special value.

Carts and wagons for transporting children on walks allow toddler treks that don't leave the caregiver with two or more weary adventurers to carry the final block. The carts or "Buggers" that attach to the back of adult bikes provide wonderful personalized bike trips for one to three children.

Places to Move Slowly: In a Japanese garden, one moves slowly along a path, eyes alert to new views, body shifting as the path changes beneath one's feet. On a lazy day, the urge to float and dawdle can become overpowering; on a grey day, the need to hold back can take over. Stone and wood paths or patterned walks that

Photograph by Jean Wallech

Photograph by Jean Wallech

Photographs by Jean Wallech

encourage deliberate motions delight children and adults.

Places to Be Human

Places to Watch, to Wonder, to Retreat: When the challenge of the climber or the commotion on the swings is too much, where is there to go to be alone or with a trusted friend or fellow

temporary outcast? Where is the cork tree for smelling the flowers? Where can I observe my next challenge? Quiet spaces scaled to child size—grottoes, nests, perches, miniature picnic tables off a beaten path—all provide wayside rests. Greenery has a calming effect.

Places to Sleep: It is common in European programs to sleep outside or on sleeping

porches. Occasionally taking naps outside provides children with memorable experiences.

Places to Eat: What makes life interesting is variation; and when outdoor eating (and cooking) is possible, children are delighted (and so are the local wildlife).

Babies Outside

Children under two belong outside. Infant and toddler playgrounds need three things: (1) soft, level surfaces with good drainage, (2) watchful maintenance for items dangerous to mouth, and (3) adults—staff and parents—who have a conception of babies as active learners capable of enduring the bumps and spills of childhood and who enjoy being outside themselves. With these three things, a small grassy area or deck can be simply transformed into a sensory-motor learning site using planks, boulders, wading pools, branches, tires, and fabric. Greenman (1985)

Places to Be Diapered and to Go to the Bathroom: Access to the bathroom or diaper table will determine the amount of outdoor play.

Places to Discover: "I do not know what I may appear to the world; but to myself I seem to have been only like a boy playing on the seashore, and diverting myself in now and then finding a smoother pebble or a prettier shell than ordinary, while the great ocean of truth lay all undiscovered before me" (Issac Newton).

Taking advantage of nature, the busy city life behind the fence, the machinery of bikes or hinges or pulleys, the aerodynamics of kites—allows great discoveries even in small areas.

Photograph by Francis Wardle

This Is My Rock
by David McCord

This is my rock
And here I run
To steal the secret of the sun;

This is my rock
And here I come
Before the night has swept away the sky;

This is my rock,
This is the place
I meet the evening face to face.

Photograph by Jean Wallech

Places that Feel Different: Sunny and shady spots, breezy spaces, still spaces, what Moore et al. (1979) call favorable micro-climates.

Creative and Constructive Play

Places for Building: Snow forts and lean-tos, milk crate walls and cardboard castles. The outdoors is a place for children to build shelters and barricades, sculptures and vehicles. With good storage and garbage control, a workyard is possible for encouraging construction with or without tools, with drift wood and planks, canvas, boulders, blocks and crates, tires, and rope. Skeletal structures—platforms, dead trees, A-frames, ladders, hurdles, and bench-like structures— are skeletal in the sense that children can add to them if ladders, planks, canvas, and other loose parts are available. Eye screws and cleats can be attached to make them more adaptable.

Places for Machines: Digging machines, wind machines, waterwheels, clothesline pulleys, trucks, and wagons.

Places for Creative Expression: The outdoors is a natural site for art. Walls provide easels and perhaps even canvases. Wood, stone, fabric, plastic, and metal provide the raw material for sculptures that play with color, light, and sound. Sidewalk painting, water painting, alternating water and sand, rock and wood environmental art that alters miniature landscapes allow children to discover and express their relation to life and beauty.

Places to Pretend: Here I am king of the forest, there a pirate, now a race car driver, a super hero, a frontier mother, a tiny rabbit. Where can I roam, walk the plank, save the citizenry, keep my baby safe, or find a good carrot? Children like the realism of a stripped down car or boat.

But structures that only vaguely represent other things or settings benefit from an ambiguity that allows children's imaginations to take over. The tower that can be a space ship or eagle's nest; the log that's either shark or horse or alligator; the clearing in the bushes or the roofed area that serves as jail, fort, house, or store, all are far superior to expensive castles or rockets or concrete turtles.

Photograph by Jean Wallech

Photograph by Shawn Connell

Abstract concrete forms rarely are popular with children. Log animals are easy to make and young children enjoy them.

Environmental Play

Places to Dig: Digging, burying, making mud, making ditches and rivers, finding life. Earth science!

"People murder a child when they they tell him to keep out of the dirt. In dirt there is life."
George Washington Carver

Multiple sand areas and a digging area can be accomplished using timbers or a truck tire for boundaries. (Concrete curbs will keep water from draining out.) The sand under climbing

---

Mirrorment
by A. R. Ammons

Birds are flowers flying
and flowers perched birds.

and jumping areas will be used by children if insufficient sand areas exist; this creates a danger. Covers prevent animals from using sand as a litter box, but sand can be cleaned and should in any event be regularly replaced. Sea sand or fine commercial sand allows children to shape and mold.

Watery Places: Water that reflects shadows and faces and flashes rainbows, water that hides life and bits of past life, water that moves and makes music with its gurgles and burbles and drips and splats water that is still. e. e. cummings described the world of springtime as "puddle-wonderful" and "mud-rich." Is there anything more wonderful than water to a child of any age?

Water creates ice to crack and mud to squish, tendrils to seep through the grass or sand. Water ferries twigs and leaves and paper boats. Water cools us, runs off our bodies, and enlivens our skin. Water fills our cups and jars and pots. Bird baths, outdoor water tables, elevated streams, splash pools, fountains, sprinklers, and wading pools bring water to a

Photograph by Jean Wallech

playground. Key considerations are always safety (no water depths over 8 inches, children in water always must be supervised, and beware of slippery surfaces), health (standing water carries germs and left will breed mosquitoes), access and drainage (where does the water come from and run off to), and clothing (how wet can children get).

Places for Growing

"Thank God for the Grass that grows through the cement."
Pete Seeger

Growing things allows children to experience the life cycle, to anticipate change in seasons, and to tend and care for life. Gardens, flower patches and boxes, herb gardens, trees, vines, shrubs, and weeds (which to a child are simply flowers in the wrong place) provide beauty, life, and loose parts. Leaves and twigs become boats and stew, little people and airplanes.

Spring Rain
by Marchette Chute

The Storm came up very quick
It couldn't have been quicker.
I should have brought my hat along,
I should have brought my slicker.

My hair is wet, my feet are wet,
I couldn't be much wetter.
I fell into a river once
But this is even better.

A Memory
by William Allingham

Four ducks on a pond
A grass-bank beyond,
A blue sky of spring,
White clouds on the wing:
What a little thing
To remember for years—
To remember with tears!

Photograph by Francis Wardle

Photograph by Jean Wallech

Photograph by Francis Wardle

Places for Animal Life: Adults tune out the lively world around them and beneath their knees. The outdoors everywhere is the playground of creatures strange and mysterious to children: squirrels and birds, worms and bugs. A living landscape encourages life. A protected outdoor setting that allows the tending of rabbits and ducks, and even larger animals, is a wonderful laboratory for children.

Places for Collecting and Carrying: Leaves, pebbles, shells, dandelions, bottle caps, bugs (all to be collected); wood, trays, water, rocks (all to be carried); sacks, backpacks, and toolbelts.

Places for Measuring: How much rain fell? What's the temperature? How fast is the wind? How long is that shadow?

Sheltered Play

Shelter from rain, wind, snow, and too much sun can make the outdoors accessible most of the time. The overhang of a roof, canopies, the underside of a high deck, leafy trees, and lawn umbrellas can allow children to be outside in rain or excessive sun. Berms and evergreens, storage sheds, walls, and snow drifts can offer windless pockets.

Adult Places

Adults play a variety of roles on a playground: overseer, nurturer, and participant.

The adult traffic flow is patterned by where the logical adult perches are and what there is for adults to do. Adults will sit or lean on something: if not benches, then stoops, stumps, tables, or the lower rungs of climbers. They will also seek out sun or shade, depending on the weather.

> ### Mud
> ### by Polly Chase Boyden
>
> *Mud is very nice to feel*
> *All squishy-squash between the toes!*
> *I'd rather wade in wiggly mud*
> *Than smell a yellow rose.*
>
> *Nobody else but the rosebush knows*
> *How nice mud feels*
> *Between the toes.*

Placing adult perches in the areas where the most supervision is desired or at the best vantage point, or on the fringe of *child turf*, helps structure staff behavior. The angle of seating structures the vantage point. Adults often congregate together on playgrounds. This can be encouraged or discouraged by the available seating.

Photograph by Nancy P. Alexander

Analyzing Play Space

Planning Environments for Young Children: Physical Space by Sybil Kritchevsky and Elizabeth Prescott (1969) is a small, extremely useful book on planning physical spaces, particularly small play yards. They devised a simple system for analyzing play space. Space is divided into: (1) a play unit which contains something to play with, and (2) a potential unit which is simply "some empty space which is surrounded in large part by visible or tangible boundaries. For instance an empty table, the empty corner of a room or a yard, a shady area under a tree or umbrella, are all potential units to which it is easy to add play material of one kind or another."

Play units can be classified by the kinds of activities they encompass and complexity, "the extent to which they contain potential for active manipulation" (p. 11). The three classifications for play unit complexity are **simple**—one obvious use and no subparts like a swing; **complex**—two subparts like a sandbox with scoops, or materials that allow for manipulation or improvisation or unpredictability like art activities; and **super units**—complex units with one or more additional play materials. The classification system developed makes it easy for programs to calculate how many play opportunities are really available in the playground.

Planning Environments for Young Children also discusses layout and pathways in terms useful to teachers.

Following illustration is from page 21.

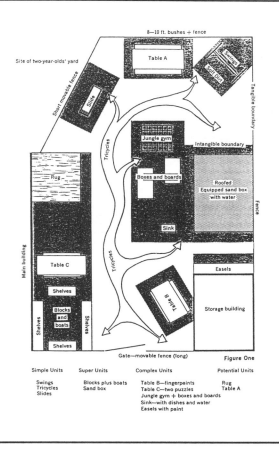

Figure One

Simple Units	Super Units	Complex Units	Potential Units
Swings	Blocks plus boats	Table B—fingerpaints	Rug
Tricycles	Sand box	Table C—two puzzles	Table A
Slides		Jungle gym + boxes and boards	
		Sink—with dishes and water	
		Easels with paint	

Platform climbers, porch swings, and some other equipment lend themselves more to adult use as active models than dome climbers, animals swings, and so on. Log and stone benches that allow sitting, and are not too comfortable will help to structure adult positioning.

Playground Planning

It is easier to list outdoor places good for children than to develop good outdoor space. The following are the important considerations in developing the space:

Criteria for Outdoor Space

1. Size and Amount to Do

For playgrounds to incorporate active motor play, 100 square feet per child is a reasonable playground minimum. Smaller playgrounds have to parcel out experiences to other outdoor areas like sidewalks, parks, and vacant lots.

Kritchevsky and Prescott (1969, p. 15) used the analogy of musical chairs to describe the implications of how much there is to do on a

playground. If a yard has 30 play places, for 10 children there are 3 places per child, for 30 children, 1 place per child. The goal in musical chairs is to eliminate children; in this analogy it is to provide each child with a chair.

"In a game with 20 chairs and 10 children (2.0 chairs per child), when the music stops children can easily find an empty chair without help. If there are 10 children and 15 chairs (1.5 chairs per child), some children probably will have difficulty finding an empty chair. The closer the number of chairs to the number of children, the more likely it will be that a teacher will need to help the children find empty chairs. . . . However, if the teacher wants the children to listen to their own *inner music*, further difficulties are introduced. . . . If several children want to change chairs in close succession, the demands on the teacher and the limitations on the children will be extreme." The moral is clear—the less choice, the more burden placed on children and adults. At least five play spaces per child seem necessary for an adequate playground.

2. Safety and Risk

Well planned, supervised outdoor play areas are necessary for children to challenge themselves and to take risks without threat of serious injury. Most playground accidents are the result of falls, bumps, and blows.

The cause of most accidents is not equipment failure as often as poor playground design, equipment selection and use, and maintenance. Often, safety problems are due to not anticipating all **the actual risk that will occur:** older children using a railing as a balance beam or younger children playing in sand under a climber. A play area has to be scaled to the developmental capabilities of the users.

Layout: Motor equipment, particularly moving equipment, needs adequate staging areas and routes in and out. A major danger from swings, seesaws, and similar equipment is collision due to inadequate pathways. Poor zoning that puts younger children in proximity to action-packed areas and sand and water near concrete both create dangers.

Crowding: Everything becomes dangerous if there is a crowd of active young children. Safety when using all climbers, ladders, high slides,

---

Falls and Surfaces

A child can receive a concussion from an impact force of 50G (50 times the force of gravity). Consider the height of fall needed to achieve a 50G impact (Mason, 1982, p. 67):

Surface Material	Height of Fall for 50G Impact
Concrete	less than 1 foot
Asphalt	less than 1 foot
Packed earth	about 2 feet
Standard rubber tile	about 4 feet
Double rubber tile	about 8 feet
Wood chips (6 inches deep)	about 10 feet
Sand (12 inches deep)	about 12 feet

---

trike paths, or tools depends on the absence of crowding.

Boredom: Children will add risk and daring in order to cope with boredom. They will jump off inappropriate equipment like slide ladders, play chicken, and test the limits of people and things. The predictability of a swing that delights a three year old holds little fascination for many five year olds who are eager to vary the experience by standing or lying on the swing. Boredom and crowding are lethal combinations.

Surfaces: Falls on a hard surface are the single most common cause of serious accidents. Children need to soar; they also need a gentle landing.

Equipment: Slides need a well railed debarkation platform, side screening along the length of the slide so children do not roll off, a run off lip at the bottom and no large gap between the lip and the ground, a soft ample landing area, and

Photograph by Francis Wardle

protection from direct sun. **Climbers and platforms** need adequate vertical railings to prevent climbing higher than anticipated, alternate routes up and down, and thoughtful designs that do not encourage leaping from piece to piece (e.g., from a slide to a ladder). **Swings** should be rubber, clearly bounded, and allotted ample area. **Seesaws, carousels, and upright concrete culverts** might as well be avoided. Some **spring equipment** is unsafe and should be carefully checked, both in terms of the potential for injury due to crushing body parts between springs and the severity of the bouncing or whipping action.

All equipment needs to be checked for exposed bolts and nails, sharp edges or seams, and gaps that may lead to choking or trapped limbs. Gaps may be the result of poor installation that leaves a space between platforms and ladders or slides. Poor installation that results in inadequate anchoring, exposed concrete, or other problems is frequent. Less expensive equipment designed for home use wears quickly and presents more safety problems.

Repair and Maintenance: Glass or metal buried in sand, exposed concrete pilings, worn metal chain links, loose bolts. All playgrounds need continual monitoring and maintenance. Safety comes from alertness to potential dangers. Sand areas need to be raked and cleaned or replenished.

Supervision: Adults need to set the expectations for safe and cooperative play, including the acceptable use and storage of loose parts and tools and taboos on use of motor equipment. They need to teach children to take safety concerns seriously.

Pests and Plants: All potential plantings should be checked both for toxicity and for their ten-

---

Playground Safety Checklist

☐ **Supports:** Equipment is secure in the ground, not movable.

☐ **Foundation:** Footings are not exposed. Concrete is solid and slopes downward to keep water from pooling around the metal.

☐ **Bolts, Nuts, Screws, Nails, Other Hardware:** No pieces are missing, loose, or exposed. Pinch or crush points are covered. There are no open S hooks or other hooks and no exposed nails.

☐ **Rust:** No rust is visible.

☐ **Wood:** There are no splinters, cracks, rotting, or sharp ends.

☐ **Metal:** Slide beds and other metal parts are shaded from the sun.

☐ **Ropes:** There is no fraying or damage and no loose connections.

☐ **Tires:** No water has collected. There are no exposed wire ends.

☐ **Sharp Edges:** There are no sharp edges on any metal; metal tubing ends are closed.

☐ **Holes and Gaps:** All ring holes or gaps between parts are either too small for a child's head to enter (generally under 3 inches) or large enough for a body to pass through (over 10 inches) to prevent strangulation. There are no gaps to trap limbs.

☐ **Equipment and Parts:** All equipment is age-appropriate with no heavy swing seats. Slides and climbers have appropriate railings.

☐ **Surface:** A non-abrasive, appropriately cushioned surface is under the entire structure.

☐ **Location:** Structures are 6 feet away from walls, fences, and pathways.

☐ **Litter:** The area is free of glass, sharp objects, animal feces.

☐ **Boundaries:** Fencing or other barriers zone play areas.

dency to attract pests—bees, spiders, rats, and so on. Rats nest in ivy and spiders in the Southwest find the inside of tires inviting.

3. Maintenance

Wonderful landscapes have to be mowed, watered, and tended. Sand needs replacing and raking, wood requires replacement and repair, asphalt patching, and so on. The planning process has to take the kind of daily, weekly, and seasonal maintenance necessary into consideration.

4. Appropriateness for All Users

This includes the children enrolled whose interest and talents change over time and use; the adults who use the area with children as supervisors or playmates; adults who maintain or deliver to the area; and adults and children who use the area when the program is not in session, whether it is sanctioned or not.

5. Cost

Start-up, maintenance, and staffing costs need to be considered. In traditional playgrounds almost all the costs are incurred in start up. Adventure playground costs are mainly in staffing and in some materials.

6. Ease and Comfort of Use

Even more than indoors, the quality of storage; the ease of access, set up and clean up; and the perception of the amount of *hassle* involved will determine the value of the area to the users. Outdoor spaces that are uncomfortable because of temperature, wind, or other weather factors; landscape; or use factors will receive limited use.

7. Change

On traditional playgrounds, change is limited to the weather and the children's development. On adventure and environmental playgrounds, change is built into the landscape, the materials, and the expectation that constructing, adapting, destroying, and growth cycles are integral to day-to-day existence.

8. Aesthetics

Children and adults do not have the same aesthetic sense. Children are attracted to bright colors; they see the beauty in the creative disorder of loose parts and dandelions. Adults rarely agree; often a major obstacle to adventure or environmental play is adult objection to a *junky* or *weedy* appearance. Zoning, fencing, compromising, and understanding can reconcile the two standards.

Playground Layout

Pathways, boundaries, zoning of related activities, and the right mixture and amount of activity areas will determine the quality of outdoor play.

Circulation Patterns

The traffic flow should be smooth, safe, and continuous from the point the child enters the outdoor area. It should encourage all children to explore to the limits of their capacities. Moore et al., after studying numerous settings recommend "looped circulation," traffic patterns with no long *runways*, visible activity areas along the loop for children to choose from, and major paths clearly differentiated from activity areas. "The environment should allow for activities to flow and move actively and continuously with multiple branches and alternatives at crossroads

and decision points." Children should be able to see choices ahead after ending an activity. The looped pathway branches off into secondary circulation patterns between activities that can lead to sequences of graded challenges. (Moore et al., p. 510-3).

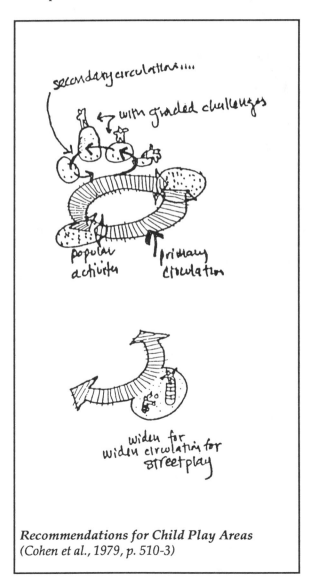

Recommendations for Child Play Areas (Cohen et al., 1979, p. 510-3)

Zoning

Active play needs to be well separated from other areas. Activities of interest to younger children should be zoned together. Sand areas need access to water, and they need to be separated from hard surfaces. Sand on wood or hard surfaces creates dangerous slippery spots. Bathrooms and drinking water in a central location makes life easier. Art areas belong close to the building, water, and storage.

Activity Areas

Clear boundaries, clear and sufficient entry and exit space to prevent accidents, and logical placement are important.

Pathways

Pathways themselves can be a major site for learning and exploration. Changing the surface from dirt to cobblestone, colored brick, half logs, wobbly planks, catwalks, raised stones, bridges, and so on provides motor challenges and opportunities for sensory exploration. Hauling a wheelbarrow load or toddling along is a very

Photograph by Nancy P. Alexander

different experience on a bumpy or raised surface than on a flat one.

Meandering pathways that rise and fall add interest. Varying the railing to include wood, metal, chain, slats, or rope changes the experience as does including plantings, walls, or poles that create semi-enclosed stretches. Pathways should widen and narrow to accommodate the traffic and wheeled vehicles.

Fencing and Barriers

Chain link fencing is common, relatively inexpensive, and easy to install. It is an effective barrier. Aesthetically drab with overtones of incarceration, it can be livened up by incorporating wood or colored fabric into the the fence. It provides little sense of seclusion.

Wood fencing is aesthetically more appealing and can be designed to seclude. It is more expensive and requires more regular repair.

Appearance and Reality

Fencing has a physical and psychological reality. One playground had a simple, elegant, wooden two-rail fence, by no means an impassable barrier. But because it was a clear taboo to go on or over the fence, children quickly accepted the fence as an imposing barrier, as the designer knew they would. The fence served its physical purpose of keeping children in.

But the adults, staff, and parents, never felt completely comfortable with the fence, never totally believed that children would respect the fence. Whatever the reality, they never felt that the children were secure behind an obviously permeable barrier, and thus the adults were always anxious. The designer hadn't anticipated the psychological reality; the fence was later replaced.

The Landscape

All play areas have *landscapes*. Even an asphalt rectangle with weeds in the cracks encounters the issues of climate, drainage, safe surfaces, and the passage of time.

• **Climate:** The landscape affects the need to keep warm, cool, dry, and wind-free at various times of the day and year.

• **Drainage:** Where does the water go that runs off the building when snow melts? How will rain water escape the sand pit or the area under the swings?

• **Safe Surfaces:** What does it feel like at the end of a 2 foot fall? a 4 foot fall? on a skidding knee or elbow?

• **Passage of Time:** How many seasons will it last? How much tending does it need?

An important concept to consider in thinking about outdoor landscapes is Moore's concept of micro-climates, "areas which deviate from the general climate on a regular basis" (Moore et al., 1979, p. 801-1). Protection from excess wind and the sun-shade mixture are the two critical factors. Creating pockets of sun and shade, of breeze and stillness, is possible if daily and seasonal wind and sun factors are taken into account.

Candlestick Park, an expensive baseball stadium in San Francisco is inhospitable to baseball because of its location. It almost guarantees windy, cold, foggy nights and serves as a warning that these factors are sometimes overlooked. Child scale allows boulders, shrubs, berms, and small walls to serve as windbreaks and small trees and awnings to provide shade.

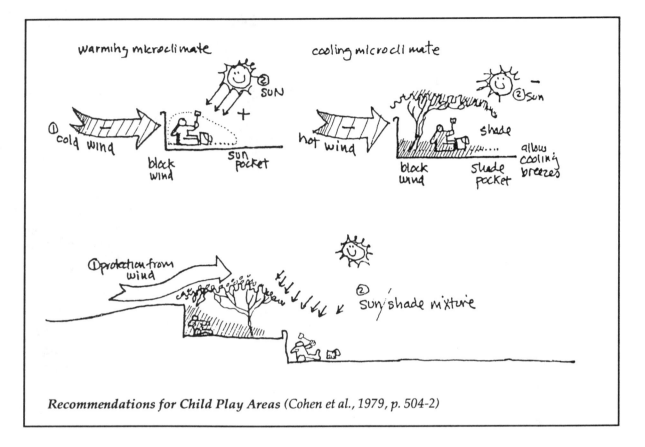

Recommendations for Child Play Areas (Cohen et al., 1979, p. 504-2)

Drainage

Poor drainage will render a playground useless (although not to children who thrive on puddles and mud). When the sun comes out, everyone wants out. It is preferable if the play yards slope away from the building. The effects of landscaping and building renovation on natural drainage patterns need to be thoroughly considered before any changes are made.

Exposing drainage by *creating stream beds* allows children to understand how the environment works. Concrete curbs around sand areas will seal in the water and impede drainage.

Drainfields can be created under sand areas and other recessions (e.g., under swings) by providing layers of gravel under the sand. Decks and platforms will salvage bad drainage areas.

Surfaces

Securing our footing, cushioning our falls, carrying off the rain, cradling our bodies, carrying our vehicles—we expect a lot from our surfaces. In addition, we want low maintenance and pleasing aesthetics. A variety of surfaces are necessary to accommodate drainage, wheel toys, climbing, and lounging.

Photograph by Shawn Connell

Grass: Grass is wonderful aesthetically. It feels and looks great, holds life, and is soft for low falls and tumbles. Even dried out brown grass is an acceptable ground covering.

Grass needs to be maintained and will not last in high traffic areas or areas that are not big enough to sustain pathways. Grass can present drainage problems in areas with heavy precipitation or in shady areas. Dew may make grass unusable for infants and toddlers during the morning in some climates (although vinyl tablecloths and blankets can overcome damp grass).

Sand: Coarse construction sand is the most versatile surface. When adequately supplied and distributed, sand provides protection from falls and good drainage; and it requires minimal maintenance (although in some areas cats present a problem). Sand needs retaining timbers, logs, or walls to separate it from other surfaces. Sand needs to be 8 to 12 inches deep to cushion falls; it loses much of its shock absorbency in cold weather.

Pea Gravel: Coarser than sand, pea gravel provides good shock absorbency and drains well. Cats are less attracted to pea gravel than sand. While it blows around far less than sand, it may tend to be thrown about, requires daily raking to distribute, and is harder to walk on than sand.

Wood Chips and Pine Bark: Wood chips and pine bark absorb energy and are often adequate in drier climates. They tend to scatter and foul up lawn mowers unless well bounded. Wood chips do rot in wet climates, and pine bark is a poor walking surface. Moisture robs wood materials of their energy absorbency.

Wood: Decks and platforms allow immediate use after rain.

Asphalt: Preferable to concrete, asphalt dries more quickly than sand and grass and is useful for riding toy and ball areas. Too hard for climbing areas, asphalt can become unpleasantly hot and sticky in the summer.

Dirt: Dirt mixed with clay and sand provides an adequate hard surface in climates with limited rainfall, but results in more clothing stains.

Synthetics and Rubber Matting: Various *safety turfs* differ in absorbency. At double-thickness they offer good protection but are expensive. Their prime use is on hard surfaces under large motor equipment where sand is not feasible.

Tire Mulch: It is not appropriate for very young children and is susceptible to fires.

Photograph by Jean Wallech

Contour

Hills and berms can provide sites for slides, tunnels and caves. In themselves they provide interest and motor challenge. They are useful for screening views and providing a sense of enclosure, high vantage points without risk, low valleys or trenches, and creating amphitheater

---

After a Freezing Rain
by Aileen Fisher

The brittle grass
is made of glass
that breaks and shatters
when we pass.
It clinks against
the icy rocks
and tinkles like
a music box.

Photograph by Jean Wallech

effects. A berm can shield from the wind without cutting sun. If a hill or berm is too small or steep (a slope more than 1 to 3), retaining grass may be difficult.

Children—as opposed to adults—love holes, ditches, and pits. All require good drainage and good traffic patterns to work.

Planting Trees and Shrubs

Vegetation provides shade and windbreaks and cools the air. It attracts wildlife, provides loose parts (leaves, cones, and twigs), provides landmarks, creates and defines pathways and grottoes, and builds in seasonal change and beauty.

When planting, consider:

Health and Safety: Check all plants with the local poison control for toxicity of any part or form of the plant.

Hardiness and Growth Rate: Small shrubs that look like twigs in the winter and young trees are not a bargain at any price, because they are likely to fall victim to childhood exuberance or thoughtlessness. Avoid plantings that need careful handling.

Play: Low branching deciduous trees can be used for climbing; shrubs can create grottoes and mazes. Dandelions and prairie flowers are a problem for whom (depending on location— perhaps the neighbors)?

Seasonal Variation: Deciduous trees don't block sun in the winter; they do provide shade in the summer. Evergreens provide color, windbreaks, and sound conditioning all year. Trees and shrubs and flowers that bloom at different times can provide continuous color.

Balance: A balance of color, smell, size, form, texture, and other qualities is pleasing to the senses. Pine cones, crab apples, blossoms, leaves, and peeling bark provide different loose parts.

Harmony: It is easy to get carried away with variety. Planting plans need to have a sense of unity and proportion. Contrast and variety must be carefully planned as part of a harmonious whole.

Trees, shrubs, and plants in a children's setting require thoughtful placement and protection. Watering new plantings is critical, and regular tending has to be built into the program.

Stone

The Chinese sometimes regarded rocks as the earthly counterpart of clouds. At the same time they saw in stone the quality of unchangeable solidity which the human character so often

Photograph by Jean Wallech

lacks. Smooth stones and rounded boulders add color and texture and define the landscape in the same manner that vegetation does.

Rock boulders can create stepping stones and places to sit, retaining walls to scale, boundaries for sand areas. Boulders and shrubs create semi-secluded grottoes—places for infants and toddlers to go in and out, over and through. Large rocks that children can move become the raw material for small sculptors and architects.

Wood

"Wood is universally beautiful to man. It is the most humanly intimate of all materials. Man loves his association with it; likes to feel it under his hand, sympathetic to his touch and to his eye."
Frank Lloyd Wright (1941, p. 117)

Photograph by Shawn Connell

Properly treated, wood wears with dignity; the scars of use have a friendly quality unlike cracked plastic, worn metal, or pockmarked concrete. Dead trees and stumps can become sculptural climbing structures, bridges, walkways, railings, and lean-tos. Branches, lumber, and driftwood can be loose parts for the child architect and sculptor. Live trees may support platforms and swings.

In some hot, wet climates, like in Florida, softer woods deteriorate much more quickly.

Storage and Loose Parts

Convenient outdoor storage can transform the most barren playground. Wading pools, hoses, and sprinklers create a water playground. Add pipe, tubing, and containers, and it becomes a laboratory. Wheelbarrows, planks, rope, blocks, crates, panels, and lumber pieces

create a construction playground. With ladders, sawhorses, hurdles, and planks, children create new climbing experiences from old jungle gyms. Foam blocks and pillows create soft spaces. Wheels and tires, balls, and cylinders become the stuff of rolling and transportation. Parachutes and fabric create Christos and Wonderwomen. Storage allows loose parts, and loose parts create learning opportunities.

Multiple storage cabinets or boxes, close to the point of use, eliminate the organizational

problems of a single storage shed or room. Storage sheds, however, can be incorporated into platforms and anchor bridges.

Commercial Playground Equipment

There are now a large number of manufacturers of playground equipment. The advantage of buying manufactured equipment is the assumption that many hours have gone into the design process to ensure safety and durability. Companies are well aware that any design flaws

Photograph by Jean Wallech

will result in their being liable for claims. One can purchase anything from a single swing to a super unit playground—with multiple slides, swings, platforms, and ramps. Some companies will put together modules to meet the requirements of a specific site. Purchasers can choose between wood and metal, logs and boards, plastic and fiberglass, natural and colored materials.

The major problem with using commercial equipment does not lie with the equipment, but with the assumption that the equipment is the playground, rather than pieces of the playground. Even the most wonderful multistructure super complex unit is limited. There are no loose parts or water, the equipment applies to a limited age range, and in some cases opportunity for creative dramatic play is restricted. Spending the entire playground budget on pieces of commercial equipment plunked on sand or grass is a common phenomenon.

Companies worth looking into:

Landscape Structures/Mexico Forge (Route 3, 601 7th Street. South, Delano, Minnesota 55328) also offers unlimited combinations and configurations. This company emphasizes bright colors

and offers components of plastic, metal, and unpainted natural wood. They are planning an innovative line of modular *working* play walls.

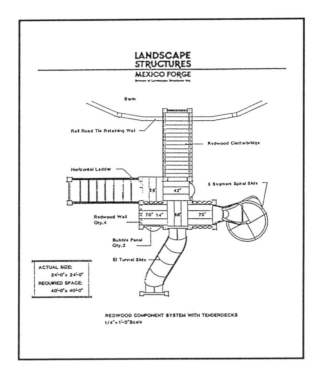

Kompan (80 King Spring Road., P.O. Box 3536C, Windsor Locks, Connecticut 06096) makes spring animals, platforms, and play equipment with a very different look—brightly colored marine-plywood and rounded shapes.

Children's Playground Inc. (P.O. Box 370, Unionville, Ontario, Canada L3R 2Z7) has an entirely modular approach and will help you put together the structures that will work for a particular setting. You can choose between climbing walls, platforms, bridges, and slides made out of different materials (rope, tires, wood, metal, plastic) and in different sizes.

Building Playgrounds

For the price of commercial play installation, far richer playgrounds can be built using natural and scrounged materials. The satisfaction that comes from a participatory design and building process is evident. But building swings, slides, and climbers that are safe and developmentally appropriate, and designing landscaping that lasts are not tasks for well meaning amateur carpenters and gardeners to tackle alone. At a minimum, one should take advantage of the books available and, if in any doubt, proceed very cautiously. Advice from local nurseries and landscape architects is often essential.

Unfortunately, insurance companies are often unreceptive to non-commercially designed equipment. One has to be prepared to mount a case for the safety of any building or renovation.

Adapting Outdoor Space—Making Do

It is discouraging that most programs have to make do with limited outdoor spaces. Some programs have to make do with plain lawns, tiny yards, or even parking lots. But even the worst space can be improved. Some piece of the outdoors is always available to work with:

Assess Your Own Resources. Can the sidewalks be trike paths; the front yard an environmental yard; the side of the building an art wall, a sound wall, a mechanical center, or a ball stop? Flower boxes, washtubs, and bird feeders are a beginning.

A storage shed, storage boxes, or storage carts will allow children to transform the area.

Complement Neighborhood Resources. If there is a traditional park nearby and program

The Nuts and Bolts of Playgrounds

For anyone contemplating designing play areas or outdoor equipment, the works of Paul Hogan are invaluable. **The Nuts and Bolts of Playground Construction** (1982) is a treasure chest of ideas, insights, and details about the ins and outs of playground design. There are hundreds of pictures from play areas around the world, detailed drawings, and the wisdom that comes from extensive experience. Careful use of these books can prevent costly mistakes and accidents caused by ill conceived plans.

Hogan runs the Playground Clearing House, Inc. (26 Buckwalter Rd., Phoenixville, PA 19460) which distributes books and audio-visual materials. The Clearing House provides design, project management, lectures, and general consultation services. It specializes in community participation and the use of recycled materials.

Other works that provide very useful hands-on information:

Ellison, Gail. **Play Structures**, Pasadena, CA: Pacifics Oaks College, 1974.
Friedberg, Paul. **Handcrafted Playgrounds**, NY: Vintage Books, 1975.
Frost, Joe, and Barry Klein. **Children's Play and Playgrounds**. Boston, MA: Allyn and Bacon, 1979.
Hewes, Jeremy. **Build Your Own Playground**. Boston, MA: Houghton Mifflin, 1975.
Mason, John. **The Environment of Play**. West Point, NY: Leisure Press, 1982.

Photograph by Jean Wallech

Exercises

1. What were your happiest moments as a child out of doors?

2. List all the things that absolutely cannot take place outdoors. Now list all the things that would be enhanced by taking place out doors.

3. Consider a plot of land 6 feet by 10 feet and develop an environmental learning area. What learning might take place in each season?

4. Go to any playground and determine the traffic flow, the risks of serious injury, and the variety of play experiences actually available to a two year old, four year old, and six year old.

5. Observe a child on a front stoop, a side walk, or in a back yard with *nothing to do*. What does he or she do?

space is limited, why take up all the available space with traditional equipment? A small playyard could become a workyard and the site for adventure and environmental play; the park and sidewalks the large motor area. If a field is nearby, use it.

Forced to make do with a vacant lot a block and a half away, the Glendale Child Development Center in Minneapolis purchased an old mail cart at a salvage store and filled it with planks and sawhorses, wheel toys, parachutes, and whatever other loose parts seemed to work. A truckload of sand, an arrangement with a neighbor for use of a hose, and permission to snow fence an area made a decent playground.

Community Playthings' six-child carts, and ample use of wagons, strollers, and backpacks, resulted in frequent use.

Adapt What You Have. Consider jungle gyms as iron skeletons; use canvas, parachutes, rope, wood, and loose parts to create variations. Add a canopy or awning to create a rain play space. Use tents to create new play possibilities. A platform around a tree, a 4 by 6 foot landing extended to an 8 by 12 foot deck, an overhead trellis for vines, or a cable to attach a swing—most programs have some options. Adding logs, stumps, or boulders creates new places, new textures, and new motor experiences.

— Chapter Fourteen —

Changing Spaces, Making Places

Change seems like it should be so easy. Armed with enthusiasm and good ideas, we can transform the classroom or center into the setting we **now** feel it should be. Unfortunately, beyond minor adjustments, it is rarely so simple. Whatever has been occurring has been happening for a reason.

The status quo—*the way we do things here*—has a logic, however strange it may seem. Child schedules, staff schedules, meal schedules, and carefully worked out scheduled assignments of common space usually mold the structuring of time. The structure of space flows from the allocation of physical resources and the way people and groups have used the resources over time. The physical arrangements and routines that seem self-defeating to an outside observer usually are grounded in the working out of solutions to past or present problems. However, neither rationales nor the results of past decisions may have been reconsidered for a while.

In one program materials were organized to accommodate a very short staff person and remained that way two years after the staff person left. In another the daily schedule was designed to facilitate part-time shifts, and much of it remained the same despite a change in staffing patterns that eliminated the part-time routines. In a center where turnover of head teachers was high in three of the five classrooms, the two other classrooms acquired most of the choice furnishings. A casual comment from a licenser, "I think couches have to be fireproof," or a director, "Dramatic play works better by the window, don't you think?" may play a major role in the environment for years to come.

There are three major reasons why change is so difficult. One is that people do what they know how to do, and most of the time they believe in what they do. Second, in an institution, the individual's actions and desires are meshed with the actions of others. There is always a strong pressure to continue present behavior; to do otherwise may alter the daily routines or challenge the beliefs or desires of others.

The third block to change is that change takes time, two kinds of time. Time away from children is the most precious resource in child care. Time to think, meet, plan, work through problems, and develop collegial relationships with other staff is scarce or non-existent in many programs. It is easier to continue to do things the way they are done, since there is rarely time to work through any complexities.

The other kind of time is time to sustain change, which often requires stability of people and material resources over time. If staff turnover or fluctuating revenues is a problem, planned change is more difficult.

Understanding that major change is complex and time consuming is important, because often the result of a failed attempt to change is to blame the idea. In a toddler program struggling to develop divided space and individualized learning opportunities, changes in staff and the director's erratic attention due to assorted crises stalled change. When the same ideas came up a year later, the perception of some staff was, "We tried that and it didn't work." Change happens when it is believed in, when the timing is right, and when there are resources to sustain the change (Greenman and Fuqua, 1984).

A Participatory Process

"Social design is working with people rather than for them; involving people in the planning and management of the spaces around them; educating them to use the environment wisely and creatively to achieve a harmonious balance between the social, physical, and natural environment; to develop an awareness of beauty, a sense of responsibility, to the earth's environment and to other living creatures; to generate, compile, and make available information about the effects of human activities on the biotic and physical environment, including the effects of the built environment on human beings. Social designers cannot achieve these objectives working by themselves. The goals can be realized only within the structures of larger organizations, which include the people for whom a given project is planned."
Robert Sommer (1983, p. 7)

Child care is a group process. Changes always involve others, whether moving a piece of furniture or building an addition. The more extensive the change, the more individuals are involved. There are those who may have to sanction, approve, or ratify change—administrators; funders; fire, safety, health, and licensing regulators; insurers; and others in authority. There are those who have to effect the change—purchasers, builders, staff, and so on. And finally, there are those who have to live with the change—staff, parents, children, and community. All come to the process with different perspectives, desires, and roles to play.

A participatory process in planning, design, and implementation does not have to mean an endless, egalitarian process, culminating in a compromise end product that serves no one well. Nor does involving teachers and parents (and children) in designing or implementing changes necessarily mean having to cater to current desires and interests and skill levels. What is important is that their perspectives and their needs are laid bare. Human experience is the foundation of good design. The more the design process takes into account the blend of roles, attitudes, and behaviors the space will encompass, the better the chance for designs that work.

Involvement in the process can take many forms. Two obvious levels are observation and interviewing. Paying attention to how the adults and children go about their daily lives, using the spaces and materials, adapting or accommodating to the particularities of the space provides critical data to decisionmakers. Asking them why they do what they do—make the children wait, use or don't use certain spaces, stay inside—and how they feel about the space adds to the information. Going further

and asking for their ideas, their wish lists, is useful and may prove surprising information.

An architect, sitting on the floor with a serious looking four year old, asked the child what she wanted in the room. "Some place to sit with my mom when she comes so we can talk and get my snow pants on and point at my friends"—certainly a reasonable design issue not addressed in

---

Involving Others

To develop a design for an earth-art project funded by a small community arts grant, a small group of staff and parents with artistic and landscaping skills and an understanding of health, safety, and play issues developed a set of design criteria. Then parents, staff, and community adults and children were invited to play a role:

PARENTS AND STAFF ARE INVITED TO:

A Design Happening: A Chance to Play Artist and Landscaper
(No special talent required beyond interest and enthusiasm)

The Glendale Child Development Center Playground
Saturday, June 28
9:30 to 1:00 (or any piece of that time)

What we will do is this: come up with a design for the stream and splash pool (and whatever else the spirit leads to) on the center playground. How, you ask, will we do this? By stimulating alternatives, brainstorming, "watching the river flow," and transferring ideas to paper.

Come for the morning or a piece of the morning. **CHILDREN WELCOME** (and any interested friends and neighbors). We will have the playground set up for children, REFRESHMENTS, and promise no coerced manual labor. (Only rain, not drizzle, will postpone the event.)

many buildings. Asking children questions like where they like to go and where and when they get excited or frustrated or sad helps adults understand their perceptions of space.

In some instances, a decisionmaking committee or design jury works well. If the goals and design criteria are clearly expressed, asking those who either have a special expertise or a large stake in the result to decide between

alternatives is different than having the committee come up with the design.

Participation in the implementation of change invests people in change. It is unsettling for all of us to be moved or to deal with changes. Incorporating a role for children, staff, and parents in the process of planning, building, or moving hastens the settling process. Children can be involved in moving furniture or the contents of a cubby, making pictures or maps of the new and old spaces, adding new decor or dismantling old.

Participation also empowers people. Good teachers, parents, and competent children need to see themselves as environmental designers, capable of adapting environments to accomplish goals.

Change always has allies and obstructionists. A participatory process need not give undue consideration to nay sayers. Clear ground rules about the nature and extent of participation is necessary to avoid misunderstandings. Brainstorming sessions and wish lists raise unrealistic hopes, unless it is clear that ideas and wants will be winnowed down as competing factors like cost and other needs come into play. Clearly explaining the rationales for the eventual decisions, why this course of action was taken or this equipment purchased, is critical for participants to feel that their participation was taken seriously.

Participants: Architects and Designers

The value of good architects and designers is in the way they think and what they know. The knowledge of how built space works as a network of systems and the different alternatives of arranging spaces, managing flows, relating to the outside, creating moods and

---

Out of this process, two design concepts emerged—and a design jury was selected to decide which to develop. Following the refinement of the design, again all were invited to work with skilled individuals to implement the design:

> ### WANT A CHANCE TO PLAY GOD? <u>OR</u> SIMPLY HELP DO SOMETHING NEAT?
>
>
> *"Sunday in the Park with George"*
> (and Jim, Bruce, Butch, Rich, Bonnie, Bill, Jan,
> and hopefully a host of others)
>
> *The Glendale Child Development Center Playground*
> *Sunday, October 19*
> *9:00 to 5:00 (or pieces of that time)*
>
> What we will be doing is this: laying stone like a jig saw puzzle to create the splash pool bed and the stream. It will be a fun chance to do something creative and beautiful that we hope will make your child's childhood at Glendale even more special. No special skill is required and not everyone needs a strong back.

"Why Didn't You Talk to Us First?"

In the "Political Collapse of a Playground," Mayer Spivak (1974) chronicles the short life and death of a wonderful adventure playground which was planned with the children in the community. For weeks the children and play leaders planned the playground they wanted. This was followed by weeks of collecting materials and creating the playground.

Two days after the playground was completed, it was bulldozed, blacktopped over, and replaced by conventional metal playground structures. Most of the community (many of them parents) were not at all pleased with the unsightly, unplayground looking playground. With a minimum of dispatch, public officials had it redone.

A playground is a community place, and all members of the community have to be considered as participants, even those who only pass by or see it from their windows.

---

behavior patterns, and the range of materials available is what they bring to the process.

Directors and teachers are often limited by what they have experienced in the way of child care spaces and program models. They rarely know many alternative ways of developing space. Visiting other programs and reading design resources can help overcome this. What program staff should know and be able to articulate to other participants is what the goals of the program are and how the adults and children in the program behave in the present space. Combining their knowledge with that of architects and designers increases the chances that the space will work with a minimum of the unanticipated side effects that haunt many programs.

"The architect is very well known and has done schools and other children's settings, but I don't know about this," said a worried child care director, indicating the blueprints she was holding. "This" was a site for a downtown child care program for children under five years old with no drop off parking, a space-consuming library, a mini-amphitheater, and very little meeting or storage space. Luckily, this building wasn't built; but others have been—high sealed windows; tiny play yards; out-of-scale rooms; and intriguing, but unworkable layouts.

Averting disaster requires architects who listen to early childhood professionals and directors who observe and listen to teachers and parents and children and who are not afraid to assert their views. It is when architects **know** and directors **know** or are silent that there are problems. Professional arrogance or arrogance of authority or status, combined with time constraints, leads to problems—problems that may never be openly acknowledged.

When a building, a design, or a bright idea doesn't work the way it was intended, the failure may be blamed on the users—staff and children. This is a common problem in architecture and design (and of course applies to the advice of experts in almost any endeavor). Worse, the users may accept the failure as their own, which has happened in a number of *state of the art* child care facilities. Those architects or designers didn't return to assess the outcomes and have gone on to build new versions of flawed designs.

These failings are compounded by the difficulty in balancing form and function, a tension inherent in design. Architects and designers are usually much more sensitive than others to the form of things, the aesthetic affects of designs. This is both necessary and positive; our lives are enriched by beauty and forms that challenge us to think. But there has to be a balance.

The styling director for Ford Motors, George Walker, when criticized for the sleek door frame design that was difficult to cope with in an era of stylish hats, replied: "It's hard to believe anyone would mind getting his hat knocked off for the sake of a clean line." An interior designer's reaction to her stylized graphics being partially covered with storage cabinets in a nursery school echoed Walker's, "Can't they do without a few materials and appreciate the design?"

Builders

Contractors and skilled craftsmen bring to the process specific knowledge. In some cases it may simply be the skills on how to do the job that you have spelled out, (e.g., build this stairway). Real craftsmen bring an understanding of the craft and join the collaborative design process, helping to determine the best way to accomplish goals ("Have you thought about a ramp or a spiral staircase?"). Success depends on recognizing what they know and don't know.

Not all carpenters can design or adapt plans to ensure structural integrity. Like most architects and designers, it is unwise to assume any builders will have knowledge of children's behavior or child scale or understand the program context. The design criteria for use and safety is the child care professional's responsibility and must be clearly expressed.

One volunteer carpenter, hoping to save the program money on an expensive platform, built horizontal rather than vertical railings, not realizing that child climbing desires dictate vertical railings. Another thoughtfully changed dimensions on dividers because the director who designed them didn't take into account that wood comes in 4 by 8 foot sheets and that there would have been considerable waste of wood. The latter case, fortunately, made little difference in design. In either case, more communication at the time of design would have resulted in better, more cost-effective structures.

In nearly every community, there are people doing carpentry or other skilled labor who would relish the chance to actually practice their craft and build something interesting or creative. Finding and latching on to these people has transformed a number of programs. Working collaboratively, over time, results in blending perspectives and coming to recognize mutual talents and limitations. It is then that the best work is done.

Licensers, Inspectors, and Fire Marshals

All programs must satisfy the standards of fire, building, safety, and health regulations. In most states, there are additional requirements for obtaining a license. In some areas, there are not only state regulations but county and municipal codes. All of these requirements are designed to set a baseline floor of quality and safety below which no provider of children's care may drop.

The officials who inspect and sign off on whether or not programs comply with the standards have considerable power. It is important to understand their perspective. Health, safety, and fire inspectors are usually very single-minded. They have a set of codes to enforce; failure to do so in a strict manner may result in danger to people and in liability claims against them and their municipality. How compliance with one regulation (panic bar fire doors) may affect other safety issues (keeping children in and burglars out) often is not a concern that the official who regulates the program can take into account. A fire inspector's focus is on fire.

The codes may be rigid, the department or the individual may be inflexible, or there may be

Photograph by Jim Greenman

some give and take. From experience, there are always programs that seem to generate some flexibility. What sets them apart? Usually one or more of the following:

• A positive relationship with the regulator.

• A positive relationship with the powers that be to whom the regulator must pay attention.

• An ability to understand the perspective of the regulator.

• An understanding of what the regulations are intended to accomplish.

• An ability to articulate the need for flexibility, taking into account the regulator's perspective.

Everyone responds to respect, personal attention, a little flattery, and prompt attention. Everyone also wants to minimize the hassles in their daily work. One center always got the leeway it needed from a particularly *by the book* health inspector because staff took his concerns very seriously and acted like they welcomed his presence as an educational event (and offered him lunch). In those instances when they needed flexibility, they always understood his position and recognized that his hands were tied (even if they weren't). They respectfully insisted that they would have to seek other recourse, either from his supervisor or from the city council member they had cultivated. He often relaxed his stand as a favor to them or put in a good word to his supervisor.

At times both the best and worst programs simply ignore some regulations. In some areas, soft furniture that is not completely fire retardant; paper on the walls; all plant and animal life; the use of corridors, however wide, for any play or storage; and carpeting have been banned for

health and safety reasons. Living is a threat to health and safety! But ignoring or circumventing regulations puts an extra responsibility on a program to be knowledgeable about what the regulations are intended to accomplish. All of those aforementioned items have a logic. Some plants and animals are dangerous. Some program use of a corridor could cost lives in an emergency. All providers have the responsibility to take the threat of fire, infectious disease, poisoning, and other safety issues as seriously as the inspectors charged to enforce codes.

A Goal Based Process

Ideally, every organization, and sub-units of that organization, would have a process for planning and evaluating. Good organizations (and good designs) stem from having a clear sense of purpose and a process that applies intelligence, expertise, and observation to accomplish the goals.

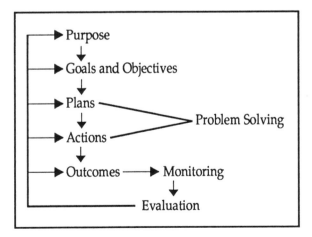

The planning process is important, whether planning a building, a classroom, a bridge, or an art corner. The complexity of planning stems from the reality that there are always a lot of

desires and needs to be turned into goals. There is also a mix of motivation, energy, ability, competing interests, and distractions that make it difficult to keep one's focus on the things that really matter.

The planning process is interactive. One is always considering one objective or design criteria against another, exploring how outcomes affect each other. Often, efforts work at cross purposes, the implicit goal of smooth efficiency clashing with goals such as children's independence. If the process outlined above is fundamental to the way that both the organization and the individuals think and behave, chances are increased that priorities will be kept in the forefront of the program's consciousness.

Making change usually begins with deciding what really matters. What are the most important goals? Often a useful next step is simply getting out people's feelings about the work.* What do people find rewarding? What's driving them crazy? What's missing? This will probably raise a host of issues far beyond the issues at hand. Sorting out the conditions or issues that seem to have some hope of being addressed from the insoluble ones is the final step before problem solving.

---

*In a chapter entitled "The Civilizing of Ruby's Center: How It Began," Jones and Prescott, in **Dimensions of Teaching—Learning Environments II: Focus on Day Care** (1978) describe the process of a director initiating change in a program with a settled staff that needs a lot of change. As the book goes on to discuss the environmental dimensions, the authors return again and again to Ruby's program as the process of change continues.

Once goals are established, feelings are out on the table, and problems are identified, the planning process can be applied to space, equipment, routines, and the expectations of adult and child interactions. Goals and objectives can be translated into design criteria for a building, space or piece of equipment.

Design criteria establish the requirements the design must adhere to. These may pertain to cost, size, use, safety factors, or storage. Some examples:

Infant Nap Room Design Requirements

• Sleep 12 babies
• Adult rocking chair
• Quiet, white noise
• Diapering area with sink
• Dimmable lights
• Ventilation, high humidity
• Linen storage
• Countertop or shelf space
• Communication/display space
• Visual and auditory monitoring

If licensing requires specific furnishings (e.g., 12 cribs), that would be the first design criteria.

Playground Climber Design Requirements

• Fit in 20 x 20 foot area
• Safe for children 24 to 60 months
• Provide developmental range of climbing experiences
• Provide variety of climbing experiences
• Two different exits
• Graded challenges
• Easy adult access
• Wide visual access
• Incorporate sliding
• Adaptable with ladders and planks

• Low maintenance
• Aesthetically pleasing to parents
• Encourage social play

Climate may dictate a choice of materials—wood instead of metal or some plastics in a very cold climate.

Platform Railing Design Requirements

• Restrain children from falling
• Adult and child visual access
• Unable to be used for climbing
• Allow adults physical access to children
• Allow use of furniture on loft

In this case, given the concern for visual access and the desire to have furniture on the loft (which children could stand on and thus fall over a low railing) and since cost is not a factor, a plexiglass railing may be the best solution.

A Creative Process

Improvement begins because someone has identified a problem or a situation that could be made better. Effective problem solving takes the form shown in the box below.

Problem solving has a creative side and an analytical side. Generating many possible solutions requires creativity. Determining whether the solutions work or what new problems the solutions may entail requires analysis. Nearly every solution to one problem generates other problems. The trick is to find the solution with the most easily resolvable or most inconsequential problems.

Design is just another version of problem solving. One tries to meet a number of criteria and anticipate all the effects of a particular design. Two examples of problem solving follow in the box on the next page:

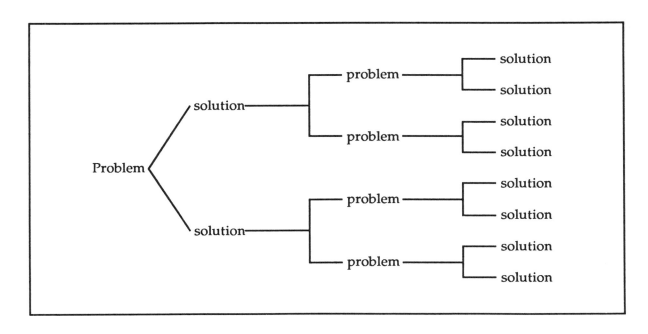

Problem 1: Loft Design

A toddler loft is being designed to give a room more and better space. Problem: What sort of entry and exit on to the loft?

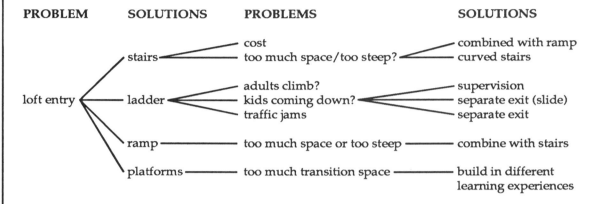

After going through this process, it is possible that no solution is satisfactory. It may be necessary to redefine the situation. Perhaps the loft is not necessary. Are there other alternatives to accomplishing what the loft was to accomplish?

Problem 2: No Meeting Space

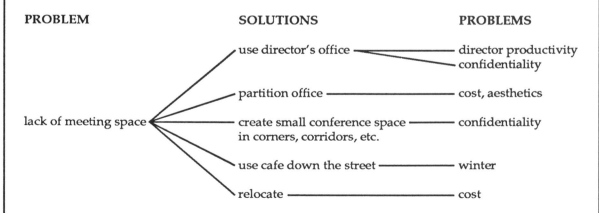

In this example, adopting aspects of some of the proposed solutions might make the most sense: use the cafe and the director's office at times and partition one part of an office.

Each solution above will generate problems of territoriality, productivity, and confidentiality.

The creative side of problem solving involves tossing out preconceptions and thinking of all sorts of solutions—some fanciful, some impractical, some simple. While most are ruled out, some may fit or contain the germ of an idea that may work. The analytical side requires examining each solution in the clear light of day—Why won't this work? What side effects will it generate? Often this process benefits from time—time for ideas to incubate, time to flesh out and illuminate ideas and issues. You can't get a creative idea from an act of will. The non-rational part of the brain needs to search among the apparently disconnected bits and pieces of information stored to make a new connection.

Both aspects benefit from experience. Past experience with similar situations helps generate possible solutions and project subsequent problems. The most creative thinkers are able to apply ideas and lessons learned from wide ranging, seemingly unrelated situations to find ideas.

Visiting other children's programs (good and bad), analyzing what they do and why, and seeing how they address environmental problems provides a store of experience. Keeping journals and idea banks as people make observations about their daily experiences can ensure that good ideas aren't dropped simply because the timing is wrong.

Problem Solving/Design Tools

Models are a useful tool in design. When designing space capsules, NASA builds full scale models and then pays careful attention to

Matrixes

Matrixes are a useful tool for applying goals to content areas or environments.

ACTIVITY AREAS

GOALS	EATING	BATHROOM	CUBBY	ART	MANIPULATIVES	DRAMATIC	BOOKS	PLAYGROUND	HALLWAYS
INDEPENDENCE									
SENSE OF SECURITY									
SAFETY									
SOFTNESS									
SMALL MOTOR									
LARGE MOTOR									
SELF-EXPRESSION									
RECEPTIVE LANGUAGE									
EXPRESSIVE LANGUAGE									
WRITTEN LANGUAGE									
NON-SEXIST									

what astronauts bump into, knock over, or can't reach. Scale models allow designers to see the relationship between parts and the overall context. Art supply stores have cardboard, balsa wood, clay, and other materials for building models.

Scale drawings are essential for serious planning of layouts. Graph paper is invaluable for drawing to scale.

Creative Implementation

Environmental change begins with a vision. What if the room had couches and plants and lots of open storage instead of just these tables and high cabinets? We need an infant-toddler playground, a place where babies can be outdoors and use all their powers. Imagine a new building instead of this church basement, with windows and offices and some classrooms. Wouldn't it be wonderful if we had a Community Playthings infant cart?

The first step is taking a vision and making it a collective vision, selling it to whoever needs to share the vision to make it real—staff, parents, or funders. A model, a drawing, a photograph, an eloquent description—combined with a clear description of the benefits—sells visions. Many efforts falter at this point; the vision is never made compelling in either words or pictures.

With a shared vision, convincing skeptics, or fundraising, or marshalling the time and energies of key people becomes far more likely. Once the vision has a reality of its own, sooner or later, with enough determined efforts, it may well happen.

Who's going to do it? Where are we going to get the materials? Who's going to pay for it?

These are usually important questions whether the issue is a new playground, new curtains, or redoing the storage room. Can we use parents or volunteers or hustle the materials?

Some decisions boil down to money. If there is no cash available or all the money is restricted—tied to labor or materials or a certain time period—the choices are dictated. Some decisions stem from institutional restrictions about purchasing or employment, the dictates of insurance agents, or an obvious lack of human resources—time, people, expertise.

Hustling, Scrounging, and Doing It Yourself

"The human race built most nobly when limitations were greatest and, therefore, when most was required of imagination in order to build at all. Limitations seem to have always been the best friends of architecture."
Frank Lloyd Wright

There is much truth to Wright's comment. Necessity is the mother of invention. But when imagination or energy flags, great limitations result in poverty, deprivation, and distress. Good children's programs have so often turned trash into treasure that the idea of actually being well endowed with resources seems unreal.

All things being equal (but they never are), settings that are partly the product of the community's labor (children, staff, parents, community) and recycled and found materials are more rewarding and meaningful. The expertise, time, and resources, however, to a large extent will determine whether they work. There are many bad volunteer-built playgrounds, unsafe cabinets, pillows that fall apart, and creative but hard to use furnishings. There are also, in the hectic world of working parents,

many parents who value their time more than their money, as well as people who simply prefer new, purchased materials. Before jumping into *let's do it ourselves* projects, ask yourself:

Do we have access to the expertise we need?

What resources do we have?

Do we have the time?

Is there the real interest and potential for follow-through?

Why not pay skilled others or buy commercial equipment?

Making It Work

"Don't look back, look now."

After a few months, the new rocking chairs are in the basement, the platform appears empty most of the time, the traffic patterns seem once again to have been designed by the Marx brothers despite the new room arrangement, and the director is ready to fire the staff or drown herself in drink. After so much work!

Changing to improve is rarely a finished effort. Staff changes and negative side effects crop up—*the children's fingers were pinched by the rocking chair*—and soon there is a reversion to the safe and familiar. Or the means become ends and obtaining the means is assumed to have achieved the goals. The goal of equipment is the experience the equipment offers **when used as intended**—rocking, spatial variety, smooth traffic flow—in the cases mentioned above. A science corner is difficult to achieve. Even more difficult is ensuring the developmentally appropriate experiences the science corner is intended to facilitate.

Flexible space or equipment is not the same as flexible use. Staff have to understand the potential for use and be committed to providing the experiences the space or equipment can provide. Without staff understanding and commitment, the space or equipment often *won't work* because the tinkering and shaping necessary won't happen. Training and supervision, as staff come and go, become more important as the creativity and flexibility the setting demands increases.

When something is not working, there is a danger of just writing off the effort, particularly by those who were lukewarm to begin with or who were not brought into the process. The failure goes into the center's historical record. "Oh, last year we tried that (a room arrangement, a sign-in sheet, a garden, a self-help routine). It doesn't work." But why? —bad timing, poor resources, inadequate training (Did staff know how to use it? Why to use it?), or parent resistance; or did it work for the children but was a pain in the neck for some staff?

The creative planning process extends after the changes take effect. Monitoring and evaluation is a critical step to ensure that the environmental goals are met. Even if something is working, knowing why will aid future efforts. The real why may be unintended positive side effects—staff or parent enthusiasm, the way children chose to incorporate the change into their lives.

One teacher rearranged her room every six months, each time finding great benefits in the new arrangement. After a few months she would become dissatisfied and redo it again. It took her some time to realize that the arrangement she ended up with was far less important than the process. She, her staff, and the children would get excited and discover and rediscover the potential of equipment and furnishings. This resulted in renewed interest in teaching and learning, not in the particular arrangement.

Monitoring means paying attention to what is really happening; how people are behaving and feeling; what the experiences of children, parents, and staff actually are. Observation and polling are the major ways to monitor. If a space is problematic, observation can be made about how the same people use the space at certain times, how different people use the same space, how use changes over time. Individual children or adults can be *tracked*, observed closely to uncover patterns and relationships. Areas can be mapped or written or visual *snapshots* taken at various times of the day to determine traffic flows and space usage. As video equipment becomes very affordable and *user friendly*, it is becoming an important monitoring tool.

Space can be analyzed from the physical perspective of all the different users, in terms of size, strength, motions required. It is very informative to mentally and, where possible, physically put oneself *in the shoes* of another. What does the world look and feel like on the floor of the infant room?

Because people seek the right fit for them, their actions will reveal problems and needs. Bottles placed casually on a diaper table reveal a need for surfaces on which to place temporarily discarded bottles or for training caregivers to put bottles elsewhere.

Polling can be simply asking an adult or child what they are doing or feeling and why— what they like and don't like. Interviews, discussion meetings, written questionnaires all provide important data as to what is happening beyond **our** perceptions, colored by our interests, biases, and limited views.

Photograph by Jim Greenman

There will always be problems. Looking for trouble will produce trouble. Solving a problem will create new problems, which is why evaluation criteria and keeping all the criteria in mind is so important.

Conclusions

We make places all the time. When we open a window, move a chair, or add a light, we are making a space a place for us. We also adapt to spaces all the time; we accommodate to poor lighting, bad air, cramped conditions.

Humanity's greatest strength is also a potentially fatal weakness; human beings may die off because of our willingness and ability to accommodate to environmental dangers created by modern man.

It is important that children experience places as made,—as living systems that are the result of choices, trade-offs, and compromises. Children and adults do not have to accept places passively. Nor do we have to unthinkingly impose a constricted vision on place after place until sensibilities dull at the grey, safe uniformity of it all.

Children's environments can be places for living and stage settings for many of the experiences of a full and productive childhood. They can be places where children and adults exercise their powers as placemakers and problem solvers and cooperative human beings.

Exercises

1. Evaluate a setting in terms of how it works for parents, for new children, for janitors.

2. Develop a goal matrix for a learning center and for a care routine.

3. Develop the design criteria for a piece of learning equipment you want invented.

4. Develop at least five solutions for a given problem. Analyze the solutions for side effects.

— References —

Allen, Lady of Hurtwood. **Adventure Playgrounds for Handicapped Children**. London: James Galt, 1974.

Allen, Lady M. **Planning for Play**. London: Thames and Hudson, 1968.

Almy, M., P. Monighan, B. Scales, and J. Van Hoorn. "Recent Research on Play: The Teacher's Perspective," in L. Katz, **Current Topics in Early Childhood Education, Volume V**. Norwood, NJ: Ablex Publishing Co, 1984.

Aronson, S. "Infectious Disease Control in Child Care," **Child Care Information Exchange**, December 1984.

Ashton-Warner, S. **Spearpoint**. New York: Random House, 1972.

Ashton-Warner, S. **Teacher**. New York: Simon and Schuster, 1963.

Barker, R. G. "From Ecological Psychology to Eco-Behavioral Science," in E. P. Willems and H. L. Rausch, **Naturalistic Viewpoints in Psychological Research**. New York: Holt, Rinehart & Winston, 1969.

Bemelmans, Ludwig. **Madeline**. New York: Viking Press, 1937.

Bengtsson, A. **Adventure Playgrounds**. New York: Praeger, 1972.

Benjamin, J. **Grounds for Play**. London: Bedford Squire Press, 1974.

Bettelheim, B. **The Children of the Dream**. New York: Avon, 1970.

Bettelheim, B. **Surviving and Other Essays**. New York: Alfred A. Knopf, 1979.

Bronfenbrenner, U. **The Ecology of Human Development**. Cambridge, MA: Harvard University Press, 1979.

Brown, M. **Good Night Moon**. New York: Harper and Row, 1947.

Bruner, J. S. "Organization of Early Skilled Action," **Child Development**, 44, 1-111, 1973.

Caplan, F., and T. Caplan. **The Power of Play**. Garden City, NY: Anchor Press/Doubleday, 1974.

Caplan, R. **By Design**. New York: Saint Martin's Press, 1982.

Cherry, C. **Creative Play for the Developing Child**. Belmont, CA: Pitman Learning, 1976.

Cherry, C. **Think of Something Quiet**. Belmont, CA: Pitman Learning, 1981.

Clifford, R. "Early Childhood Environments in Child Care Centers in the United States." Presentation at 1986 NAEYC Conference, Washington, DC.

Coates, G. **Alternate Learning Environments**. Stroudsberg, PA: Dowden, Hutchinson, and Ross, 1974.

Coelen, C., F. Glantz, and D. Calore. **Day Care Centers in the U.S.** Cambridge, MA: Abt Associates, 1978.

Cohen, U., A. Hill, C. G. Lane, T. McGinty, and G. Moore. **Recommendations for Child Play Areas**. Milwaukee, WI: The School of Architecture and Urban Planning, University of Wisconsin–Milwaukee, 1979.

Cohen, U., T. McGinty, and G. Moore. **Case Studies of Child Play Areas and Child Support Facilities**. Milwaukee, WI: The School of Architecture and Urban Planning, University of Wisconsin–Milwaukee, 1978.

Coles, R. **Migrants, Sharecroppers and Mountaineers**. Boston, MA: Little Brown, 1972.

Coles, R. **Uprooted Children**. New York: Harper and Row, 1970.

Dattner, R. **Design for Play**. Cambridge, MA: MIT Press, 1969.

Dean, J. **Room to Learn**. New York: Citation Press, 1974.

Deasy, C. M. **Design for Human Affairs**. New York: John Wiley and Sons, 1974.

Doman, G. **How to Multiply Your Baby's Intelligence**. New York: Doubleday, 1984.

Douglas, M. **Purity and Danger**. New York: Praeger, 1966.

Dylan, B. "Ballad of a Thin Man." Los Angeles, CA: Warner Bros., 1965.

Dylan, B. "Like a Rolling Stone." Los Angeles, CA: Warner Bros., 1965.

Eble, K. **A Perfect Education**. New York: Macmillan, 1966.

Educational Facilities Laboratory. **Places and Things for Experimental Schools**. New York: Educational Facilities Laboratory, no date.

Elkind, D. **The Hurried Child**. Boston, MA: Addison-Wesley Publishing Co., 1981.

Elledge, S. **E. B. White: A Biography**. New York: W. W. Norton, 1984.

Ellison, G. **Play Structures**. Pasadena, CA: Pacific Oaks College, 1974.

English, H., and A. English. **A Comprehensive Dictionary of Psychological and Psychoanalytical Terms: A Guide to Usage**. New York: Longman, 1958.

Environmental Criteria: MR Preschool Day Care Facilities. College Station, TX: College of Architecture and Environmental Design, Texas A and M University, 1974.

Erickson, E. **Childhood and Society**. New York: Norton, 1950.

Erickson, E. **Toys and Reasons: Stages in the Ritualization of Experience**. New York: W. W. Norton and Co., 1977.

Evans, R. **Jean Piaget: The Man and His Ideas**. New York: E. P. Dutton Co., 1973.

Ferguson, J. "Creating Growth Producing Environments for Infants and Toddlers," in E. Jones (editor), **Supporting the Growth of Infants, Toddlers, and Parents**. Pasadena, CA: Pacific Oaks College, 1979.

Feuchern, Peter. **The Book of Eskimos**. 1963.

Flemming, R., and R. von Tscharner. **Placemakers**. New York: Hastings House, 1981.

Forman, G. and F. Hill. **Constructive Play: Applying Piaget in the Preschool**. Menlo Park, CA: Addison-Wesley, 1984.

Forman, G., and D. Kuschner. **The Child's Construction of Knowledge: Piaget for Teaching Children**. Washington, DC: NAEYC, 1983.

Friedberg, P. **Handcrafted Playgrounds**. New York: Vintage Books, 1975.

Frost, J., and B. Klein. **Children's Play and Play Grounds**. Boston, MA: Allyn and Bacon, 1979.

Gandini, L. "Not Just Anywhere: Making Child Care Centers into Particular Places," **Beginnings**, Summer 1984.

Gauldie, S. **Architecture: The Appreciation of the Arts**. London: Oxford University Press, 1969.

Gonzalez-Mena, J., and D. Eyer. **Infancy and Caregiving**. Palo Alto, CA: Mayfield Co., 1980.

Grahame, Kenneth. **The Wind in the Willows**. New York: Holt, Rinehart and Winston, 1980.

Greenman, J. "Babies Get Out," **Beginnings**, Summer 1985.

Greenman, J., and R. Fuqua. **Making Day Care Better: Training, Evaluation and the Process of Change**. New York: Teachers College Press, 1984.

Hainstock, E. **Teaching Montessori in the Home—The Preschool Years**. New York: Random House, 1968.

Hall, E. **The Hidden Dimension**. Garden City, NY: Doubleday, 1969.

Hewes, J. **Build Your Own Playground**. Boston, MA: Houghton Mifflin, 1975.

Hill, A., C. Lane, U. Cohen, G. Moore, and T. McGinty. **Abstracts on Child Play Areas and Child Support Facilities**. Milwaukee, WI: The School of Architecture and Urban Planning, University of Wisconsin–Milwaukee, 1978.

Hiss, T. "Experiencing Places," **New Yorker Magazine**, June 22, 1987, pp. 45-68; June 29, 1987, pp. 73-86.

Hogan, P. **The Nuts and Bolts of Playground Construction**. West Point, NY: Leisure Press, 1982.

Hohmann, M., B. Banet, and D. Weikart. **Young Children in Action**. Ypsilanti, MI: High Scope Press, 1979.

Holt, J. **What Do I Do Monday?** New York: E. P. Dutton, 1970.

Illich, I. **Deschooling Society**. New York: Harper and Row, 1970.

Issacs, S. **Childhood and After**. New York: Agathon Press, 1970.

Issacs, S. **The Nursery Years**. New York: Schocken Books, 1968.

Jacobs, J. **The Death and Life of Great American Cities**. New York: Random House, 1969.

Joffe, C. **Friendly Intruders: Child Care Professionals and Family Life**. Berkeley, CA: University of California Press, 1977.

Jones, E. **Dimensions of Teaching-Learning Environments: Handbook for Teachers**. Pasadena, CA: Pacific Oaks College, 1973.

Jones, E. **Dimensions of Teaching-Learning Environments II: Focus on Day Care**. Pasadena, CA: Pacific Oaks College, 1978.

Jones, E. **Joys and Risks of Teaching Young Children**. Pasadena, CA: Pacific Oaks College, 1978.

Katz, M. B. **Class, Bureaucracy, and Schools**. New York: Praeger, 1971.

Kidder, T. **House**. Boston, MA: Houghton Mifflin, 1985.

Kritchevsky, S., E. Prescott, and L. Walling. **Planning Environments for Young Children: Physical Space**. Washington, DC: NAEYC, 1969.

Laing, R. D. **The Self and Others**. London: Tavistock, 1969.

Lederman, A. **Creative Playgrounds and Recreation Centers**. New York: Praeger, 1959.

Liljestrom, R. Quoted in **Report on Preschool Education**, November 8, 1977, p. 7.

Loughlin, C., and J. Suina. **The Learning Environment: An Instructional Strategy**. New York: Teachers College Press, 1982.

Lowenfeld, M. **Play in Childhood**. London: 1935.

Mason, J. **The Environment of Play**. West Point, NY: Leisure Press, 1982.

Massad, C. "Time and Space in Space and Time," in K. Yamamoto (editor), **Children in Time and Space**. New York: Teachers College Press, 1979.

McCall, R. **Infants**. New York: Vintage, 1980.

Mead, M. **Blackberry Winter: My Earlier Years**. New York: William Morrow, 1972.

Milne, A. A. **Winnie-The-Pooh**. New York: Dell Publishing Co., Inc., 1926, 1954.

Montagu, A. **Growing Young**. New York: McGraw-Hill, 1981.

Montessori, M. **The Absorbent Mind**. New York: Holt, Rinehart and Winston, 1967.

Moore, G., U. Cohen, and T. McGinty. **Case Studies of Child Play Areas and Child Support Facilities**. Milwaukee, WI: The School of Architecture and Urban Planning, University of Wisconsin–Milwaukee, 1978.

Moore, G., C. Lane, A. Hill, U. Cohen, and T. McGinty. **Recommendations for Child Care Centers**. Milwaukee, WI: The School of Architecture and Urban Planning, University of Wisconsin–Milwaukee, 1979.

Morris, W. **The Home Place**. New York: Scribner, 1948.

Nelson, G. **On Design**. New York: The Whitney Library of Design, 1979.

Newman, O. **Defensible Space**. New York: Collier, 1973.

Newman, R. "Short People." Los Angeles, CA: Warner Bros., 1977.

Nicholson, S. "How Not to Cheat Children," The Theory of Loose Parts, in G. Coates (editor), **Alternate Learning Environments**. Stroudsberg, PA: Dowden, Hutchinson, and Ross, 1974.

Noren-Bjorn, E. **The Impossible Playground**. West Point, NY: Leisure Press, 1982.

Olds, A. Quoted in "Fine Details: Organizing and Displaying Materials," **Beginnings**, Summer 1984.

Olds, A. "Planning a Developmentally Optimal Day Care Center," **Day Care and Early Education**, Summer 1982.

Osmon, F. **Patterns for Designing Children's Centers**. New York: Educational Facilities Laboratory, 1971.

Peller, L. "The Children's House," reprinted in **Man-Environment Systems**, Vol. 2, No. 4, 1972.

Perin, C. **With Man in Mind**. Cambridge, MA: MIT Press, 1970.

Pettygrove, W., and J. Greenman. "The Adult World of Day Care," in J. Greenman and R. Fuqua (editors), **Making Day Care Better**, 1984.

Piaget, J. **To Understand Is To Invent**. New York: Viking, 1974.

Polloway, A. **The Urban Nest**. Stroudsberg, PA: Dowden, Hutchinson, and Ross, 1977.

Pragnell, P. "The Friendly Object," **Harvard Educational Review**, 39 (4), 1969.

Prescott, E. "Is Day Care As Good As a Good Home?," **Young Children**, 1978, 33, pp. 13-19.

Prescott, E. "The Physical Environment—A Powerful Regulator of Experience," **Child Care Information Exchange**, April 1979.

Prescott, E. "The Physical Setting in Day Care," in J. Greenman and R. Fuqua (editors), **Making Day Care Better**, 1984.

Prescott, E., and T. David. "The Effects of the Physical Environment on Day Care," ERIC Document No. 156-356, 1976.

Prescott, E., and E. Jones. **Day Care As a Child Rearing Environment, Volume I**. Washington, DC: 1972.

Prescott, E., E. Jones, and S. Kritchevsky. **Day Care As a Child Rearing Environment**, Vol. II. Washington, DC: NAEYC, 1972.

Provenzo, E., and A. Brett. **The Complete Block Book**. Syracuse, NY: Syracuse University Press, 1983.

Rahim, J., and G. Moore. "Selecting an Appropriate Location for an Early Childhood Development Center," **Day Care Journal**, Vol. 1, No. 2, Fall 1982.

Relph, E. **Place and Placelessness**. London: Pion, 1976.

Riley, S. "Some Reflections of the Values of Children's Play," **Young Children**, 28 (3), pp. 146-153.

Rudolph, N. **Adventure Playgrounds**. New York: Teachers College Press, 1975.

Rybczynski, W. **Home**. New York: Viking, 1986.

Selye, H. **The Stress of Life**. New York: McGraw-Hill, 1978.

Silberman, C. **Crisis in the Classroom**. New York: Random House, 1970.

Sommer, R. **Personal Space: The Behavioral Basis of Design**. Englewood Cliffs, NJ: Prentice Hall, 1969.

Sommer, R. **Design Awareness**. San Francisco, CA: Rinehart Press, 1972.

Sommer, R. **Tight Spaces: Hard Architecture and How to Humanize It.** Englewood Cliffs, NJ: Prentice Hall, 1974.

Spivak, M. "The Political Collapse of a Playground," in Gary Coates (editor), **Alternate Learning Environments,** 1974.

Stills, S. "For What It's Worth." Los Angeles: BMI Music, 1969.

Suransky, V. **The Erosion of Childhood.** Chicago, IL: University of Chicago Press, 1982.

Tarkington, B. **Penrod.** New York: Grosset and Dunlap, 1965.

Taylor, A., and G. Vlastos. **School Zone: Learning Environments for Children.** New York: Van Nostrand Reinhold Co., 1975.

Thoreau, H. **Walden.** New York: Signet, 1960.

U.S. Department of Housing and Urban Development. **A Playground for All Children, Book 3.** Washington, DC: U.S. Government Printing Office, 1976.

Weber, L. **The English Infant School and Informal Education.** Englewood Cliffs, NJ: Prentice Hall, 1971.

Wechsler, L. "Profile: Harold Shapinsky," **New Yorker Magazine,** December 16, 1985.

Weikart, D., L. Rogers, C. Adcock, and D. McClelland. **The Cognitively Oriented Curriculum.** Washington, DC: NAEYC, 1971.

Weinstein, C., and T. David. **Spaces for Children: The Built Environment and Child Development.** New York: Plenum Press, 1987.

White, B., and J. Watts. **Experience and Environment.** Englewood Cliffs, NJ: Prentice Hall, 1973.

White, E. B. **Letters of E. B. White.** New York: Harrow, 1977.

Williams, T. **Night of the Iguana.** New York: New Directions, 1962.

Willis, A., and H. Ricciuti. **A Good Beginning for Babies.** Washington, DC: NAEYC, 1975.

Wilson, F. **The Joy of Building: Restoring the Connection Between Architect and Builder.** New York: Van Nostrand Reinhold Books, 1979.

Wohwill, J., and G. Weisman. **The Physical Environment and Behavior: Annotated Bibliography and Guide to the Literature.** New York: Plenum Press, 1981.

Wright, F. L. **On Architecture.** New York: Grosset and Dunlap, 1941.

Wright, O. **Frank Lloyd Wright: His Life, His Work, His Words.** New York: Horizon Press, 1966.

Yamamoto, K. **Children in Time and Space.** New York: Teachers College Press, 1979.

— Poetry Acknowledgements —

"After A Freezing Rain" from **Out in the Dark and Daylight** by Aileen Fisher. Text copyright © 1980 by Aileen Fisher. Reprinted by permission of Harper & Row, Publishers, Inc.

"April Rain Song" copyright © 1932 by Alfred A. Knopf, Inc. and renewed 1960 by Langston Hughes. Reprinted from **The Dream Keeper and Other Poems** by Langston Hughes, by permission of Alfred A. Knopf, Inc.

"Automobile Mechanics" from **I Like Machinery** by Dorothy Baruch. Permission granted by Bertha Klausner International Literary Agency, Inc.

"Barter" reprinted with permission of Macmillan Publishing Company from **Collected Poems** by Sara Teasdale. Copyright © 1917 by Macmillan Publishing Company, renewed 1945 by Mamie T. Wheless.

"Books Fall Open" from **One At a Time** by David McCord. Copyright © 1965, 1966 by David McCord. By permission of Little, Brown and Company.

"Chinese Checker Players" from the book **The Pill Verses the Springhill Mine Disaster** by Richard Brautigan. Copyright © 1968 by Richard Brautigan. Published by arrangement with Delacorte Press/Seymour Lawrence. All rights reserved.

"Doors" from **The Complete Poems of Carl Sandburg**, copyright © 1950 by Carl Sandburg; renewed 1978 by Margaret Sandburg, Helga Sandburg Crile and Janet Sandburg. Reprinted by permission of Harcourt Brace Jovanovich, Inc.

"Fletcher Avenue" from **Worlds I Know and Other Poems**. Copyright © 1985 Myra Cohn Livingston. Reprinted with the permission of Margaret K. McElderry Books, an imprint of Macmillan Publishing Company.

"The Frost Pane" from **One At a Time** by David McCord. Copyright © 1925 by David McCord. First appeared in **The Saturday Review**. By permission of Little, Brown and Company.

"The Fury of Overshoes" from **The Death Notebooks** by Anne Sexton. Copyright © 1974 by Anne Sexton. Reprinted by permission of Houghton Mifflin Company.

"Halfway Down" from **When We Were Very Young** by A. A. Milne. Copyright © 1924 by E. P. Dutton, renewed 1952 by A. A. Milne. Reprinted by permission of the publisher, E. P. Dutton, a division of NAL Penguin Inc.

"Happiness" from **When We Were Very Young** by A. A. Milne. Copyright © 1924 by E. P. Dutton, renewed 1952 by A. A. Milne. Reprinted by permission of the publisher, E. P. Dutton, a division of NAL Penguin Inc.

"A Lazy Thought" from **JAMBOREE Rhymes For All Times** by Eve Merriam. Copyright © 1962, 1966, 1973, 1984 by Eve Merriam. All rights reserved. Reprinted by permission of Marian Reiner for the author.

"Little Girl, Be Careful What You Say" from **The Complete Poems of Carl Sandburg**, Revised and Expanded Edition, copyright © 1950 by Carl Sandburg, renewed 1978 by Margaret Sandburg, Helga Sandburg Crile and Janet Sandburg. Reprinted by permission of Harcourt Brace Jovanovich, Inc.

"Mediterranean Beach, Day After Storm" from "Love: Two Vignettes." Copyright © 1966 by Robert Penn Warren. Reprinted from **New and Selected Poems 1923-1985** by Robert Penn Warren, by permission of Random House, Inc.

"Mirror, Mirror" from **Miracles** edited by Richard Lewis. Copyright © 1966 by Richard Lewis. Reprinted by permission of Simon & Schuster, Inc.